Copts at the
Crossroads

D0731683

Copts at the Crossroads

The Challenges of Building Inclusive Democracy in Contemporary Egypt

Mariz Tadros

The American University in Cairo Press
Cairo   New York

CONCORDIA UNIVERSITY LIBRARY
PORTLAND, OR 97211

First published in 2013 by
The American University in Cairo Press
113 Sharia Kasr el Aini, Cairo, Egypt
420 Fifth Avenue, New York, NY 10018
www.aucpress.com

Copyright © 2013 by Mariz Tadros

Some of the material in this book appeared previously in articles by Mariz Tadros published in the *Middle East Research and Information Project*: "Egypt's Bloody Sunday," 13 October 2011; "A State of Sectarian Denial," 11 January 2011; and "Behind Egypt's Deep Red Lines," 10 January 2010. Reproduced by permission.

All rights reserved. No part of this publication may be reproduced, stored in a retrieval system, or transmitted in any form or by any means, electronic, mechanical, photocopying, recording, or otherwise, without the prior written permission of the publisher.

Dar el Kutub No. 13835/12
ISBN 978 977 416 591 7

Dar el Kutub Cataloging-in-Publication Data

Tadros, Mariz
    Copts at the Crossroads: The Challenges of Building Inclusive Democracy in Egypt / Mariz Tadros.—Cairo: The American University in Cairo Press, 2013.
    p.   cm.
    ISBN 978 977 416 591 7
    1. Egypt—History
    2. Copts
    962

1 2 3 4 5   17 16 15 14 13

Designed by Adam el-Sehemy
Printed in Egypt

To Dr. Khairy Abdel Malek, Dr. Ra'if Yanni,
Dr. Marie Assaad, and Akram Habib

In memory of the late Dr. Samer Soliman, professor, activist,
and co-founder of Egyptians Against Discrimination

Contents

Acknowledgments

This book would not have been possible without the support of many people. First and foremost I would like to thank my husband, Akram Habib, for his immense contribution in developing the ideas and arguments presented in this book and in challenging me to dig deeper, probe further, and question everything. My deepest gratitude goes to my parents, Fikry and Mary, for their unfaltering encouragement and support.

This book benefited immensely from the very capable research assistance of Robeir el Fares, the assistant editor in chief of *Watani* newspaper and one of the most influential Coptic writers and activists in Egypt today. Chapters 6 and 8 relied heavily on interviews undertaken by El Fares. I owe Hani Morsi, doctoral student at the University of Sussex's Institute of Development Studies (IDS), my deepest thanks for his research assistance in collating the quantitative data that was then synthesized and presented in chapters 2 and 7. I am deeply indebted to Dr. Sinout Delwar, Dr. Ra'if Yanni, and the Coptic Culture Centre at al-Dahir, Cairo, for sharing with us the database of all the press articles published on sectarianism from 2007 onward. I owe much to all the informants and interviewees who gave me of their time and shared all that they have in both formal and informal capacities. I would like to thank Chris Toensing, editor of the *Middle East Research and Information Project* (MERIP), for kindly allowing me to reprint some articles that appeared in the magazine. A special thank you to Richard (Dick) Douglas for his incomparable editing skills and substantive commentary. I would like to thank all the members of the "participation tribe" at the IDS for their constant support and my friends in Cairo, in particular Lilian Awad and Faiza Rady, for their constant encouragement.

Many thanks to the anonymous reviewers, whose comments and suggestions were immensely helpful for the refinement of this manuscript. No words can do justice to the editing work that the very capable Nadia Naqib and Jasmina Brankovic dedicated to the manuscript. A special thank you is also due to Neil Hewison and Randi Danforth for their exceptional efforts in bringing this manuscript to light in a timely manner. All disqualifiers apply.

Preface

Copts are at the crossroads. Egypt is at the crossroads. The entire region is in the remaking. Pope Tawadros II was named as the 118th pope of the Coptic Christian Orthodox Church in November 2012, four months after President Muhammad Morsi was elected as Egypt's president, the first leader to rule over Egypt after President Mubarak's reign of thirty years and the country's first leader to come from within the ranks of the Muslim Brotherhood, a movement that was formed over eighty years ago to demand the instatement of an Islamic government. Pope Tawadros II is the successor to Pope Shenouda III, who reigned over the Coptic Church for forty years. Pope Tawadros II will preside over one of the oldest churches in the world, believed to have been formed around AD 48 by St. Mark the Evangelist himself upon his visit to Egypt. Today the Copts number around eight million, or ten percent, of the Egyptian population, representing the largest Christian minority in the Middle East. The pope also presides over a burgeoning Coptic diaspora of significant size in the United States, Europe, Canada, and Australia. Pope Tawadros II will have a tight balancing act to follow: to adopt a charismatic leadership like that of his predecessor, while pursuing genuine internal church reform.

Egypt is at the crossroads. The 25 January Revolution of 2011 which led to the ousting of President Mubarak was supposed to rid Egypt of authoritarian rule and put the country on the path of a transition to democratization. Yet the revolution, this book argues, was hijacked by the Supreme Council of the Armed Forces (SCAF), which arrived at a political settlement with the Muslim Brotherhood, the strongest, most organized political force on the scene at the time. This informal political settlement granted the Muslim Brotherhood political concessions to facilitate a fairly smooth accession to political power in return for securing the army a 'safe exit' from power—in other words, impunity from accountability and protection from budget transparency. At the time of writing, two years have passed since the 25 January 2011 revolt, yet the catchcries of the revolution, "bread, freedom, and dignity," are as far from realization as ever. The economic situation deteriorated dramatically after the revolution, with many Egyptians suffering from new economic hardships, including acute shortages in cooking gas cylinders and with daily electricity cuts running to several hours. As for freedom, new restrictions on the press and the media inhibit freedom of expression, while controls over human rights organizations and assaults on non-Islamist coalitions undermine freedom of association. Police brutality, one of the factors that drove many Egyptians to rise up to demand their human dignity in the revolution, has resurfaced.

Egypt is in transition, but transition to what no one can quite tell. The Muslim Brotherhood had vowed to adopt policies in recognition of the representation of all political, civil, and religious forces, yet this had not materialized. New forms of monopolization of power by the Muslim Brotherhood's Freedom and Justice Party (FJP), which has assumed political power, are reminiscent of the ways of the former ruling National Democratic Party, particularly in its latter days when it was informally run by Gamal Mubarak, the son of the ousted president. One of the most important benchmarks of a new political order, the Egyptian constitution, has failed the litmus test of recognizing full equality of all citizens, irrespective of religion, gender, class, and ethnicity.

The Coptic Orthodox Church is at a crossroads in its relationship with the new Islamist-led government. Bishop Pachomious, the acting pope from March 2011 until November 2012, had avoided open confrontational tactics with the new Islamist regime, while being quite vocal in his demand for a more proactive stance on the part of the government in dealing with the escalating violence and assaults waged by Salafis and other Islamist groups against the Coptic citizenry. Yet unlike with the previous regime, where there was some degree of clarity as to the points of entry to backdoor policy-making processes (for example, through Zakariya Azmi to relay messages to President Mubarak), at the time of writing, the policy-influencing processes in relation to President Morsi remain opaque. Will Pope Tawadros II seek to forge an entente with President

Morsi as had his predecessor with President Mubarak, or will he seek to remain at an arm's length as had Bishop Pachomious in relation to SCAF and subsequently Morsi? Will the new pope adopt a pacifist approach or pursue strategies of resistance and confrontation? This book provides the political-historical background of Church–state relations necessary to situate the new modes of engagement that will unfold between the two new leaders—the leader of the Coptic Orthodox Church and the leader of post-revolutionary Egypt—and explains the wide node of power configurations in which they are embedded.

Egypt's Coptic citizens are at a crossroads themselves. After participating side by side with their fellow Egyptians in the 25 January Revolution there were high hopes that the banner of "Muslim, Christian, One Hand" raised during those eighteen days of the uprising would mark a new phase in Egypt's history. There was a firm hope that the revolution would represent a break with a past—one characterized by a buildup of sectarian tension over the previous forty years, which culminated in the bombing of a church in Alexandria on 1 January 2011 that left twenty-five dead and over two hundred injured, an act allegedly attributed to the State Security Investigations apparatus (SSI). Yet, as this book illustrates, sectarian violence against Egypt's largest non-Muslim minority has taken a turn for the worse, in terms of both the frequency of incidents (increasing from 45 incidents in 2010 to 70 in 2011 to 112 in 2012) and their level of atrocity (the crushing of peaceful protesters by army vehicles in a systematic manner, the cutting off of a citizen's ear, the expulsion of citizens from their villages and towns, and the imposition of taxes on Copts in return for their survival are but some examples). There have been multiple reactions from the Copts of both a flight and a fight nature. One response has been the exodus of an unknown number of Copts from Egypt. Another has been the withdrawal of Copts from elements of societal participation. Another response has been the emergence and growth of Coptic civil society and attendant forms of activism.

Against the backdrop of the burgeoning of a deeply active post-revolutionary political society in Egypt there appeared a number of Coptic movements, coalitions, and initiatives, most notably the Maspero Youth Movement, which has contested and defied both SCAF and the Islamists and sought to hold them to account for their violation of citizens' rights, in particular those of the Copts. Such emerging movements, although they are seen by the wider polity as being driven by sectarian motives, in effect serve to amplify the voices of Coptic citizens in their demand for their rights vis-à-vis the government and society. Such movements also challenge the role of the Coptic Orthodox Church as the sole political representative of Copts in relation to the state. In effect such movements may create new spaces for Coptic citizens to directly contest the status quo without requiring the mediation of the Church.

Copts are also at a crossroads vis-à-vis the internal reform of the Coptic Orthodox Church. Pope Tawadros II is expected to revamp the power configuration within the church institution in relation to the different tiers of leadership. The pope faces a challenge from Coptic groups that demand a new system of governance to deal with requests for divorce and marriage, which lay exclusively in the hands of Bishop Paula under his predecessor's reign. He also faces pressures from internal groups who demand new systems of accountability and transparency, and an increased role for the laity in church governance and management structures.

In short, this book is written at a particularly dynamic moment in Egypt's history. It sounds alarm bells on the emergence of a non-inclusive political order premised on majoritarianism that threatens the very fabric of Egyptian society.

15 January 2012

Introduction
A Future of Crescent without Cross?

This is the end of sectarianism in Egypt: from now on there will be no more conflict between Muslims and Christians. Or so some who participated in the 25 January Revolution in 2011 that led to the ousting of President Mubarak believed. The lifting of the Crescent and Cross high in the sky, the Qur'an and the Bible, the hymns and Friday prayers, were all compared to the 1919 Egyptian revolution against British colonial rule, that other historical juncture celebrated by Egyptians as the apex of national unity.

Yet the high hopes that the ousting of an authoritarian leader would lead to a transition characterized by justice, equality, and freedom were in many ways, eighteen months on, dashed. As Egypt held its first post-Mubarak presidential and parliamentary elections, many argued that the country was successfully meeting its milestones for building a democracy. Perhaps from a liberal democratic procedural viewpoint, Egypt was ticking the right boxes. However, from a substantive point of view, the foundations laid were not those of an *inclusive* democracy. Sectarian violence against non-Muslim minorities such as the Christians, Baha'is, and even Muslims such as the Sufis grew by 30 percent from the previous year and doubled from 2008/2009. In Upper Egypt, local religious and community leaders were laying down conditions for the reconstruction or renovation of a church, which they deemed should occur without the external symbols of a Christian place of worship—no cross or bell, please. In Cairo, the protests against sectarian assaults in which demonstrators held aloft crosses and religious symbols were seen by many passersby and by wider public opinion as a provocation to Muslim sentiment—how could they raise the Cross high in the country of Islam?

As sectarian violence escalated and new configurations of power brought Islamists into parliament, many Egyptians wondered whether there was a place for the Cross alongside the Crescent.

This book is about the challenge of building an inclusive, as distinct from a majoritarian, democracy in Egypt. It seeks to make a contribution to the literature on transitions by analyzing the tensions between majoritarian democracy and inclusive democracy, with its greater focus on the substantive experiences of marginalized citizens. *Copts at the Crossroads* argues that the tyranny of majoritarian democracy can seriously undermine social cohesion and generate new inequalities, even if it appears to be following 'milestones' on the path to democratization.

This is a historical juncture for Copts, for Egypt, for the region, and for the world because of a number of major political transformations, and hence the aim here is to explore the positioning of, and dynamics of, change influencing the Arab world's largest religious minority, the Copts, over the past fifty years, with a particular focus on the 2000–2012 period. Religious and ethnic minorities had been in a general state of insecurity in the Middle East for some time, but this unease was exacerbated by the revolts that shook the Arab world from the end of 2010 onward. It is important to note that the kind of political settlement that unfolds in Egypt and its implications for religious pluralism will have a ripple effect beyond Egypt's national borders. In Syria, for example, many Christians became weary of supporting the revolutionary forces as Christian refugees flooded in from Iraq and as they heard (and watched) what was happening to the Christians in Egypt. At the top of the *People under Threat* report for 2012 are countries from the Middle East such as Syria, Libya, Yemen, and Egypt, which have risen significantly in the ranking of countries at risk of mass killings. The report notes that the opening up of political spaces has created a situation in which minorities are scapegoated. "The huge changes taking place across the Middle East and North Africa, while increasing hopes for democratization, represent for both religious and ethnic minorities perhaps the most dangerous episode since the violent break-up of the Soviet Union and the former Yugoslavia," suggested Minority Report's director, Mark Lattimer.[1] It has been estimated that some 350,000 Copts left Egypt in 2011, although there is no methodologically sound means of verifying this.[2]

While there is a copious amount of literature on the Copts in Egypt and in the diaspora,[3] almost all of it tackles the period prior to the 25

January 2011 Egyptian uprising. This book covers the period prior to and after the revolution, up to the presidential elections of May–June 2012. Hence, in addition to analyzing the power configurations existing in the decades before the 25 January Revolution, it also examines questions such as: "Why was the show of national unity at the time of the ousting of Mubarak followed by an escalation of sectarianism? Did sectarianism indeed increase and, if so, why and how?"

The intended focus here are the relations among the state, the Church, Coptic citizens, and civil and political society against the backdrop of a growing diversification of actors, a change in the country's political leadership, a change of leadership within the Church, and the transformations occurring in the region more widely.

Although by no means exhaustive, it seeks to engage with the micro- and macro-dynamics of power relationships, therefore involving more visible sources of power (high-ranking political officials, Church leaders) as well as backstage but highly influential players (the State Security Investigations apparatus, the diocesan bishops). Elements of these relationships have been explored in some of the literature, but often in isolation. For example, there is a substantial body of literature focusing on the state–church relationship (most recent examples of which include al-Bishri 2011; Labib 2012; Sultan 2008; Tadros 2009b; Taha 2010; al-Sheikh 2011), relationships between the Coptic Orthodox Church hierarchy and its followers (Shafik 2011; Zakhir 2009; al-Baz 2005; Zayan 2011; Ghobrial 2008; Beshay 2010; Kamal 2012), or the relations among Copts, the state, and society (the most recent of which include 'Abd al-Fattah 2010; Riyad 2009; Abu Ghazi 2009; Hassan 2009; Ashmawy 2009; Hassan 2010; Khalil 2010; Guindy 2010; Shobki 2009; Baraka 2011; Bebawy 2006; Van Doorn-Haarder and Vogt 1997). In this book, I attempt to disentangle the multiple relationships existing across several levels rather than focus exclusively on one set.

Moreover, a multidisciplinary approach is adopted here, one that draws on history, politics, sociology, and anthropology. The methodology, for example, combines a case study of the micro-level dynamics of engagement as well as insider-informant perspectives on what is happening on the ground with macro-political analysis captured through semi-structured and open-ended interviews and secondary data analysis as well as quantitative analysis of incidents of sectarianism from 2007 to 2012 (see methodology section on page 16).

Copts at the Crossroads seeks to bring in the perspectives of actors whose voices have conventionally been sidelined. It is argued throughout the book that there is a dominant narrative that has assumed hegemonic proportions with respect to the story of sectarianism in Egypt. Leach and Dry (2010) suggest that one way to understand how a particular society reacts to crises is through an examination of the narratives explaining them, since narratives are more than stories; they are stories "with purposes and consequences." The hegemonic narratives on the nature and causes of sectarianism are often elitist in their perspectives and tend to mute the voices that reflect stances that conflict with theirs. In this book, there is an attempt to capture counter-narratives because by restricting ourselves to dominant narratives, the nuances of what is happening beneath the surface are missed. A record of alternative narratives is also important as a means of reflecting the proliferation of Coptic activist voices that has taken place in the past five years in particular, and to reflect the emergence of political and social movements and groups, some of which have identifiable constituencies and mobilizational power.

The narratives I have sought to capture are those with a different reading of the experience of the Copts across different historical phases (chapter 1), the narratives of those who led and participated in the uprisings (chapter 6), those who interpreted and reported on sectarian events (chapters 5 and 7), and even Copts who joined Islamist parties (chapter 10). All of this is a consistent reminder that Copts are not a homogeneous group with a common worldview and agenda. By presenting these voices, we are breaking the monopolization of representational power that decides whose views are conveyed and whose are necessarily sidelined or muted.

Transitions from Authoritarian Regimes and Social Cohesion

While the interpretation of the political transformations in Egypt needs to be contextualized in terms of the country's own historical and political trajectory, nevertheless, the literature on transitions is very relevant to this critical juncture in Egypt's history. Remnants of former authoritarian regimes may take time to be dismantled, and democratization hardly ever follows a linear path. Furthermore, a transition from a dictatorial regime may produce different kinds of political orders. For minorities in religiously and ethnically plural societies, the new political order may produce an inclusive democracy or a tyrannical one. Transitions from authoritarian rule in ethnically and religiously heterogeneous societies have been known to exacerbate ethnic tensions. Democratization processes in Africa, Asia, and Eastern Europe in deeply divided societies spawned in some instances high levels of violence (Johnson 2002). Some countries, such as Yugoslavia, disintegrated into political violence; others, such as Romania, were able to avoid that pathway, despite the fact that both countries are characterized by a high degree of ethnic heterogeneity.

It is not the intention here to review the literature for a blueprint of how sectarian conflict can be avoided in times of transition, since the constellation of factors, both agential (the kind of actors and leadership) and structural (contextual and historical factors) are context-specific in how they produce different power configurations. However, it is noteworthy that countries that have undergone transitions without an escalation of sectarian tensions, such as Romania, Bulgaria, and Slovakia, all shared one common political strategy despite their very different contexts, and that is that they did not focus only on introducing democratic procedures, such as elections, and building institutions for reorganizing state–society relations, but also paid special attention to building *inclusive democracies*. The idea behind inclusive democracies as developed by Arend Lijphart (1977) is that the only way to integrate excluded groups into political orders is to introduce policies and practices that recognize difference and that accord groups representational power and the ability to contribute to state building without having to deny or negate their distinctiveness. This is critically important, because it cannot be taken for granted that political and social orders will be accommodating once authoritarian shackles are removed, or that social cohesion will be a byproduct of the process of democratization. Mungiu-Pippidi (2006: 646) succinctly summarized this as follows:

> What worked in postcommunist Europe were formulas to make unitary states more inclusive and more accountable, through the adoption of international legal standards for minorities, strong external pressure to ensure that these laws were implemented, and national cooperative politics. Individuals, however, not communities, remained the constituents of the state. This is the package that has produced successful states and fair political societies.

Romania is a good case in point because it showed a political will to integrate minorities even when other crucial elements of democratization, such as a shift to complete civilian control, were stalled. Although it took almost ten years before it was possible to talk of a democratic order, and it managed to avoid ethnic violence despite the prevalence of simmering tensions beneath the surface, Romania's difficult transition has much resonance with that of Egypt, in that the demise of the Ceaușescu dictatorship in 1989 was not followed by the instatement of a democratic system of governance. The country underwent a period of 'quasi-authoritarianism,' as substantial elements of the former communist regime remained intact and continued to exercise significant political power up to 1996, when the liberal opposition came to power (Cawther 2010). Romania also has a sizeable ethnic minority, amounting to about 10 percent of the population.[4]

Carter Johnson's study of Romania's and Bulgaria's transitions from communist rule for the 1989–99 period suggests that both Balkan countries did not experience protracted violence despite the presence of significant Hungarian and Turkish minorities in their respective populations. He argued that "it cannot be overstated that ethnic relations in these two countries have benefited immensely from the fact that they are inclusive democracies" (Johnson 2002: 8). One factor that creates an environment conducive to an inclusive political system is an electoral system based on party-list proportional representation. This encourages parties to form coalitions to reach power, making coalition-building with minorities necessary. Moreover, minorities can be represented in party proportion lists in a way that supports their integration into the wider political system. While this does not in and of itself secure minority integration, it can, if accompanied by other enabling factors, encourage enhanced political representation. Party-list proportional representation seems to have been successful in creating a political platform for Romania's largest ethnic minority—the Hungarians—who established a political party, the Democratic Union of Hungarians in Romania (UDMR), which has been successful in gaining representation in every single round of elections since the fall of communism (Protsyk and Matichescu 2010: 34).

On the other hand, while party proportional lists were a step in the right direction in Romania and Bulgaria, "this did not guarantee inclusion in government; frequently political parties either did not need the minorities' political seats to form a coalition or else opposed cooperating with the minority parties for fear of being 'ethnically outbid' by other nationalist parties" (Johnson 2002: 19). This accounts, for example, for the fact that mainstream parties, irrespective of whether they were right- or left-leaning, did not adopt an active strategy of putting forward persons belonging to ethnic minorities on their party lists (Protsyk and Matichescu 2010: 34). To counter this, and to encourage genuine political representation in both parliament and government, a system of reserved seats in parliament was instituted in the 1990 Romanian parliamentary elections to ensure representation of all of those minorities that were not successful in crossing the electoral threshold in the party-list system. The rule applied was one seat per minority and a minimum vote requirement for a minority organization to claim a seat (Protsyk and Matichescu 2010: 32). What is particularly striking about the reserved-seat system is that minorities did not need to have established political parties in order to compete for these seats. Civic ethnic organizations were able to compete for a seat as long as they received 5 percent of the vote (raised to 10 percent in 2004) .

Mihaela Mihailescu argues that, by and large, it is the participation of minorities in the political system that facilitates a non-violent transition from authoritarianism. He contends that in the case of Romania and Slovakia (with Hungarian minorities of 7.1 and 10.6 percent, respectively), "violence was averted due to the inclusion of ethnic minorities in the national political system" (Mihailescu 2008: 554). His study showed the importance of minorities' ability to form coalitions that can then use their political weight to negotiate agendas with other opposition forces. Two factors enabled this process to succeed in Romania and Slovakia. The first is that the minorities in both contexts had "coalition potential," which Mihailescu defined as "the capacity of ethnic minority parties to command stable constituencies, obtain significant electoral results, and be strategic players in the formation of any alternative governmental coalition." This proved critical in the case of the Hungarian minority in Romania (Mihailescu 2008: 561). In both countries the Hungarian minority represented a political bloc that voted for the Hungarian parties, and this gave the latter political clout and made them attractive allies to the democratic opposition in both countries, hence paving the way for interethnic cooperation.

The second critical factor was the ability of ethnic minorities and opposition parties to work around a "minimum consensus," that is, to agree on the absolute minimum terms of engagement that would take into account the political demands of the constituencies facing the different actors and to work around a formula that would balance those interests. Arrival at a minimum consensus was also made possible because the opposition parties needed allies to increase their clout. In both Romania and Slovakia, opposition parties had emerged from communist rule weak and lacking in a strong institutional base, and hence forming coalitions with ethnic minorities proved politically desirable.

An important factor identified by many analysts as helping to avert political violence in transition was the moderation of the demands of the leadership of the Hungarian minority political parties. They were ready to compromise and select their issues based on areas of consensus. This made them appealing to the other opposition parties and laid the groundwork for collaboration. In both Romania and Slovakia, ultranationalist political parties accused the opposition parties that formed alliances with the Hungarian political parties of treachery and of lacking in patriotism. To avoid losing their appeal to the wider citizenry without forgoing their alliances with the minority political parties, these parties adopted a politics of minimal consensus. In effect, it meant that

> Romanian and Slovak politicians would support Hungarians on some issues on which there was agreement, while dissenting matters would be set aside and not discussed by the partners. This tactic allowed the Romanian and Slovak oppositions to preserve the advantages of cooperation, while minimizing their costs by distancing themselves from the more radical demands of the Hungarians and thus making the interethnic relationship more palatable to their voters. (Mihailescu 2008: 575)

In Romania, Bulgaria, and Slovakia, inclusive political practices were instated despite their lack of popularity among the majority of the population and in spite of strong opposition from some political circles, such as ultranationalist political parties. However, an important factor that helped legitimize the ruling powers' inclusive politics is that the policies were established against the backdrop of the majority of citizens' desire for their countries to accede to the European Union (EU). The EU required the improvement of minority conditions as necessary proof of these countries' commitment to democratic values. Such a condition for EU accession served as a political incentive for governments to commit to minority rights and to use the EU card as justification to the majority population of why such policies were advantageous.

Egypt at the Crossroads

Situating the Egyptian case study within the broader literature on transitions and the quality of their inclusiveness would suggest that an exclusionary political order was put in place from the very moment the Supreme Council of the Armed Forces (SCAF) took over. In some ways, SCAF had the political maneuvering space to put in place the foundations of an inclusionary political system, but regrettably such an opportunity was missed. Building on the repertoire of national unity euphoria created by the eighteen days of the Egyptian uprising, SCAF could have instituted policies to promote inclusive politics. However, it lacked the political will to do so, and was discouraged from pursuing such a path by the informal settlement it had forged with the Islamists, as will be discussed below. Further, unlike the case of the Eastern European countries, there was no international 'carrot' to motivate SCAF to show a commitment to the integration of minorities. To the contrary, SCAF seemed determined to show that it was disassociating itself from its western allies, in particular the United States, which had been one of the principal international actors to have evinced an interest in the status of minorities in Egypt. Moreover, SCAF seemed to be leaning toward support from Arab countries such as Saudi Arabia, which have no interest in the status of the country's minorities.

The chronological order in which different political forces joined the uprisings is significant to an understanding of how the political settlement between SCAF and the Muslim Brotherhood and other Islamist forces came about. Youth groups such as the April 6 Movement and some political forces such as the Mohamed ElBaradei national committee orchestrated a number of major protests on 25 January, successfully appearing in places not predicted by the security forces. However, they were subjected to a ruthless clampdown for the next three days, during which many lives were lost and many people disappeared. On Friday 28 January, the Muslim Brotherhood, which had officially announced that it would not participate in the uprisings, said that it would join the revolutionaries. Late that night, the army took to the streets. From this point onward, evidence seems to suggest that there was a planned military coup against Mubarak, orchestrated by the army and led by Field Marshal Muhammad Hussein Tantawi, then minister of defense. On 4 February, Tantawi visited Tahrir Square and called upon the protesters to ask the Supreme Guide of the Muslim Brotherhood to enter into dialogue with Omar Suleiman, then Egyptian vice-president.[5] This was a highly significant step in view of the fact that the regime had never officially entered into dialogue with the Muslim Brotherhood at so high a level and had never referred to it as anything but the "the outlawed." Suleiman met with the Muslim Brotherhood with a view to forging a deal, even though the youth revolutionary forces had insisted that no deal be struck.

The Mubarak regime continued to respond to the popular uprising with methods of repression and control, but without success. On 11 February, Omar Suleiman announced Mubarak's "departure," declaring that Mubarak had handed power to SCAF. At first, the youth groups welcomed SCAF's takeover—after all, had it not been for the army's intervention against Mubarak, there would have been some very bloody massacres and possibly a civil war. However, shortly after Mubarak's ouster, the first indicators of SCAF's alignment with the Muslim Brotherhood began to appear in the form of a political settlement, that is, an agreement reflecting the fact that "the best interests of both parties are served in a particular way of organizing political power."[6] This kind of political settlement between the two parties can best be described as an informal pact, which are "uneasy arrangements between elites that find accommodation through the brokering of interests. These may stagnate, often as a result of prolonged crisis" (DFID n.d.). The informal pact established between SCAF and the Muslim Brotherhood did eventually stagnate. It culminated in a standoff in the presidential race in which Ahmad Shafiq, a former air marshal, ran against Muhammad Morsi, the Muslim Brotherhood candidate. However, it will be argued that the rules of the game brought about by this informal pact involved highly exclusionary political practices that led to the deliberate suppression of non-state actors such as youth coalitions, non-Islamist political parties, women, and religious minorities.

Evidence of the informal settlement between SCAF and the Islamists began to manifest itself in several ways. Shortly after the ousting of Mubarak, the youth revolutionary forces, a loose coalition of different groups, began to hold SCAF accountable for its failure to deliver on the youth groups' political demands by calling upon people to go to the streets in so-called *milyuniya*s (one-million-person protests) to demand their rights. The Muslim Brotherhood and other Islamists prohibited their members from joining and threatened to expel those who broke ranks and went ahead with the protests. A systematic campaign to demonize the youth groups began, instigated by both the state media, now in army hands, and the Islamists' outreach channels, primarily mosques and the media.

Specific political concessions began to be made in relation to the Islamists. Despite the fact that the Egyptian constitution prohibits the emergence of parties based on religion, all of the Islamist parties were easily registered, with no mechanisms to hold them responsible for showing compliance with the law, a theme we return to in chapter 10.

The informal SCAF–Brotherhood alliance reached its peak around the time of the constitutional amendments that were put to a countrywide referendum in March 2011. SCAF put forward a number of constitutional amendments that would in effect serve to consolidate its power while simultaneously facilitating the Islamists' accession to power. SCAF and the Islamists urged the people to vote yes on the proposed amendments in the referendum. The youth revolutionary forces and non-Islamist political parties urged a no vote. The Islamists' instrumentalization of religion was effective in mobilizing the majority to vote favorably for the constitutional amendments. The constitutional amendments stipulated that parliamentary elections should precede the writing of the new constitution, which was to be followed in turn by the presidential election.

The implications of the constitutional amendments for the configurations of power are highly significant. First, by fast-tracking parliamentary elections ahead of the writing of the constitution, the amendments by default positioned the Islamists in a privileged stance with respect to other political forces and the youth revolutionary movements. The Muslim Brotherhood had been engaged in established forms of political activity for over eighty years, with extensive outreach in its constituencies via the mosques and the welfare services provided through its non-governmental organizations (NGOs). The youth revolutionary movements and coalitions as well as new emerging non-Islamist political forces simply did not have the time to develop their party structures or constituencies quickly enough to compete. As predicted, the Islamists (the Muslim Brotherhood and the Salafis) won a majority in parliament, one with hardly any members of the youth movements that instigated the uprisings.

While the Muslim Brotherhood declared its commitment to drawing up Egypt's new constitution via an inclusive and consensual process whereby men and women, Muslims and Christians, secular and Islamist forces would all be represented, it in effect captalized on its majority status in parliament to try to impose an Islamist majority on the one-hundred-person constituent assembly responsible for drafting Egypt's post-revolution constitution. The liberal forces, together with al-Azhar University and the three churches, withdrew from the assembly in protest, and it was later declared unconstitutional by the Supreme Constitutional Court. Evidently, had the constitution been drawn up before the parliamentary elections through an inclusive process, the Islamists, who had not yet achieved a parliamentary majority, would not have been able to assume majority representation in the constituent assembly.

It can be inferred from the unfolding political situation that the terms of the SCAF–Muslim Brotherhood alliance were that SCAF would facilitate the Islamists' access to political power in return for the Islamists controlling the streets so as to undermine the revolutionary forces' resistance to military rule. Moreover, one important aspect of the deal was that in return for SCAF's role in facilitating the Islamists' ascension to political power, the latter would allow them a 'safe exit' from power, which would grant them political immunity from future prosecution.

The political exclusion of the Copts from power-sharing can be understood as one of the many outcomes of the SCAF–Brotherhood alliance. In addition to the new government's increasingly sectarian discourse and policy and practice toward Copts, the youth revolutionary forces and political movements that had initiated the uprisings were also excluded from power sharing. Moreover, women's rights experienced the worst backlash in over two hundred years. Laws giving women a modicum of rights were at risk of repeal, women's political representation in parliament fell from the previous year, and women were increasingly assaulted on the basis of their attire (Tadros 2012a). In effect, the lack of the emergence of an inclusive democratic political order is a direct consequence of the informal pact, or political settlement, forged between the Muslim Brotherhood and SCAF, a theme that we will return to in chapter 6.

Copts at the Crossroads

It was not only Egypt that was at a critical juncture but the Coptic Orthodox Church and Coptic citizenry as well. There was a reconfiguration of power unfolding within the Coptic community due to a revival in Coptic citizens' social and political activism. Another factor was the death of Pope Shenouda III in March 2012 and the question of who was going to succeed him to become the 118th pope of the Coptic Orthodox Church. Each of the two factors will be discussed separately below.

The Coptic Orthodox Church leadership's absolutist grip on the power to be the sole political representative of the Copts had been on the wane well before the January 2011 uprisings. It began with two distinct but politically weighty phenomena. One was the internal challenge to its authority, which came from two groups. The first comprised Coptic groups and actors within civil and political society that demanded internal reform and greater accountability on the part of the Coptic Orthodox Church leadership. One of the most prominent was the lay group established in 2006 and led by Kamal Zakhir that sought internal reform of the institutional running of the Church. Although Zakhir's group sought internal accountability within the Church ranks, it was also outspoken in its criticism of state policies toward incidents of attacks on Copts. The second group within the reformist camp called for reform of the Church's management of personal status affairs. This was a much smaller group than the other, with far fewer sympathizers among Copts, largely because of the very conservative social attitudes among Christian Orthodox followers toward divorce. This group was very vocal, however, and staged some prominent protests.

The second challenge to the Coptic Church leadership came from a number of groups and movements that assumed a political position on sectarian assaults on Copts at odds with that of Pope Shenouda III. Some of the leaders within that camp were also among those who advocated for internal institutional Church reform. One of the most prominent actors was the group that produced *al-Katiba al-qibtiya*, a newspaper that became widely read by Copts. While the newspaper served as a platform through which to report on incidents of assault on Egyptian citizens of Christian affiliation, out of or in parallel to it grew a protest movement that became highly vocal in publicly calling to account the state for its complicity in sectarian assaults against Copts. After the revolution, the group that formed around *al-Katiba al-qibtiya* and other similar groups coalesced into what became known as the Maspero Youth Movement. Also to emerge were a number of smaller groups, some of them offshoots from the Maspero Youth Movement. However, these were still in a nascent stage as they tried to establish a constituency among Copts and beyond.

An important phenomenon that had gained ground, in particular in the 2000s, was the political involvement of Copts in major resistance movements such as Kefaya. This reflected what was happening in Egyptian society at large: the retreat of people from political parties as a forum for political activism and their increasing participation in movements and coalitions that cut across partisan interests. In Kefaya, the movement's founder, George Ishak, a Copt, emerged as an iconic figure, the coordinator of a movement that openly challenged the Mubarak presidency and the possibility that Hosni Mubarak might pass the reins of power directly to his son Gamal. Kefaya was not only highly critical of the Egyptian government but also targeted Mubarak more personally, something which had been considered a no-go area before.

The Egyptian revolution further reshuffled the configuration of power within Coptic activist circles. First, Pope Shenouda III emerged as a highly unpopular figure in view of his earlier stances supporting Mubarak and Mubarak Junior and his directives to all bishops to instruct their parishes to tell Coptic youth not to join the 25 January uprisings. As a result, the Coptic Orthodox Church leadership in post-Mubarak Egypt entered a political cocoon—it chose to keep a low profile, at least between March 2011 and March 2012.

In tandem, the withdrawal of the Church's hegemonic power in political matters relating to Coptic citizenry and in mediating between the laity and the state also led to the emergence of a number of politically important Coptic movements. They emerged out of several forces: first, the general fervor of political activism, and, second, the escalation of assaults on Coptic places of worship, citizens, and property that catalyzed a collectivization of efforts aimed at challenging increasingly sectarian levels of polarization.

After the ousting of President Mubarak, levels of participation by Egyptians in their country's political life grew steadily. Since the Copts are not a homogeneous group, different public figures and groups gravitated toward different liberal political parties. With the exception of Rafik Habib, who was appointed deputy head of the Muslim Brotherhood-affiliated Freedom and Justice Party (FJP), most Copts joined liberal political parties. For example, prominent business tycoon Naguib Sawiris founded the Free Egyptians Party, renowned political thinker Emad Gad became associated with the Egyptian Social Democratic Party, and Amin Iskander, a political activist in the Kefaya movement, renowned for being a Nasserite, currently heads the Karama Party. The Copts' participation and involvement in these parties was high. Michael Mounir, a figure associated with the lobbying power of the Coptic diaspora, formed his own party, Hizb al-Hayat, announcing that the party is not premised on religion and is open to all Egyptians.

However, the party's Coptic membership seemed to be considerably less than that of the Free Egyptians or the Egyptian Social Democratic Party, for example. This may be indicative of the Copts' perception that the fulfillment of their aspirations for inclusion in public life is most likely to be achieved when they partake in a greater political project able to attract support from the wider Egyptian population.

In effect, the cumulative impact of the growing activism of Copts in civil and political society was to weaken the earlier understanding established between the Church leadership and the state, in which the pope was the political representative of the Copts (see chapter 3). It meant that the emerging political landscape came more to resemble that which existed before the 1950s, in which there was no monopolization of political power by any one actor and a plurality of actors with different power bases influenced the agenda-setting processes and platforms with respect to the Coptic question.

There are similarities in the new power configuration with that which existed prior to the 1950s in terms of diversity of causes and heterogeneity in the composition of movements, groups, and political orientation. However, there is also a major difference in that the new political landscape has democratized the spaces through which Copts can participate and lead. Prior to the 1950s, political leadership for Copts was mostly restricted to the *arakhna*, the elitist corps of wealthy Copts. Admittedly, there were Copts who were active in civil society organizations, but generally they did not wield as much political power. In the twenty-first century, the leadership comes from a broad-based class background. The middle class, in particular those members associated with the Sunday School Generation (see page 30), have assumed prominent leadership roles. However, Coptic activists from more modest backgrounds have also been able to assume leadership positions in various revolutionary projects. Moreover, these Coptic leaders have built a constituency using 'people power' that cuts across class distinctions (see chapter 8).

After the revolution, the death of Pope Shenouda III in March 2012 represented the other important rupture with the status quo that may lead to a reconfiguration of power in the relationship between the Church, Coptic citizenry, and post-Mubarak authorities. In terms of the relationship between the Coptic Orthodox Church and the citizenry, the death of the pope came against the background of a section of the Coptic citizenry that had become much more politically active and which therefore wished to play a more active role in the selection of the pope's successor. The law regulating the selection of the patriarch is highly controversial in terms of the criteria for nomination, who has the right to vote, and the process of selecting the final candidate himself. With respect to the criteria for nomination, lay Coptic groups objected to the idea that existing bishops presiding over dioceses have the right to nominate themselves, which they argued runs counter to the laws of the Coptic Church.

In terms of the right to vote, the hegemony of the clergy over the process has generated a sense of marginalization among the laity. Bishops are empowered to choose the lay members from their dioceses who will have voting powers. Finally, in terms of process, the committee that is charged with selecting the five to seven pre-final candidates can reject nominees without being required to offer any justification for its decisions.

The intensity of competition between the bishops and monks for the papal seat reached its peak during the first half of 2012. Never before in the history of the Coptic Orthodox Church had there been seventeen nominees (ten monks and seven bishops). The race for the papal seat took place against a backdrop of ambiguity over the role of al-Majlis al-Milli (see page 62) and much internal contention concerning the kind of leadership that would be most equipped to steer the Church through such tumultuous times.

Methodology

The methodological approach pursued in the course of my research speaks to two of the main aims of this book: to capture not only the highly dynamic relationships across the macro–micro levels, but also alternative narratives from actors whose voices have conventionally been excluded from mainstream accounts of sectarian matters. In order to do this, it was critically important to go beyond interviewing the intelligentsia, who are the conventional port of call for quotations on sectarian matters. In doing so, my position as a Coptic Egyptian woman was important in influencing this study. My social repertoires and networks within the Coptic community both in Egypt and in the diaspora provided me with insider information and access to contacts and data. I consistently used triangulation and corroboration to verify the validity and reliability of the data collected. However, my research also presented me with significant ethical responsibilities to protect vulnerable participants and communities from a possible social or security backlash. In addition to a careful review of which data were appropriate for publication and which were not, I in many instances refer to informants whose identity I have kept anonymous.

This study has relied on both qualitative and quantitative research methods. In order to interpret the number, type, and frequency of incidents involving tensions between Muslim and Christian citizens, a quantitative analysis of reports in the press between January 2008 and December 2011 was undertaken.[7] Such a time phase allowed for an examination of the pattern of sectarian incidents and their type prior to and after the Egyptian revolution.[8]

The fact that the quantitative scoping relied on press reports is not without its limitations. Two important ones can be identified here. First, it is possible that certain incidents were simply not reported in the press for reasons of self-censorship, because they were deemed unworthy of publication, or because of security orders prohibiting publication. The second limitation relates to the nature of reporting in Egypt itself. As a former journalist myself I have observed first hand that ethical principles of objective and honest reporting are not always observed. This is often the case when reporters rely on only one side of the story or when they do not take the time to go to the field in the first place and instead call one of their fellow reporters to request second-hand information. To mitigate these two factors undermining the credibility of the data, two methods of verification were used: triangulation and corroboration. Press reports were corroborated with reports appearing on relevant websites and the Internet. Further, reports in one newspaper were corroborated with others consistently throughout the process. The quantitative scoping of sectarian incidents was important in showing trends in the numbers of incidents, the types of incidents that took place, and the actors involved in them.

The qualitative research undertaken involved the use of multiple methods of data collection. In terms of secondary data, a review of the literature in Arabic and English was undertaken and complemented with an analysis of press and media content as well as a review of gray literature (think-tank reports, human rights monitoring reviews, and so on). Primary data collection methods included interviews, political ethnography, focus groups, and action research. Between January 2011 and May 2012, interviews were conducted with a wide array of actors, including political activists, members of youth revolutionary groups, members of the clergy, Coptic Orthodox Church and Anglican Church leaders, members of parliament, journalists, and political analysts. In some instances these interviews were semi-structured and formal; in others they were open-ended and took the form of informal conversations. The form of the interview selected was based on an assessment of what would make the interviewee most comfortable and at ease. Political ethnographic approaches were adopted during the four-year period in which the research took place, in order to study the changes in public space, street politics, and the dynamics of interaction between the different actors. These interviews were highly instructive in revealing the power configurations of actors influencing sectarian matters and how contextual changes are influencing and being influenced by politicized religious differences.

Six focus groups were undertaken with Coptic women living in low-income residential areas in Mu'assasat al-Zakat in Cairo and in urban and rural Minya in May 2011. The purpose of the focus groups was to generate a sense of the pulse of the street from the perspective of characters whose voices have conventionally been ignored in the study of sectarian relations as a consequence of their class, educational background, and gender.

Action research was used as a method of collecting and synthesizing data in capturing the dynamics of change experienced by the garbage-collecting communities (*zabbalin*) of Cairo. Development practitioners working in local NGOs in these communities, who happened to be from *zabbalin* families, were provided with capacity development support to undertake research and then conducted interviews with members of these communities themselves in order to capture the garbage collectors' own narratives. The information was then used to inform developmental activities in the area. Data collected through action research was corroborated through information gathered through interviews I conducted myself and through secondary sources.

Outline of the Book
In order to show the continuity in those sources of sectarian tension that strained Muslim–Christian relations from the Mubarak era (and well before that) into the post-Mubarak years, and to explain the dynamics of sectarian relations within the context of the wider social, political, and economic changes affecting the country, events and issues are presented according to the chronological order in which they unfolded.

For example, the Camillia Shehata affair is first discussed as a matter touching on Church–State Security Investigations relations in chapter 3 and its micro–macro dynamics in the context of unfolding sectarian relations in chapter 4, and is revisited when it reemerges after the revolution against the backdrop of growing sectarian strife. I therefore deliberately seek to understand incidents against the backdrop of a particular political moment and leadership, with their underlying power configuration and historical nuances.

Chapter 1 engages with some of the terms that are used throughout the book. It starts with a brief introduction to the debate of who the Copts are, discusses the controversy surrounding their numbers, and accounts for particular historical narratives and their political significance. It analyzes changing perceptions of identity, questions of positioning within wider society, and uses of the term 'minority.'

Chapter 2 offers a quantitative description of the nature of sectarian incidents—their frequency, causes, actors, and other general characteristics, for the period between 2008 and 2011. It examines the three most important triggers for sectarianism in contemporary Egypt: the transformation of non-religious small-scale disputes into full-blown communal assaults on Copts, gender relations between two people of different religious faiths, and matters pertaining to the construction and renovation of churches. While each of these issues is discussed in detail in the chapters that follow, in this chapter there is a focus on showing how an analysis of the data when corroborated with other qualitative evidence dispels many of the myths surrounding the nature of these issues, and the reasons why they have contributed to sectarianism in Egypt.

Chapter 3 discusses the changing political dynamics of Church–state–citizen relations from the 1950s up to 2004, ending with the Wafaa Constantine affair. The chapter discusses the emergence of the Church leadership as the mediator of relations between the Coptic citizenry and the state, the marginalization of Copts in civil and political society as a consequence of Nasser's centralized state policies, the Islamization of political space from the 1970s onward, and the vicissitudes in the entente between the Church and the state up to the mid-2000s. It argues that although such an entente contained some elements of the pact established between the Pope and the authorities under Ottoman rule, nevertheless, the diversification of the centers and sources of power within the state and the Church made such a pact more complex, the ability of both sets of actors to keep their side of the deal more challenging, and the ultimate outcome more ambiguous.

Chapter 4 continues the discussion of Coptic Church–citizenry–state relations from the mid-2000s onward and examines the behind-the-scenes tug-of-war between the SSI and the church leadership that arose in the wake of the vendetta that emerged after the Constantine affair. It discusses attempts by the state security apparatus to contain Pope Shenouda III, his dwindling bargaining power vis-à-vis the state, and the emergence of alternative spaces of resistance among Coptic civil actors in response to the escalation of sectarian attacks against the Copts. It covers the period from 2004 to 2011.

Chapter 5 discusses the nature of the escalation of sectarian tensions in Mubarak's Egypt. It examines the causes for the communal violence against Copts at the micro level, and the role of the SSI in the mitigation, management, and resolution of conflict. It also examines the issues around which sectarian tensions arise, that is, Christian places of worship, gender relations, and the transformation of petty fights of a non-sectarian nature between individuals into full-blown communal clashes. This is done through an examination of a number of vignettes and cases.

Chapter 6 examines the dynamics influencing the Copts' engagement with the uprisings that led to the ousting of President Mubarak. It commences with the protests following the bombing of the Two Saints Church in Alexandria on New Year's Day in 2011, which served as one of the precursors to the 25 January Revolution. It examines the high turnout of Copts as participants in and organizers of the 25 January uprisings, and analyzes what their involvement means in view of the position of the churches and other actors against the uprisings. The chapter discusses the motives behind their participation in the uprisings and their representation in the revolution before and after the ousting of Mubarak, and focuses on their own narratives of change. Finally, it offers some clues as to why sectarian sentiment resurged in such powerful ways after 11 February 2011 (the date of Mubarak's ouster).

Chapter 7 discusses the factors behind the escalation of sectarianism in post-Mubarak Egypt. It first analyzes why Tahrir Square represented a time-and-space-bound positive rupture in Muslim–Christian relations and not a point of transformation, and then documents the series of sectarian incidents that followed in 2011 and early 2012. It examines three main questions: What constellation of factors and actors has contributed to their instigation? To what extent are they reminiscent of sectarian incidents at the time of Mubarak? Do we see any patterns in how sectarian incidents are handled?

While chapter 7 ends with a discussion of how sectarianism has influenced the positioning of the Copts in the wider polity, chapter 8 is about agency in the form of resistance, subversion, and protest, and offers insights into some of the dynamics of Copts' mobilization around particular grievances. Chapter 8 provides a scoping of the actors who have participated in forms of resistance, their agendas, positioning, and relationship with the Coptic Church, Copts, and the state.

Chapter 9 presents a case study of the protests and the ensuing massacre that took place at the state television and radio building in Cairo known as Maspero on 9 October 2011. It discusses the ripple effects of the army's assault on peaceful protesters on the relationship between SCAF and the revolutionary movements, on the relationship between the Maspero Youth Movement and the Coptic Church leadership, and the question of how the governing powers deal with Coptic resistance.

Chapter 10 inverts the conventional question asked in relation to the Copts and Islamists by engaging with perspectives of different Copts' on the Muslim Brotherhood's Islamist project. The chapter analyzes why the demise of the Mubarak regime did not lead to the Copts turning a new leaf in relation to the Islamists. This is followed by a discussion of the establishment of Islamist parties and the extent to which their emergence violated the constitutional principles prohibiting the formation of religious parties. The final part of the chapter focuses on the Copts who joined Islamist parties, examines the prospects of their assimilation or integration, analyzes their profiles and reasons for joining, and inquires as to their expectations and assumptions about these parties' agendas.

Chapter 11 examines the first two elections in Egypt's post-Mubarak era in view of their centrality as 'milestones' in the transition from authoritarianism to democracy. The elections were in reality displays of deep sectarianism, for while they were heralded as marking a new phase in Egypt's history, their sectarian nature, it will be argued, seriously jeopardized the possibility of building an inclusive order, not only in terms of electoral politics but also in terms of social cohesion more broadly. The chapter also raises the question of whether Islamist parties that purport to be civil actors while simultaneously deploying Islamic references do not in fact represent an oxymoron.

The concluding chapter highlights emerging trends and possible scenarios for future configurations of power and their implications both for Copts and for the prospects of building an inclusive democratic order for Egyptians. It examines the possible future of the entente between Church and state, the dynamics of Coptic protest movements, and the kinds of political orders that the transition may produce and their impact on the extent of integration or exclusion of Copts in the wider polity.

1 | The Copts of Egypt

The Copts through Coptic Lenses

The word 'Copt' derives from the Greek word *Aigyptos*, meaning 'Egyptian.' Until the Arab conquest of Egypt in the seventh century, the word 'Copt' meant 'Egyptian,' which was synonymous with the word 'Christian,' since it was the religion of the majority of the Egyptian populace at the time. The Arabs subsequently used the word *Qibt* (Arabic for 'Copt') to refer to the inhabitants of the Nile Valley (Hassan 2003:17).

Many Arab and Muslim scholars have devoted considerable attention to the study of the Copts and their origins and history, including Ibn al-Kandi (n.d.), al-Mas'udi (1916; 2005), Abul Ja'far (AH 1407), and Abu Zulak (1999).

The socio-political use of the word 'Copt' is highly significant. In this book, the terms 'Copts' and 'the Coptic community' refer to Egyptians of a Christian origin, irrespective of whether they are living in Egypt or abroad. While recognizing the diversity of political affiliation, class, gender, and denominational affiliation within the group to which the terms apply, the use of the terms 'Copt' or 'Coptic community' does assume that there is a common identity based on being an Egyptian Christian.

Use of the terms would suggest exclusionary overtones, since Egyptian Muslims would not be able to claim that they are Copts. A minority of Egypt's intelligentsia, such as Sheikh Gamal Fawzy, professor of history and Islamic civilization at Cairo University, have sought to affirm the idea that all Egyptians—whether Muslims or Christians—are Copts,[1] a position first adopted by renowned intellectual Lutfi al-Sayyid in the nineteenth century (al-Sayyid 1937; 1945). Al-Sayyid was vehemently opposed by those who sought to affirm Egypt's Islamic character, such as Dr. Ilham Shahin, professor of creed and philosophy at al-Azhar University, in *al-'Ilmaniya fi Misr wa ashhar ma'arikuha*. In her book, she launched an attack on al-Sayyid for assaulting Islam by saying "Egypt is for Egyptians." Another example is Sayyid Hussein al-Afani, a Salafi writer, in his book *A'lam wa aqzam fi mizan al-Islam*.

Today, there are many Egyptians, such as members of the political party Misr al-Umm, who adopt this stance, but the notion does not have much currency in mainstream narratives, where references are almost invariably to "Muslims and Copts," not Muslims as Copts, for reasons we will discuss below.

The political association of the word 'Copt' with 'Christian' is very much embedded in history and in different representations of the history of the Coptic people through time and space, and often the narratives change depending on the audience. For example, in many written historical accounts by prominent Coptic historians and public figures, the history of the Copts begins with ancient Egyptian history, since they believe that the Copts are direct descendants of the pharaohs (Eskarous 1910; Mankarious 1913; Roufeilah 1898; Lajnat al-Tarikh al-Qibti 1922; Yuhanna 1983).

Brief History

It is beyond the scope of this book to provide a detailed description of Coptic Egyptian history, of which there are hundreds of excellent scholarly accounts. The outline I give here is intended to provide the minimal background necessary for understanding the changing trajectory of the Copts within the current socio-economic and political dynamic of the modern state of Egypt. It is noteworthy that, historically, when Egypt's situation was poor, so, too, was that of the Copts, and vice versa, when the country flourished, so the Copts' fortunes rose as well. However, this is not to suggest that religious identity played no qualifying role in the experience of the Egyptians. While all suffered or prospered at different times, there were particular instances where Copts were subject to forms of repression that were specifically associated with their religious status. The history of Coptic Egyptians can be divided broadly into five phases, as described below.

From conversion to the Arab conquest (AD 48–641)

The late renowned Coptic scholar Aziz Sorial Atiya argues that, ethnically, Copts are neither Semitic nor Hamitic but Mediterranean. He argues that there is some truth to the claim that they are direct descendants of the ancient Egyptians because "it is clear that their religion kept them from mixing with the successive waves of invaders from other faiths" (Atiya 1968: 16). It is significant that most accounts of the 'Coptic nation,' or *umma*, do not begin with the conversion of Egyptians to Christianity but go back much earlier, to the ancient Egyptians. This is because the notion of the Copts' lineage being tied to the pharaohs is central to the representation of their identity and sense of self, a theme to which I return later. Christianity is believed to have spread in Egypt through St. Mark, one of the Four Evangelists, in AD 48 (see, for example, Shenouda III 1975; Atiya 1968; Yuhanna 1983). Mark is regarded by the Coptic Church and its followers "as the first in their unbroken stream of 116 patriarchs" (Atiya 1968).

What followed, however, was a phase of intense persecution during the Roman occupation of Egypt. Yet, it is also during the fourth century that monasticism was founded in Egypt, from whence it spread to the rest of the world, representing an important contribution to Christianity as a whole (Toson 1996; Youannes n.d.). From a cultural point of view, the Coptic era commenced in the second century with the invention of the Coptic alphabet and the flourishing of Coptic art, music, and language. Most historical accounts place the Coptic Orthodox Church at the center of the preservation of Coptic heritage, in which it plays not only a spiritual but also a cultural and political role. In particular, Coptic Christianity acquired an international standing due to the Catechetical School of Alexandria, which "was undoubtedly the earliest important institution of theological learning in Christian antiquity. Its members were responsible for the formulation of the first systems of Christian theology and for some of the most monumental works of exegesis" (Atiya 1968: 33). Its fame spread not only for its theological standing but also for being a center for learning in a broad set of subjects in the humanities, sciences, and mathematics.

Following the period of intense persecution under the Romans, the natives of Egypt, the majority of whom had converted to Christianity, fell under another phase of intense persecution, most notably that of the Byzantine Era (311–641). Against the backdrop of an intense theological dispute between the Monophysites and Monothelites, commonly known as the Melkites, the patriarch of the Coptic Church, Benjamin, had to flee the Melkite colonialists who ruled over Egypt, his period of exile lasting for more than a decade.

From the Arab conquest to the end
of the Ikhshidid period (AD 641–969)

The year 641 marked the conquest of Egypt by Amr ibn al-ʿAs. He established a new covenant with the Christian Egyptians, the covenant of dhimmitude, and recalled Patriarch Benjamin from exile. The Copts did not resist the Arab conquest and in fact brought religious enfranchisement from the Melkites (Abd al-Rahman n.d.; Ibn Abd al-Hakam 1922; Soliman 1988; al-Metentawy 2002).

This period in Egypt's history was characterized by a certain degree of religious tolerance because the country's new rulers were not so much interested in religious obliteration as they were in the extraction of important natural resources for the sustenance of other parts of the Islamic caliphate. For those who resisted conversion to Islam, a *jizya*, or poll tax, was imposed on all able-bodied adult Christians barred from military service (Atiya 1968: 83). As the rulers who followed Amr ibn al-ʿAs raised the poll tax and increased the exploitation of Egypt's resources, this created a strain on both the finances of the native population and on agricultural land.

Between 739 and 773, there were five rebellions by Christians against the growing financial burdens being imposed upon them, with, in some instances, Muslims joining on their side. These rebellions and others ended with bloody repression, the most famous of which was the Bashmuric uprising of 829–30.

Fatimids and Abbasids (AD 969–1250): A period of decline

Atiya summarizes the period of the Fatimids for the Copts as follows: "The real grandeur and subsequent decline of the Coptic nation in Islamic times took place under the Fatimid Caliphs, who invaded Egypt from Tunisia in 969 and held it until 1171" (Atiya 1968: 87). The first ruler, al-Muʿizz li-Din Illah (932–75), looked favorably upon the Copts, and his successor al-Aziz bi-llah al-Fatimi (975–96) further raised the status of Copts, who prospered under the rule of both men and assumed prestigious positions of governance. This period of religious revival ended with the coming to power of Caliph al-Hakim (985–1021), a tyrant whose thirty-six-year rule was one of the worst in Egyptian history for Christians and Jews, and for Muslims, although not with the same intensity and brutality as that experienced by religious minorities (Mahmoud 1982; 1995).

For Christians, al-Hakim "enforced distinctive dress on Christians, whom he commanded to wear a five pound cross and on Jews who had to hang a heavy bell round the neck. Christians were dismissed from the administration and their churches were ordered to be demolished by letting loose the mob on them" (Atiya 1968: 89). According to al-Maqrizi (1998: 774), al-Hakim wrote to the prefects to empower Muslims to demolish churches, and in the period from 403 to 405 more than thirty thousand churches were demolished and their internal possessions plundered and endowments appropriated.

It is also during the twelfth century that the Coptic language, which had been allowed to thrive side by side with the Arabic language, was repressed and its usage severely contained (see Omar 1970: 19–55; Ishak 1997; 2001).

The practice of requiring Copts to walk while brushing against the wall as a sign of lower status also emerged during this phase, out of which came the popular Egyptian expression associated with Copts of *yamshu gamb al-hiit* (walking next to the wall).

The period that followed witnessed the First Crusade (1096–99), which, according to Atiya, "proved to be one of the greatest calamities that befell the communities of eastern Christians" (Atiya 1968: 92). This, he argues, was due to the fact that the Muslim rulers' antagonism to the holy wars of the Cross fueled their hostility toward all who venerated the Cross (Atiya 1968: 93). Numerically, the Fatimid period also saw a significant drop in the number of Copts, as large numbers converted to Islam.

Mamluks and Ottomans:
Dark ages for Muslims and Christians (AD 1261–1805)
Between the end of the Fatimid period and the rise of the Mamluks in 1261 were a few decades of chaos in which governance did not seem to be in the hands of one particular ruler. The Mamluk period from 1261 onward can be considered a dark age for Muslims and Copts alike, for Egypt suffered a decline in its political, economic, and social conditions (see Philipp and Haarmann 1998; Kassem 1994). It was one of the worst periods in Egyptian history, one characterized by intense persecution of Copts (Zaklama 1931; Zukhur 1993). It was also a phase that saw the degeneration of the Coptic Orthodox Church, in terms of both its international standing and its internal development.

Egypt became one of a number of satellite states within the broader Ottoman Empire in 1517. The millet system was instituted, which gave the Coptic Church's hierarchy substantial freedom to govern its followers.

However, this was also a period during which heavy taxes were levied upon Copts, Christianity was forced out of Nubia (southern Egypt) through terrorism and stealing, Pope Mark IV was imprisoned, and Copts were required to wear distinctive dress, all of which culminated in an atmosphere of insecurity for both Muslims and Christians (Malaty, in Makari 2007: 47–48).

From the rule of Muhammad Ali
to the 25 January Revolution (1805–present)

The era of Muhammad Ali has often been described as the beginning of the formation of the modern Egyptian state.[2] Particular attention was given to modernizing the country's agricultural base, raising standards of health and education, and putting an end to the predatory relationship that existed between Egypt and the Sublime Porte. Against this back-drop, Copts witnessed a renaissance, as over the course of several decades there was a shift in their status from one of dhimmitude to citizenship (Afifi 1992; Milad 1983; El Howeiry 2002; Winter 1992; Armanios 2011). The renaissance was also partly attributable to changes within the Coptic population, as a class of Copts became enriched as overseers of lands and possessions and their administrative abilities enabled them to excel. Under the rule of Khedive Sa'id Pasha (1854–64), the *jizya* was dropped and permission for Copts to be conscripted into the army was granted in 1855. When the first ever parliament was established in 1866, Copts were represented and voted in by both Muslims and Christians, suggesting that one more facet of Islamic governance—the prevention of Christians from assuming leadership or decision-making powers over Muslims—was removed. Muhammad Ali's grand modernization project also entailed the building of strong political and commercial relations with Europeans, and in the process European missionaries entered Egypt through Catholic missions beginning to gain ground in 1852 and Protestant ones in 1854.

In both instances, Protestant and Catholic missionaries were charged with working primarily among non-Christians, but they ended up taking the short cut and focused on converting Copts instead (Atiya 1968: 112–13). This they did through the provision of services, education in particular. The threat of conversion from Coptic orthodoxy generated a knee-jerk reaction within the Coptic Church, which faced the challenge of reforming itself quickly and sufficiently to compete with the

European missionaries (Richter 1910). In this sense a counter-reform movement emerged in response to the missionaries' work (Atiya 1968: 112–15) to address the Coptic Church's stalled progress, which had become particularly acute during the Mamluk era. Education and acculturation for the Church's clergy and laity became one of its top priorities. Peter Makari notes that "historical and contemporary tensions among the Christian communities exist over doctrine, social motivation, and political agenda" (Makari 2007: 42). And, indeed, there are those among the Coptic Orthodox Church leadership who have never overcome their deep sense of resentment for the Protestant Church for having captured some of their followers. Nonetheless, as will be argued in chapter 6, the 25 January Egyptian uprising created the conditions for solidarity across the followers of both denominations.

The ruler in Egypt privileged Catholics and Protestants in order to gain favor and secure interests with Europeans, both politically and commercially. Gradually some of these privileges were extended to Coptic churches. This represented a double-edged sword, because on the one hand it meant the granting of certain concessions that were not previously enjoyed, while on the other hand it meant that Copts' rights, given that they were an indigenous population with historical roots in and ties to the land, were being displaced as the term *galiya*, conventionally used to refer to foreign communities, was deployed to describe them instead.

The emergence of a nationally organized leftist movement in the 1920s had a major impact on the stratification of Copts and the forging of a space for an alternative positioning for a Copt. Until then, the Copts could be divided into three strata, the *arakhna* (elites), the clergy, and the general Coptic population. The elite class always had strong relations with the Coptic Church, even while it contested the Church's powers. Because of their wealth, members of the elite played an influential role in the Church and in politics (such as Habib al-Masri Pasha, Morcos Hanna, and others). The elite class has conventionally come to comprise the Majlis al-Milli to this day (see page 62) and until 1950 it played an active role in the political life of the nation as well. The second stratum comprised the general population that followed the Coptic faith and was subservient to the Coptic Church. Another class emerged as a consequence of the leftist movement, the members of which were not preoccupied with the internal matters of the Coptic Church but who were not necessarily opposed to the Church. What distinguished them was their commitment to secularism, and their strength came not from their wealth necessarily but from their political thought on matters of state and society. They came to comprise the Coptic intelligentsia. The founding members of this class include personalities such as George Henein, Fawzy Habashy, Ramsis Yunan, and Anwar Kamil. Examples from the generation that followed include Salama Moussa, Abou Seif Youssef, Youssef Karam, and Anwar Abd al-Malik—all renowned thinkers who played an influential role in the leftist movement.

After the 1952 Revolution (a period covered in chapters 3 and 4), the *arakhna* lost much of their wealth and subsequently their influence within the Coptic Church, yet the Coptic intelligentsia continued to grow. This class plays an important role in the country's affairs to this day, both politically and socially. The *arakhna* continue to be represented in the Majlis al-Milli, membership of which is still largely determined on the basis of wealth. It has, however, as a consequence of the Church–state entente lost much of its influence over the internal reform of the Coptic Church. Alternatively, a movement emerged in the 1940s, known as the Sunday School Movement, whose members were made up of *arakhna* and clergy intent on reforming the Coptic Orthodox Church. It has produced a generation of Coptic leaders such as Kamal Zakhir, who have led the lay movement calling for greater accountability, transparency, and a voice for the non-clergy in the Church.

What will be argued in the coming chapters is that as a consequence of the revival of a Coptic civil and political society in the final years of Mubarak's rule and in the wake of the 25 January uprising, another reconfiguration of power relations may be in the making within the Coptic community.

The Politics of Numbers

The issue of the population of Copts as a percentage of the total population is one of those unsettled questions that has stirred intense political debate, because of the absence of adequate census data and because of questions regarding the credibility of the data available.

On the question of availability, the last nationwide census, taken in 1986, indicated that Copts made up 5.6 percent of the population. Since then, there has been no official census to establish their number today. The credibility of the data has been questioned by Coptic scholars and activists, who have raised concerns as to whether the data collectors' officers sometimes show bias and, for example, mark Christians as Muslims to deflate the former's number.

More recently, the Central Agency for Public Mobilization and Statistics (CAPMAS) announced that there are no more than 4.6 million Copts, which is in line with the Pew Research Institute's estimate of Copts' numbers today.[3] According to the Pew Institute, the percentage of Muslims in Egypt is 94.7 percent, meaning that non-Muslims constitute a little over 5 percent of the population. It bases its estimate upon the Egyptian Demographic Health Survey of 2008, which surveyed 10,000-plus women aged 15–49 who had been married, and of whom 5 percent were Christians. However, even the Pew Institute acknowledges that there may have been a deliberate underrepresentation of Christians, although it nevertheless maintains that the percentage is not much higher in view of the lower fertility rate among Copts in comparison to the rest of the population.[4]

What is clear is that both CAPMAS and the Pew Institute are basing their estimates on a number of assumptions, the most important of which is that there has been a decline in the number of Copts across the years due to emigration and lower population growth rates. In view of the sharp sectarian sentiment characterizing the contemporary Egyptian context, this can only serve to deepen mistrust on both sides. For Islamists, it is further evidence that the Copts are exaggerating their number in a bid to demand disproportionate power, while for Copts, deflating their numbers is seen as part and parcel of a political project aimed at undermining their presence and weight in the country.

The government is to blame for a lack of transparency in releasing credible data on this question. If national censuses are costly and their data-collecting process brought into question, there is a simple, straightforward way to arrive at credible data: the civil registrar. All Egyptians generally do follow the officially required procedure of registering newborns at one of the health offices affiliated to the Ministry of Health. Deaths are also registered. Both documents bear the religion of the person. By deducting the number of deaths from the number of those whose births are registered, it should be possible to arrive at a fairly accurate representation of the number of Christians in the country. The failure to release such data simply adds fuel to the fire of rumor and suspicion.

Islamist writers such as Muhammad Selim al-'Awa, Muhammad Emara, and Tarek al-Bishri do not believe that the official numbers may suffer from bias, hold that they are 'scientific,' and argue that they are a true representation of the size of Coptic citizenry in Egypt. Al-Awa suggests the percentage of Coptic citizens in Egypt is 6 percent,[5] while Muhammad Emara suggests that the figure is that of the 1986 census, or 5.9 percent of the population. Emara and al-Bishri both suggest 6.24 percent based on the 1976 census (El Bishri 2005). Abu al-'Ila Madi, the founder of al-Wasat political party, has also suggested that the percentage of Copts does not exceed 6 percent.[6] It is important to note that the figures cited by these Islamist writers are based on censuses taken in 1976 and later, at a time when President Anwar al-Sadat was encouraging the Islamization of Egypt and was in a battle with then Pope Shenouda III. In 1978—one year after the release of the 1976 census in 1977—Sadat put the number of Copts at two million. Coptic activists in the diaspora accused Sadat of fabricating the number. A political crisis exploded in 1977 when during a meeting between Pope Shenouda III and President Jimmy Carter in the United States, Carter spoke of the Copts in Egypt as numbering seven million. Carter's statement drew deep anger from Islamists, although Jehan al-Sadat's autobiography is revealing on this matter. Sadat writes about the 1977 commissioning of a high-level parliamentary committee to investigate sectarian matters, which subsequently published the well-known Oteifi Report. She notes,

> During a month, Anwar proposed a political solution to religious violence and appointed a committee of Muslims and Copts in parliament to investigate reports on sectarian tension, and after he studied the results of the committee's investigation, Anwar took a just position toward the sectarian problem and to retrieve the trust of *6 million Copts in Egypt* (al-Sadat n.d., author's emphasis).

The Coptic Orthodox Church's own estimate is that Copts constitute 20 percent of the total population.[7] Bishop Morcos, the spokesman for the Coptic Church, has announced that the number of Copts is between ten and twelve million, thus constituting about 15 percent of the Egyptian population.[8] More recently a prominent Coptic figure, Tharwat Bassily, who was also a member of the Majlis al-Milli, said in an interview in January 2012 with *al-Ahram* that the total population of Copts was 18,565,484 as of January 2012. Given that CAPMAS's official figure for the total population is 81,395,000, this would suggest that Copts represent 22.81 percent of the population.[9]

Judge Selim Naguib, a former member of the International Court of Justice, believes that the 20 percent estimate is probably closer to the real figure because it is based on the number of baptisms certified in the Church. However, Naguib also gives reasons for why the Coptic population may be diminishing, which would therefore account for a smaller percentage figure than that cited by the Church. These include: lower birth rates among Copts; the emigration of Copts to Australia, Europe, and the United States, estimated to be around two million since emigration began in the 1960s and until the 1990s (Khalil 1999: 34–35); and conversions from Christianity to Islam, estimated to number around 15,000 annually.

Muhammad Hassanein Heikal, the prominent intellectual and one-time editor-in-chief of *al-Ahram*,[10] estimated that Copts comprise about 11.6 percent of the population (Heikal 1983: 19). Heikal's figure is probably the most realistic, given that he based it on the census undertaken at the time of Nasser, meaning during a phase in Egypt's recent history when there is no reason to assume that there was a political will to deflate the figure. Moreover, Heikal's figure seems to be the most convincing in view of the fact that the Church's own estimate (roughly 20 percent) does not account for the factors cited by Naguib above. The numbers question has grave political ramifications on all aspects for public life, as will be shown below.

The question of the percentage of the Coptic Christian population would be inconsequential were citizenship the framework through which rights and duties are mediated. However, citizenship, as will be shown in the next chapters, has been more rhetoric than reality in Egypt for a large number of people. In times of acute political transformation, when there was a heightened debate surrounding Egypt's identity, the numbers question has assumed center stage—for example, when Sadat was reframing his own identity and that of Egypt in Islamic terms during the 1970s, and, more recently, against the backdrop of Islamists' ascent to political power following the ousting of Mubarak.

In the power struggles that ensued in post-Mubarak Egypt, the number of Copts as a percentage of the Egyptian population came to the fore once again in three regards. First, if Copts were to be awarded representation in policy-making positions or the right to build more churches, should this not be commensurate with their size in society? Second, if the numbers of the minority are small, should they not comply with the will of the sweeping majority? Third, to what extent does the Coptic population represent a significant influencing bloc and under what circumstances?

The first question was raised against the backdrop of the poor representation of Copts in parliament, and in particular the numbers that should be represented in the national committee responsible for drafting Egypt's new constitution. The second question was concerned with growing references to the Islamic *marja'iya* ('reference') as reflecting Egypt's identity, and the necessity of recognizing that this view speaks for the majority of the Egyptian population. The third question became very significant in light of the presidential race between Muhammad Morsi and Ahmad Shafiq in 2011, when it was believed that Copts would vote en masse for the non-Islamist candidate (that is, Shafiq). In this particular instance the political weight of the Copts lay not in their numbers but in their ability to mobilize into a single bloc.

In terms of demographic distribution across Egypt, Saad Eddin Ibrahim proposes, based on the 1976 census, that Copts are more concentrated in Upper Egypt (10.8 percent) than in Lower Egypt (2.3 percent) (Ibrahim 1996), as well as concentrated in cities, such as Cairo. Islamist thinkers such as Muhammad Emara seem to agree on this point, suggesting that Copts tend to be demographically concentrated in Cairo and Upper Egypt (in particularly Minya and Asyut), where they make up 20 percent of the population. Historically, certain suburbs, such as Shubra in Cairo, and certain villages in Upper Egypt have been home to a high concentration of Copts. However, nationwide, segregation of Christians and Muslims in terms of residence has not been the norm and they have lived side by side as neighbors in building blocks, informal settlements, and village houses. However, my own ethnographic research in urban settlements such as Bulaq al-Daqrur in Cairo (2004) and in villages in 2011/2012 suggests that religion is increasingly playing a role as a determinant of residential abode. More and more, Muslim and Christian property owners are inclined toward leasing their property to members of their own faith. In post-January 2011 Egypt, informants living and working in Upper Egypt have noted that there has been some voluntary relocation of Christian families in hamlets or villages where there is a handful of them to bring them to live close by their relatives in urban areas such as 'Izbit al-Nakhl or al-Marg in Cairo or in large towns. The informants pointed out that the reasons are primarily to do with increasing religious discrimination, for example, Muslim employers no longer wishing to offer work to Christians, sustained pressure to convert, or a rising sense of threat to personal safety and well-being. Since this relocation has been happening with handfuls of families moving quietly and over time rather than en masse at one particular point, much of it has simply not been captured by the press, human rights monitoring groups, or Coptic lobby groups. However, the fact that it is taking place quietly and gradually does not preclude its potential cumulative impact. It is important to note that this geographical relocation, whether temporary or permanent on the part of many Coptic families coincides with other forms of socio-economic differentiation, for example, less engagement between Muslims and Christians as pupils at school and students at university, less interaction as co-workers, and more cautious interactions with neighbors who are of a different religion. This is not to suggest that such changes are happening across all of Egypt. To the contrary, deep-seated bonds of neighborliness, friendship, fellowship, and solidarity exist across all social classes, genders, and backgrounds. However, it is to suggest that in instances where voluntary or involuntary, temporary or permanent relocations on the part of Copts is occurring, there are often other ties that are being severed. Such demographic transformations, if they become more permanent, will no doubt have serious political implications.

To Be or Not to Be a Minority: That is *Not* the Question

Seteni Shami argues that the word 'minority' was first used in the early 1920s when the Egyptian public was debating whether the new Egyptian constitution should include specific language concerning the protection of minorities (Shami 2009: 153). By 1922 Egypt had gained independence from Britain although there remained areas in which Britain retained absolute control, including the defense of the interests of foreigners and minorities (Shami 2009: 164). An instrumentalization of Copts allowed external powers to justify interventionist policies in Egypt. Shami argues that in contemporary Egypt, under the international human rights framework, which has shifted the discourse from that of the protection of minorities to minority rights, the debate continues to be deeply influenced by a questioning of whether the agenda of minority rights is driven by interventionist goals. In other words, championing the rights of Copts is frequently seen as a potential invitation for outside powers, the United States in particular, to interfere in Egyptian affairs. In the case of Egypt, this debate has been deeply embedded in a wider discussion regarding the United States' role in monitoring religious freedoms in the global South. Thus, as Shami suggests, in contemporary Egypt, one century later, the discussion of whether Copts are a minority continues to be deeply influenced by questions of foreign interventionist designs and national resistance (Shami 2009: 166).

I argue that there is a need to distinguish between a minority in the descriptive sense, that is, explaining the condition or state of being a minority, and a minority as a claims-making label. Copts are a minority in the numerical and political sense. In other words, not only does their affiliation to Christianity make them a minority in terms of number, but their status and their 'othering' also makes them a minority. If we resort to the definition of the Office of the United Nations Human Rights Commissioner, Copts qualify as a minority:

> A group numerically inferior to the rest of the population of a State, in a non-dominant position, whose members—being nationals of the State— possess ethnic, religious, or linguistic characteristics differing from those of the rest of the population and show, if only implicitly, a sense of solidarity, directed toward preserving their culture, traditions, religion, or language. (Office of the United Nations High Commissioner for Human Rights 2010)

All the above-named factors apply in the case of the Copts: being in a nondominant position, possessing religious characteristics distinguishing them from the rest of the population, and having a collective sense of awareness of their particular identity and heritage.

However, the fact that many Copts in Egypt are aware of their particular identity and positioning as a minority does not mean that they choose to represent themselves or wish to be labeled by others as such. In fact, in none of the public claims making by Copts in Egypt was the banner of a minority raised. The reasons are many. Certainly, for the Coptic intelligentsia, they are aware of the highly controversial implications of using a term associated with western instrumentalization. However, it would seem that there are other reasons that discourage many Copts from using the term 'minority' for claims making. Use of the term would suggest that they are marginal to the mainstream, which would only add to their sense of exclusion.

The term 'minority' would also suggest that their rights should be proportional to their minority status. Further, by representing themselves as a minority, they would play into the Islamist discourse of being protected as *ahl al-dhimma*, that is, as a religious community that is protected by the majority Muslims (Galal 2012: 47–48). The discourse propounded by many leading Islamist writers, such as Muhammad Moro and the late Sheikh al-Ghazli, that Copts are the happiest minority in the world is a salient one. As a result, activists who advocate for Coptic rights often frame their claims in terms of the rights of all Egyptians, as opposed to the rights of a religious minority, to equal treatment.

The fact that many Copts opt out of identifying themselves as a minority does not suggest, however, that they believe that their status is equal to that of Muslim citizens or that their religion is not a differentiating factor. The words 'discrimination' and 'persecution' have featured prominently in many of the narratives of Coptic citizens with whom I have spoken. Nonetheless, this does not make Copts a passive locus for the exercise of hegemonic power, for their agency is expressed in multiple forms, including open resistance and subversion, in response to being denied full citizenship rights.

A dual discourse is adopted by the Coptic Orthodox Church to deal with this:

> The Christian identity promoted by the Church has not only rejected the designation of Copts as a minority, and as second-class citizens, but has also endorsed Christianity as a primary identity without compromising Egyptianness, positing the former as an integral part of the latter. This simultaneity is achieved through a combination of social activities, religious narratives and practices. (Galal 2012: 51)

Galal talks about how stories of martyrs and saints feature prominently in Copts' stories, and embedded in such stories is their agency in negotiating their own identities:

> The saint and martyr stories are stories about sufferings representing experiences of the minority that cannot be fully conveyed, either because the majority are not able to sense or acknowledge them or because the official memory is not able to contain them. Like the national unity narrative, the official memory needs the minority experience to be silenced. (Galal 2012: 55)

To speak of minority experiences through stories about the saints and martyrs, as part of a grand Coptic Orthodox Christian narrative, constructs individual suffering as universal, as the struggle against inhuman violence and hence against inhumanity, rather than the struggle against a specific historical—Roman or Muslim—sovereign (Galal 2012: 56).

The following chapters suggest that Copts have been exposed to religious discrimination, here defined as discourses, policies, and practices that differentiate between people on the basis of their religious affiliation, whether individually or collectively. It is argued that there are instances in which they have been exposed to persecution, defined here as a systematic and insidious form of discrimination against persons or a group. The phase following the 25 January uprising and throughout the first year of transition qualifies as a period of persecution (though there are instances that reflect this during the preceding thirty years as well).

Identity Matters

In the conceptual framing in the previous chapter, it was argued that inclusive democratic systems offer the greatest prospects of recognizing and addressing pluralism. What will be argued here is that the most inclusive identity marker, the one that has created the ripest conditions for Muslim–Christian cooperation in the contemporary history of Egypt, has been that of Egyptian nationalist identity. It is argued that while pan-Arab and Islamist identities have claimed to be inclusive, in practice they can be highly assimilationist, the common grounds for their universal identity resting on the denial of Coptic identity, if to a greater or lesser degree.

Coptic identity and conceptions of the Coptic *umma*

The earliest books by Coptic authors available (dating back to the advent of book publishing in the eighteenth century) all describe the basis of Coptic identity as being a common ancient Egyptian heritage, which is based in turn on notions of historical roots in the land and ties to the civilization, to a heritage dating back thousands of years.

This is, for example, the line of argument presented by Tawfiq Eskarous, a Coptic Egyptian lawyer and historian, in *Nawab' al-Aqbat wa mashahirahum fi al-qarn al-tasi' 'ashar* (Exceptional and Famous Copts of the Nineteenth Century). Eskarous was renowned for founding one of the oldest and most important Coptic civic associations, Gam'iyat al-Nash'a al-Qibtiya. It is also presented in Youssef Mankarious' *Tarikh al-umma al-qibtiya fi sanawat min 1893–1912* (The History of the Coptic Nation in 1893–1912); by Ramzy Tadros, the author of *al-Aqbat fi al-qarn al-tasi' 'ashar*) (The Copts in the Nineteenth Century); as well as by Yacoub Nakhla Roufeilah, historian, linguist, writer, and founder of *al-Watan* newspaper, and the author of *Kitab tarikh al-umma al-qibtiya* (A History of the Copts). It is supported by Isis Habib el Masri, one of the few female Coptic scholars and author of the eleven-volume *Tarikh al-kanisa al-qibtiya* (The History of the Coptic Church).

This notion of the Coptic *umma* has been salient in Coptic scholarship for at least a hundred years, if not more. However, the implications of this sense of being grounded in ancient Egyptian history can be either inclusive or exclusive. The mainstream discourse adopted by Coptic historians is that this presents a common Egyptian history binding together all Egyptians, Christian and Muslim.

At the same time, this affinity to the land and the celebration of a phase in history preceding the Arab conquest can also be transformed into a supremacist, exclusionary discourse that refers to Copts as the original inhabitants of the land and others as having lesser claims to it. An example of such a discourse appears in an interview in the widely read newspaper, *Al-Masry Al-Youm* (15 September 2010), with Bishop Bishoy (see page 93), one of the most powerful figures, second to the pope in the Coptic clerical hierarchy. It is also a discourse adopted by some Copts living in the diaspora, such as the late Shawky Karas. However, the discourse of guests and rightful original inhabitants does not have much currency, whether among the Coptic intelligentsia in Egypt or among the Coptic population at large.

When Egypt was under British rule (1882–1952), a political project aimed at promoting *al-umma al-misriya* (the Egyptian nation) emerged, championed by Ahmad Lutfi al-Sayyid, known as the father of Egyptian political liberalism. Al-Sayyid's vision was of an Egypt independent from both British colonialism and the caliphate (unlike Mustafa Kamil's vision, which saw Egypt as part of the Islamic caliphate).[11] In 1907, he established a political party, al-Umma al-Masriya, which attracted many Egyptians and was premised on the notion of the Egyptian *umma* being founded on a distinct Egyptian identity and heritage, Egyptian colloquial Arabic, and ancient Egyptian civilization. Taha Hussein (1889–1973), the renowned literary figure and intellectual, also championed the idea of an Egyptian nation state, categorically pitting it against the notion of its incorporation into the Islamic caliphate. Again, his followers were both

Muslims and Copts. The political project of an independent Egyptian nation state was revived in the 1970s in the aftermath of the peace accord signed by President Anwar al-Sadat with Israel, which led to the expulsion of Egypt from the Arab League. Prominent Egyptian writer Tawfiq al-Hakim (1898–1987) and Coptic intellectual and writer Louis Awad (1915–90) championed the notion that Egyptians are not Arabs. When Arab leaders sought to punish Egypt for the peace treaty with Israel by expelling it from the Arab League, al-Hakim wrote a highly controversial article in *al-Ahram* newspaper entitled *al-Hiyad* (3 March 1987), in which he argued that Egypt should assume a nonpartisan stance, empathizing with neither Israel nor the Arabs, and insisted that Egypt should not be represented as Arab. His article generated a fierce and decades-long debate among intellectuals about Egypt's identity.

Pan-Arabism, which reached its apex under Gamal 'Abd al-Nasser, was not championed by the Coptic intelligentsia or population at large, yet Copts did not vehemently oppose it in the way they opposed pan-Islamic identity. One can divide the Copts' engagement with pan-Arab identity into roughly three categories. The first category are those who see a tension between their Coptic Egyptian identity and Arab identity insofar as the latter does not recognize the national specificity of Egyptian culture and history. For these Copts, the Arabization of Egypt represented the repression or containment of Egyptian Coptic identity. Hence, they find it difficult to identify themselves as Egyptian Copts and Arabs simultaneously. This discourse has been openly adopted by many of the writers of *al-Katiba al-qibtiya*, who see the Arab entry into Egypt as a case of invasion, not emancipation. It is also the unstated assumption held by many Copts, even if they do not publicly express it, although there are exceptions, such as Kamal Farid Ishak, a lecturer at the Coptic Studies Institute in Cairo and author of *Mihnit al-hawiya al-qibtiya wa mihnit al-lugha al-qibtiya*.

The second category of Copts are those who identify themselves as Copts but who believe that their identity is reconcilable with the Arab identity. Examples include the late Pope Shenouda III and Milad Hanna, the writer and former minister of housing who served as a member of parliament under President Sadat. Generally, this group of Copts has tended to occupy leadership positions of high public import, and hence their discourse has tended to be outwardly oriented vis-à-vis the wider public. Their identification with Arab identity has manifested itself in their championing the Arab cause. For example, Pope Shenouda became known as the "Pope of the Arabs" in recognition of his role in championing the Palestinian cause and the Arab right to Jerusalem. Pope Shenouda argued that "belonging to one identity binds the Egyptian people, our absolute loyalty to the civilization that binds together all the Arab people" (Shoukry 1991: 130). For Milad Hanna, the Egyptian personality is the cumulation of "layers of civilization on top of each other" (Hanna 1993: 18). In his well-known *al-A'mida al-sab'a li-l-shakhsiya al-misriya* (The Seven Pillars of the Egyptian Personality) Hanna puts forward the notion that throughout Egypt's long history, the Egyptian personality has come to be shaped by a new melding of identities: the ancient Egyptian, the Coptic, the Arab, the African, and the Mediterranean. It is also worth noting that these leaders all come from what became known as the Sunday School Generation (see page 30).

The third category comprises pan-Arab intellectuals who happen to be Copts. Their primary allegiance is to pan-Arabism and they have sought to reconcile both identities by subsuming their Coptic identity to Arab nationalism. Unlike the Sunday School Generation, they were not significantly represented by the Coptic Orthodox Church and their Coptic Christian faith was not a significant identity marker. Examples of this category in the public sphere include Abou Seif Youssef and Ghaly Shukry.

Pan-Arabism only became a political project under Gamal 'Abd al-Nasser in the 1950s and 1960s (although it remains an influential strain of Arab political thought). The 1950s and 1960s were a phase during which most Copts withdrew from public life, as did many Muslims, as a result of the overall repression of civil and political society. Nonetheless, this was, by and large, a period of assimilation rather than integration. A pan-Arab identity required the subsumption of Coptic and Egyptian identity, and insofar as it meant solidarity with Arab nations on the basis of a common civilizational background, language, and geography, it was not considered as threatening to Coptic identity as the Islamic identity because it did not seek to actively suppress it. On the other hand, the more pan-Arabism became infused with the notion of a common religion, and the more its advocates invoked Islam as its central tenet, the more likely Copts became to disengage from it.

Egyptian Islamic identity has been consistently represented by most Copts as threatening to their Coptic Egyptian identity. Very few Coptic thinkers have espoused the idea of Coptic allegiance to an Islamic heritage. Among the notable exceptions is Rafik Habib. Habib never claimed to represent the Copts, and his profile and inclinations are at odds with those of the majority of Copts, who believe that he is more representative of the Islamist ideological wave. For a start, Habib was born into a Protestant family while the majority of Christians in Egypt belong to the Coptic Orthodox Church. Second, he is identified as an Islamist thinker in view of his defense of the Islamist civilizational project and his unstinting support for the Muslim Brotherhood. It is fair to make the generalization that the majority of Copts have no faith in the Islamist project. Habib does not have a following among Copts. He is not regarded with reverence or as a role model. In fact, many leading Coptic intellectuals told me in confidence that they believe that Habib's identification is more with the country's Muslim identity than the Coptic one.

It has also been widely circulated that Makram Ebeid, the renowned Coptic politician and one-time Wafd Party secretary general, championed the notion of allegiance to Islam as a national identity and Christianity as a personal faith. Needless to say, the current Islamist discourse of Copts and Muslims both celebrating their Islamic heritage and civilizational background has not gained currency among the majority of Copts. This narrative, which has been widely promoted by advocates of the Islamist political project rests on a number of arguments: first, that Copts have an affinity with Islamic civilization that reflects their values and social mores; second, that Copts' identification with Islamic civilization derives from their experiences of tolerance while living under Islamic rule from the time of Arab entry into Egypt and during the fourteen centuries that followed; and third, that it is only the mantra of shari'a, not that of liberal secularism, that can guarantee their rights. Rafik Habib elaborates on this perspective in *al-Wasatiya al-hadariya* (The Civilizational Middle Ground), arguing that one cannot speak of the Arab conquest or invasion because the Arab forces did not aim to colonize other countries but to disseminate values, which gradually became part of these countries' identities until there were no longer many nations but one nation that holds to the Islamic normative framework (Habib 2010: 156). He suggests that the Islamic *umma* is a multireligious, multinational entity based on a common civilizational ethos. Although, for example, Christians and Jews would not profess religious adherence to Islam, they would nonetheless be loyal to the values of the civilization to which they belong, namely the Islamic one (Habib 2010: 157). Hence, the Muslim will have a sense of belonging to the Islamic *umma* on account of his religious affiliation and civilizational ties, while the non-Muslim feels a belonging on account of his civilizational ties. The affiliation to the Islamic civilization, argues Habib, allows for a plurality of identifications. The Egyptian can have a national identity, an Arab one, and an Islamic one, all bound together by an affinity to a common base, the Islamic civilization (Habib 2010: 158). This common base founded on Islamic civilization is not a matter of choice for non-Muslims, for they are required to be loyal to it because it embodies the values of the majority and in order to ensure the unity of the Islamic *umma*:

> Naturally we have to emphasize that the non-Muslim who refuses to belong to the Islamic civilization and wishes to be restricted to national belonging is like the secularist who wishes to fragment the Islamic *umma* and transform it into disparate nations and this amounts to a political project in conflict with the Islamist project. (Habib 2010: 220)

Certainly, Habib's perspective belongs to a prominent school of thought in Egypt, but it is one espoused by Islamists, not Copts. Habib's idea has strong resonances with the ideas of Islamist leader Yusuf al-Qaradawi on these matters. The notion of Egyptians as joined by a common Islamic identity irrespective of their personal faith fails to grasp the fact that neither the Copts' reading of their history nor their direct experience of equality or the lack of it allows them to identify with this narrative.

Fundamentally the Copts' narrative is premised on the celebration of ancient Egyptian heritage and its civilization, language, values, and philosophical contributions. It rejects the notion that Egyptians are Arab, and while seeing Islam as a religion, it believes in a secular order in which religion is valued in society but is not the basis for a political system. The emphasis on Egyptian nationalist identity is not a negation of religious pluralism but rather an affirmation that it provides the most appropriate framework for securing it without giving supremacy to any one religion over the other.

In terms of a theoretical construct, it has little appeal within contemporary discourse. However, in practice it has proven to have strong mobilizational potential. In the past hundred years the moments in which citizen activism reached its apex, namely the 1919 and 2011 revolutions, were instigated in the name of Egyptian nationalism, not pan-Arabism or pan-Islamism. It is around these two instances—1919 and 2011—that the participation of Copts in the life of the Egyptian nation flourished.

2 | Overview of Sectarian Incidents (2008–2011)

This chapter provides an overview of the frequency, type, and geographical location of sectarian incidents, their triggers, their salience, and the actors involved in them, between 2008 and 2011. The purpose of the chapter is to capture nuances and highlight patterns of sectarian dynamics. More detailed and micro-level analysis of sectarianism is presented in chapter 5 with respect to incidents that occurred during the Mubarak era, while chapter 7 applies the same level of analysis to the first year of the post-Mubarak transitional phase. It is important to note that the database available (see pages 17–18) pertains to sectarian assaults on Coptic Christians only, although there have been several other sectarian incidents against Baha'is and Shi'is and in 2011 against Sufis, on their sacred sites.

Day-to-day monitoring of the press and comparisons across different newspaper sources was undertaken to make the coverage as comprehensive and as rigorous as possible, for the period from 2008 to 2011. From 2005 up to 2011, there was a relatively expanded level of political space, which allowed for a substantial level of press freedom, albeit within constraints. During this period, press reports on government corruption and poor governance on the part of high-ranking officials increased. The press also began to report, without inhibition, on taboo social subjects (such as incest and sexual abuse) and there was an increased interest in sectarian matters. While the reporting was often biased and distorted, it meant that there was almost a full documentation of the basic information, specifically that a particular incident happened on a particular day. Journalists informed me confidentially that from 2012 they were given instructions from their editors-in-chief not to report on sectarian matters, whether actual incidents, court rulings, or any other related matter.

From the table below, it is evident that there has been a steady increase in the number of sectarian incidents over time, from 33 in 2008 and 32 in 2009 to 45 in 2010 and 70 in 2011. What will be argued here is not only that the number of sectarian incidents has increased, but also that the level of intensity of assault has increased.

Table 1: Triggers of sectarian incidents (2008–2011)[1]

Trigger	2008	2009	2010	2011	Total No.	Total Percentage of total
Escalation of small disputes/fights	11	14	1	11	37	20.56
Building/expansion of Christian places of worship	1	8	10	15	34	18.89
Muslim/Christian gender relations	4	7	9	13	33	18.33
Reasons related to Coptic converts to Islam	3	0	13	6	22	12.22
Property disputes	7	2	3	3	15	8.33
Attacks on Christian protesters	0	0	1	4	5	2.78
News/rumors of defamation of Islam	2	0	1	1	4	2.22
Christian evangelical activities	1	0	2	0	3	1.67
Other reasons	4	1	2	1	8	4.44
Untriggered (no obvious reasons)	0	0	3	16	19	10.56
Total number of incidents	33	32	45	70	180	100.00

The geographical distribution of sectarian incidents (see Table 2 on page 49) confirms some long-standing claims of areas of tension, but also reveals some difficult-to-explain phenomena. What the data confirm is that the Upper Egyptian governorates combined (Beni Suef, Fayoum, Aswan, Asyut, Minya, Luxor, and Qena) have witnessed more than half the total number of sectarian incidents. Minya in particular had the largest number of sectarian incidents (thirty-six) throughout the 2008–2011 period. Since the 1970s, Upper Egypt has been the region most likely to experience assaults on non-Muslims. There are several possible explanations for this. Upper Egyptian governorates have the lowest human development indexes, which has implications for social relations. Another explanation is that this is an area with a high concentration of Islamist activism. A third reason is that it is an area that suffers from lax security and extremely low levels of governance. A further possible explanation is that this area of Egypt has the highest concentration of Christians. This explanation is further supported by the fact that Greater Cairo, which saw the second-highest incidence of sectarian assault, has a high presence of Copts. However, this can only be a partial explanation since sectarian incidents have also occurred in communities with only a handful of Coptic families. It is likely that poor security, extreme poverty, and a high concentration of Islamist activities have combined to accentuate the possibility of sectarian assault occurring there.

The second phenomenon, which is more difficult to interpret, concerns the governorates that have experienced no incidents of sectarian assault at all. There are six governorates that fit this description: Damietta, the New Valley, Port Said, the Red Sea (Hurghada), Sharqiya, and South Sinai (Sharm al-Sheikh).The question is why.

It is notable that these governorates do not represent a regional bloc and are situated in different parts of the country. It is possible that the Red Sea and South Sinai have low incidences of communal violence because they are tourist destinations (Hurghada and Sharm al-Sheikh, both main tourist cities, are in the governorates of the Red Sea and South Sinai, respectively), which has created a cosmopolitan atmosphere and a thriving economy. Port Said also has a thriving economy due to its status as a free economic zone, as well as a relatively high human development index. As for the New Valley, it is likely that there are no Copts there or else the percentage is negligible. Most perplexing are Sharqiya and Damietta. These two governorates are worthy of examination as cases of positive deviance, as they have a very low percentage of Copts. It is unclear what constellation of factors accounts for the absence of any sectarian incidents in these two particular governorates over the period from 2008 to 2011.

A third important finding is that there were governorates that had not experienced any sectarian incidents in the three years prior to the revolution but that witnessed flare-ups in the year following. These include Aswan, Sohag, and Ismailiya. This sudden escalation of sectarian incidents is bewildering. While some of these governorates, like Sohag, had witnessed sectarian assaults before (such as the infamous incident that occurred in the village of al-Kushh, Sohag), they had not experienced any sectarian incidents in at least the three years prior to the revolution. One possible explanation for the sudden resurgence is the growth in Islamist activity and the lax security situation.

It is striking that the largest percentage of sectarian incidents is not triggered by matters pertaining to religious difference. While on the surface this may seem reassuring since it suggests that tensions do not originate in religious difference, in reality this is a disturbing finding, for it shows that the potential for everyday ordinary disputes to tranform into full-blown sectarian incidents is high. This is not to suggest that matters associated with sectarian grievances do not precipitate conflict, as will be discussed below.

The highest percentage (20.56 percent) of sectarian incidents across the four years occurred where a petty fight or dispute erupted at a local level that had no religious causes whatsoever, but as the two parties involved had different religious affiliations, the matter escalated into a full-fledged sectarian clash.

This is striking, since this major trigger of sectarian tensions is hardly ever discussed: it is not addressed in policy circles or in the realm of human rights monitoring, nor does it feature on the agendas of Coptic rights advocates, locally or in the diaspora. Yet, this finding is corroborated by focus groups I conducted in Cairo in April 2012 with Coptic women living in the squatter settlement of Mu'assasat al-Zakat. They told me that what they feared most was the eruption of fights in their alley should their sons, in the course of playing football with their Muslim friends, enter a minor dispute that would escalate into a sectarian matter. One of the boys would damn the religion of the other, who would return the insult; the adults would subsequently interfere and then quickly mobilize along religious lines.

Since there is a power differential in most communities as a consequence of the Copts being a minority, once an ordinary dispute assumes a sectarian character, the Muslim majority not only becomes mobilized against the person involved in the dispute but also pursues the collective punishment of all the Copts in that neighborhood or rural area.

Table 2: Classification of numbers of sectarian incidents by governorate and year

Geographical distribution	2008	2009	2010	2011	Total	
					No.	Percentage of total
Alexandria	2	1	5	3	11	6.11
Aswan	0	0	0	2	2	1.11
Asyut	2	2	2	8	14	7.78
Beheira	2	1	1		4	2.22
Beni Suef	1	3	2	4	10	5.56
Cairo	3	2	8	19	32	17.78
Daqahliya	1	3	1	0	5	2.78
Damietta	0	0	0	0	0	0.00
Fayoum	3	0	2	1	6	3.33
Gharbiya	0	2	0	0	2	1.11
Giza	2	1	5	3	11	6.11
Ismailiya	0	0	0	2	2	1.11
Kafr al-Sheikh	1	1	1	0	3	1.67
Luxor	0	1	3	4	8	4.44
Matruh	1	0	1	0	2	1.11
Minya	12	10	6	8	36	20.00
Minufiya	0	0	1	0	1	0.56
New Valley	0	0	0	0	0	0.00
North Sinai	1	0	2	2	5	2.78
Port Said	0	0	0	0	0	0.00
Qalyubiya	0	0	1	1	2	1.11
Qena	2	3	3	2	10	5.56
al-Sharqiya	0	0	0	0	0	0.00
Sohag	0	2		11	13	7.22
South Sinai	0	0	0	0	0	0.00
Suez	0	0	1	0	1	0.56
Total	33	32	45	70	180	100.00

An examination of the incidents that fall under this category provides us with important insights into the most significant source of sectarian strife. In terms of triggers, while the disputes are in some cases caused by crimes, in most instances they are simply heated discussions on petty matters that can occur between any two citizens, anywhere. This is significant because it shows that there is considerable sectarian antagonism simmering beneath the surface, which can be sparked off at the slightest provocation. It shows that social cohesion is under extreme strain.

The fact that local disputes between citizens become transformed into full-scale communal clashes refutes the theory widely propagated by high-ranking officials and the press that sectarian tensions are the works of "hidden outside hands." It is striking the degree to which a community can mobilize its members to punish collectively the members of another community on the basis of their religion, even when they had nothing to do with the original dispute. It is in effect about the tyrannical instrumentalization of majority status to oppress the minority.

The transformation of a small-scale disagreement into full-scale violence suggests that the absence of law and order creates a catalytic environment for an escalation of tensions with great speed and scale. It is interesting, therefore, that the escalation of tensions occurs in low-income areas where human security is lowest. In poor rural and urban areas, there is hardly a policeman to be seen and the police station assumes little or no responsibility for citizens' safety (be they Muslim or Christian).

The dynamics of these incidents also suggests the absence of resolution mechanisms to deal with small-scale local disputes. For example, if a dispute unfolds as a consequence of claims made on the same resources (be it ownership of a football or a farm animal), the fact that it can quickly assume a religious character means that people do not trust the formal avenues of conflict resolution and prefer to take matters into their own hands. Moreover, the fact that the issue then becomes about winning a battle for one's religion indicates the extent to which society has internalized a sense of threat from the 'religious other.' It suggests that social harmony is undermined by deep-seated mistrust and hostility generated by a sense that religious difference is a source of conflict. Evidently, in every case where mobs have risen against a minority, there have been Muslims who have sought to protect them, to stand up for them, and to disassociate themselves from the acts of the majority. However, they have been a minority and often paid a heavy price socially for their position.

What is particularly alarming about the fact that ordinary citizen disagreements are being transformed into full-scale communal clashes is the spontaneity and unpredictability of such incidents. Whereas, for example, in the case of the construction or upgrading of a church, policy-makers can assume the worst and take precautions to protect the premises and raise awareness of what is about to take place, one cannot readily predict that price-haggling between a vegetable seller and a shopper will escalate into full-blown sectarian strife. It makes planning against such incidents far more difficult. It may therefore require years—possibly a generation—to change the social mores, values, and ideas that each religious community has about the other.

Interestingly, many of the recommendations for addressing religious discrimination focus on institutions in the formal sphere, such as the building of churches, the allocation of high-ranking posts on the basis of merit not religion, the increased representation of Copts in the legislature, and so on (see, for example, Morcos and Fawzi 2012). Yet, citizens' experience of discrimination and persecution is happening in the informal sphere, on a community level, not through institutions but through citizen-to-citizen interaction. This is not to suggest in any way that addressing discriminatory policies, laws, and practices in the formal sphere is unnecessary; indeed, it is a priority. It is rather to say that in order for the lived experiences of the majority of Coptic citizens to improve and harmony between Christian and Muslim citizens to ensue, due attention must be given to the unpredictable, spontaneous escalation of violence emanating from ordinary day-to-day disagreements and disputes.

Christian Places of Worship: Ticking Bombs

The second greatest source of sectarian strife (18.89 percent of all recorded incidents) is the construction, expansion, or upgrading of churches, with thirty-four cases happening between 2008 and 2011. This comes as no surprise in view of the fact that Christian places of worship have already been a source of contention on a micro-community level and on a macro-policy-making level. Some of the most violent sectarian assaults are associated with the construction/upgrading of churches, such as the Maspero Massacre of October 2011, which followed protests against the incident of al-Marinab Church in Aswan (see pages 184–85). It is in essence a question of legitimacy. For many, the problem is that Copts are circumventing the law, which clearly stipulates that official permits must be obtained for the construction of churches, and they are transforming houses intended for private residence into churches. This act of resurrecting a church behind everyone's backs and then presenting the community with it as a *fait accompli* is illegal, illegitimate, and provocative to Muslim sentiment. From the writings of some Islamist thinkers (Moro (1998), for example), restrictions on the construction of churches are regarded as necessary because otherwise Christians will be trying to build a church around every corner, with a view not to having a place of worship but to boasting of having a symbol of Christianity on every street. Hence, every time a church gets torched, plundered, or attacked by mobs, there is an attempt to explain such action on account of the church's illegality, that is, it does not have a permit, it is outside the law, and therefore deserves to be treated as such. In fact, in the case of the Marinab Church in Aswan, when the youth attacked a church under renovation, the governor himself defended the youth on the grounds that their actions were taken to remedy a faulty situation.

For many Copts, since the law is discriminatory, it is illegitimate. For the Copts, the question of the right to build, renovate, upgrade, or repair Christian places of worship represents one of their most deep-seated grievances and has been the source of much advocacy work by Coptic diaspora groups. According to Bebawy (2011: 11) there are 1,460 registered churches in Egypt, and if we were to assume that there are 11 million Copts, this would suggest that there is one church per seven thousand Christians. Bebawy offers a personal anecdote to show the discrimination against building a Christian place of worship, recounting that before his mother passed away, she requested from him and his siblings that the land she owned and which they were to inherit be dedicated for the construction of a church. After her death, out of respect for her will, he proposed that the land be used to build a church and a mosque and a public library in-between and that this be called the "national unity complex." He submitted the application to the authorities on 17 March 2000, received immediate approval for the construction of the mosque and library and only received the approval for the building of the church on 24 January 2011, almost eleven years later (Bebawy 2011: 11–12).

Until 1998, the construction and renovation of churches required a presidential decree (even for restoring a collapsing ceiling), after which Presidential Decree No. 13 was issued, relegating that responsibility to governors. In 1999, Presidential Decree No. 453 was issued, delegating to local councils the responsibility of granting permits for the construction of mosques and churches. However, there remained ten rules that served as criteria as to whether a permit should be granted. These qualifying criteria were issued by Ezaby Pasha, deputy to the minister of interior, in 1934 and are as follows:

1. That the land proposed for the construction of a church be vacant and is not being used for agricultural purposes at the time.
2. That the church be away from a mosque or a Muslim shrine.
3. To verify whether the proposed church will be built in an area with a majority Muslim or Christian population.
4. If within a Muslim population, that there be no objection to its construction.
5. That the denomination in question not already have a church in the same *balda* (county or village).
6. That the distance to the closest church for this denomination be determined.
7. If the proposed place for the construction of the church is close to the banks of the Nile or a stream, that the opinion of the irrigation authorities be obtained and, if near a railway, that the opinion of the specialized authority be taken.
8. That the number of people belonging to this denomination living in the county be determined.
9. That an official record be made, showing the shops nearby to the proposed church.
10. That the application be presented accompanied by an architectural drawing and with the signature of the head of the denomination. (Bebawy 2001: 46–47)

Given Egypt's high population density and the presence of a mosque on nearly every corner, this in effect makes it impossible for any proposed church to be granted approval. These guidelines continue to be applied to the construction of churches, although mosques are not required to comply with them.

The idea of issuing a law that addresses these discriminatory provisions has been on and off the government's agenda for at least a decade. In 2005, Muhammad al-Goweily, a member of parliament (MP) and person then responsible for the complaints committee in the People's Assembly, proposed a unified law for the construction of places of worship. In 2007 and 2008, a number of MPs (including Georgette Kalliny, Ibtisam Habib, Kamal Ahmad, and Essam Ahmad) put forth proposals for legislation for places of worship. However, these proposals never saw the light of day (Mounir n.d.: 54–55).

More recently, following a spate of assaults on churches after the 25 January revolution, the Supreme Council of the Armed Forces (SCAF) put forward another proposal for a unified law on places of worship. The proposed law delegated the responsibility for approval of the construction of a place of worship to the governor and according to a number of criteria, including:

1. That approval be granted by the Ministry of Endowments or the designated person responsible for the denomination.
2. That the places of worship be proportionate to the number and density of followers in the area and according to the real need for the performance of their religious rituals.
3. That the distance between one place of worship and another belonging to the same denomination be no less than one thousand meters.
4. That the place of worship not be built on agricultural land.
5. That the place of worship be built on an area no less than one thousand meters squared in size. (Bebawy 2001: 46)

However, the Islamic Council of al-Azhar University, the world's oldest Sunni mosque–university and Egypt's premier Islamic institution, rejected the law and suggested that a law for regulating the construction of churches be issued separately.[2] The Ministry of Endowments itself refrained from approving the law. The Coptic Church did not initially reject the law, but expressed its reservations over some of the articles; however, it seems that in order to show solidarity with al-Azhar, it took a stance in rejection of the proposed law.[3] By October 2011, there was no more mention of a unified law for places of worship and it was not raised during the first transitional parliament. It will probably remain shelved until another major crisis erupts and then be shelved again once the public mood has quietened.

In practice, the legal precepts applicable during the Mubarak era were irrelevant because the 'file' of church regulation was managed entirely by the State Security Investigations apparatus (SSI). This management process relied on backroom politics among the SSI, the diocese bishop, and the local priest. The process was succinctly articulated by Judge Noha al-Zeini, who said that the standard practice was for people to seek application for the construction of a church and for the SSI to deny an official permit but allow them to convert a place into an informal house of worship. There are many churches that were denied an official permit but allowed by the SSI to function for decades in this particular way as though they were 'legal' entities.[4]

Since the SSI is a rather opaque institution (Tadros 2012a), one can only speculate as to why such a policy was pursued. There is no doubt that it enhanced the SSI's control over the community in several ways. By allowing the Church leadership to establish a church without granting it an official permit, it entered into a pact with it, so in return for the construction of its church, the Church leadership had to cooperate. In other words, the clergy are grateful for being allowed to have a church and yet by virtue of the latter's informal status, they remain vulnerable and susceptible to attack at any point. There is also another reason why the SSI might want to pursue the strategy of "allowing the church to exist on the black market" and that is to avoid the wrath of the Muslim community. It also means that it can turn the tables against the Church or threaten to do so, thus wielding the power to pursue a divide-and-rule strategy between Muslims and Christians when it so wills (see chapter 5 for further details on the securitization of the sectarian file).

Ironically, the partial withdrawal of the SSI from the governance of the sectarian file following the ousting of Mubarak did not lead to a more harmonious relationship between Muslims and Copts on a local level. The SSI, at the very least, did not mind the building of churches, as long as their strict instructions were meticulously followed. It was through this informal mechanism that an unknown number of churches were built during the 2000s. However, after the fall of Mubarak, it was the Islamists who replaced the SSI in 'managing' sectarian matters, and this only incurred more injustice (see chapter 7).

The Politics of Religion in Gender Relations

The third major cause of sectarian strife in Egypt, representing 33 percent of all incidents, is gender-related matters. There is a growing awareness, even among the public, of the central role gender relations play in exacerbating sectarian strife. When prominent Islamist thinker Muhammad

Selim al-'Awa was campaigning for the presidency, he claimed that he would seek to address sectarian strife, arguing that it was caused in 95 percent of cases by romantic relationships. An editorial by a prominent *al-Ahram* writer similarly suggested that behind every sectarian incident is "a woman," arguing that it is when women enter into romantic relationships they know to be forbidden that conflict between Muslims and Christians arises.[5] Political commentator and regime critic Ibrahim Eissa noted that "most of the incidents of sectarian strife in Egypt are caused by a Christian boy falling in love with a Muslim girl or a Muslim boy wanting to marry a Christian girl or something to do with relations between the opposite sexes."[6]

Whatever the reading of the nature of gender-related fallouts between Muslims and Christians, there are some common caveats to both sides' engagement with these matters. First, these discussions take place in a deeply patriarchal society, in which women's agency is severely circumscribed. Women 'belong' to families, their religion, and society. Second, both sides use human rights discourse to defend their claim to particular women, but neither side is committed to the human rights of women. Third, the discussions on gender matters shed light on a deep-seated misogyny held by both Christian and Muslim advocates. For example, famous writer Karam Gabr gives directions: if you want to know the source of sectarianism, look for the woman, for "from her the flame is ignited until it becomes a big fire that demolishes homes and streets."[7] Blaming women for sectarian troubles seems to be one approach to avoiding dealing with the causes of gender-related incidents of sectarianism.

Since 2004, when a battle began between Christians and Muslims over the religious affiliation of Wafaa Constantine, the wife of a Coptic priest (see chapter 3), and 2010, when another battle was waged over the religious affiliation of another wife of a priest, Camillia Shehata, the debate over gender-related sectarian tensions has been almost reduced to these two cases alone. It is as though there would be no gender-related sectarian strife if only everyone could be openly assured that the wives of these two priests are following the religion they desire (which is categorically assumed to be Islam). The cases of these two women have been a source of sectarian tension that has lingered on for years, literally. For example, it has been nearly a decade since the Wafaa Constantine saga and it is still fresh in the minds of many Egyptians. Shortly after the appearance of Camillia Shehata on a satellite television station, Muslim Brotherhood writer Qutb al-Arabi appealed for Wafaa Constantine to also appear on television to put everyone's minds at ease and in order that sectarian matters finally be put to rest and the nation move forward.[8]

The prominence of these two cases arises out of the intensity of reaction of both Muslims and Christians to it. One of the most tumultuous protests to have been mobilized by Coptic citizenry was in Cairo's Abbasiya Cathedral in 2004 calling for the return of Wafaa Constantine. Similarly, when Camillia Shehata disappeared, there were highly emotive protests staged by Copts in the diocese in Minya. In both cases, the protest slogans were loaded with intense animosity toward the government and the SSI in particular. On the other side, the protests staged by Islamists under the leadership of Salafis on behalf of "sister Camillia and sister Wafaa" were sustained over the course of several months and involved the mobilization of hundreds of people. In one protest, the cathedral in Abbasiya was surrounded, and chants against the pope personally and the Coptic Church were made.

The cases of Wafaa and Camillia are highly complex, and no doubt there was a level of mismanagement of cases of marital dispute by a highly patriarchal Coptic Orthodox Church leadership, with Pope Shenouda bearing primary responsiblity as the Church's patriarch. In the case of Shehata, she should have appeared on television immediately after the controversy first erupted, in which case the matter would have been settled. It may have been personal pride that prevented Pope Shenouda from taking such a measure for he may have sought to avoid being seen to bow to public opinion. It is also possible that the SSI asked him not to interfere so as not to expose its own role since they were managing the case. However, the responsibility for assuring the public that the Church was not holding Shehata against her will, by allowing her to make a public appearance, rested on the shoulders of Pope Shenouda and it was strategically a mistake for him to postpone this in the case of Camillia Shehata and not to go ahead with it at all in the case of Wafaa Constantine.

If Islamists and a significant proportion of the public placed the responsibility for the sectarian incidents squarely on the shoulders of the Church, which, they argued, behaved as though it were above the law and was a state within a state, others believed the problem lay with the personal status legislation regulating marriage and divorce affairs in the Coptic Orthodox Church. Its refusal to allow people to divorce except in case of adultery has prompted men and women to seek their own ways of escaping unhappy marriages. Karima Kamal argued that if both Wafaa Constantine and Camillia Shehata had been offered a dignified exit out of their unhappy marriages, they would not have been subjected to the immensely damaging experiences they went through and sectarian escalation would thus have been prevented (Kamal 2012). No doubt some Coptic women and men who find themselves stuck in unhappy marriages have on occasion turned to conversion, and the failure of the Coptic Church to offer solutions needs to be addressed. Some women and men have resorted to conversion to Islam as a way out of unhappy marriages when the Church has refused to allow them to divorce (Tadros 2010a).

However, what the findings of the research indicate very strongly is that the majority of gender-related sectarian incidents are not related to married women or men but are cases of protest in response to the disappearance or conversion of young, sometimes underage, girls. When a young girl suddenly disappears, her family has no way of knowing whether she left of her own free will or whether she was coerced or kidnapped. Against a backdrop rife with rumor of Coptic women being kidnapped by Muslim fanatics, the possibility that their daughter may be one of them is a source of fear. Moreover, in a society in which a family's honor rests on a girl's behavior, the disappearance of a young woman is a source of tremendous shame.

One hypothesis is that the annulment of what were known as the "guidance sessions" is the cause behind the majority of gender-related sectarian incidents. The guidance sessions were introduced through an internal memorandum by the Ministry of Interior in 1863 by Khedive Ismail Pasha and featured as one of the steps necessary for any Copt wishing to convert to Islam to ensure that the person was doing so out of his/her own free will. Although not formally legalized, they have continued to be part of the process of conversion in Egypt since then. The process of conversion has several steps: the person goes to the police headquarters (*mudiriyyit al-amn*) and declares his/her desire to convert. Someone sharing the convert's religious affiliation is notified and invited to come to the police headquarters to provide direction and guidance. A representative from the police headquarters attends to ensure the peacefulness of the session. The case is closed if the person chooses not to change his/her religion. If the person chooses to convert, however, he/she proceeds to the public notary to confirm the decision.

On the surface, the guidance sessions may appear to be an infringement of personal freedoms and anathema to the principle of religious freedom. However, the sessions served to address some of the inequalities prevalent in law and social practice. First, since it is legally possible to convert from Christianity to Islam, but not the other way around, except with extreme difficulty, the act of conversion could not be a two-way path. Second, in view of deep-seated social inequalities and the fact that a Coptic woman can marry a Muslim man but a Christian man cannot marry a Muslim woman, the guidance session served to ensure the full agency of the convert before all the parties concerned. The guidance sessions were run until 2004, when the Ministry of Interior decided to put a stop to them.

It is noteworthy that in responding to the controversy over the rules of conversion being waged at the time, the former head of the Journalists' Syndicate, Makram Muhammad Ahmad, asserted that the policy of allowing "guidance and consultation sessions" with persons wishing to convert has been practiced for seventy years, and there is no justification for stopping it "unless the aim is to foment a forced crisis."[9] It would consequently follow that the state security decision to cancel the guidance and consultation sessions in 2004 was a retaliatory measure against the loss of face they suffered in the Constantine saga. According to the Copts' press mouthpiece, *Watani*, the decision came abruptly, and the Ministry of Interior gave no explanations for its decision.[10] It is not that the SSI, argued Yusuf Sidhom, the editor-in-chief of *Watani* and one of the most vocal Coptic activists, was always entirely objective in the way it conducted these sessions, as it often intervened or sought to obstruct the meeting if it felt the person was on the verge of changing his/her mind and often denied the right to a meeting in the absence of SSI oversight but that these sessions were extremely important for ensuring that the person wanted to convert out of firm belief and that it was a decision taken out of his/her own free will.[11] Islamist writers such as Tarek al-Bishri and Islamist groups more generally have critiqued the guidance sessions for contravening Islamic precepts, which recognize a person as Muslim when she/he declares the testimony of faith, or *shahada*, namely that "there is no god but God and Muhammad is His Prophet."[12] The process of having to go through the guidance session and through registration at al-Azhar is not required in Islam, it has been argued. Yet so long as families have no way of tracing their disappeared daughters, gender-related sectarian incidents will increase and cause equally emotive reactions within communities.

In the chapters to follow, a discussion of the micro-dynamics of sectarian incidents during Mubarak's reign and after is presented by looking more closely at specific cases, and examples are given in chapters 5 and 7.

3 | The Patriarch–President Pact and the People in Between

This chapter uncovers the historical emergence of the Coptic Orthodox Church as the mediator of relations between Coptic citizenry
and the state in the 1950s, the impact of which has continued to
influence the political scene some sixty years later, during the post-Mubarak
era. The chapter argues that an entente was forged in the 1950s between
the Church leadership and the state's political leadership that provided the
Church with certain concessions in return for its political allegiance
to the regime. Such an entente may have given the Church leadership
room for maneuver vis-à-vis wider Egyptian society, but it severely constrained its ability to hold the state and its apparatuses accountable for
human rights abuses toward Coptic citizens. Historically, the period
prior to 1952[1] had also witnessed the Coptic Orthodox Church leadership forging alliances with regimes in power, but its ability to represent
Copts in relation to the state was rivaled by the presence of other Coptic
voices in civil society, such as the Majlis al-Milli. From 1952 onward,
the state encouraged the emergence of the Coptic Church leadership
as the undisputed voice of the Coptic community while inhibiting the
presence and power of Copts in civil society.

A set of propositions regarding the dynamics and nature of the
entente are put forward here. First, there is a multiplicity of actors, both
within the ranks of the Coptic Orthodox Church's leadership and within
those of the state and its various apparatuses, who have influenced the
entente. In other words, there is a need to go beyond an analysis of the
Church as composed of clerics with a homogenous stand and of the state
as espousing a unified agenda vis-à-vis the Coptic Church. This approach
also displaces the representation of the relationship between the pope

and the president as a recapitulation of the old millet system under the Ottoman reign, under which "the Patriarch retained responsibility for administering communal affairs, and for relaying communal concerns to Ottoman officials" (Sedra 1999: 224), because in reality, beneath the veneer of single political wills on both sides (Church and state) there are multiple contending wills at play.

Second, there is much deliberation as to whether a political role for the Church is desirable or not, and how to distinguish among the realms of the political, civil, and spiritual. Highly influential Islamist writers such as Muhammad Selim al-'Awa, for example, have argued that the politicization of the Coptic Orthodox Church's role has had a detrimental impact on national unity (al-'Awa 2006). Others, however, such as writer and Coptic activist Magdi Khalil, have argued that the leadership of the Coptic Orthodox Church has pursued a patriotic rather than political role.[2]

The third proposition is that Coptic citizens have, by and large, not benefited from such an entente; to the contrary, it has harmed their interests.

The Emergence of an Informal Entente/Contract

Of particular significance to the study of contemporary relations between the Church and the state in Egypt is the impact of the establishment of Nasser's regime on the political relations among the state, the Coptic Church, and the Coptic laity. The policies institutionalized during Nasser's era affected the balance of power between the ecclesiastical and lay orders within the Coptic Orthodox Church. Until the nineteenth century, the Coptic Orthodox Church wielded much authority as the representative of Copts. However, members of the Coptic laity became more influential in Church matters and Church–state relations in the nineteenth century. These lay members came from a class of educated Copts who rose to influential positions in government and who became prosperous landowners. Their status and wealth empowered them to play an active role in shaping the policies affecting the Coptic community. Their lobbying culminated in the establishment of a consultative council, the Majlis al-Milli, in 1874, which was composed of lay Copt members, who were to participate in the governance of the affairs of the Coptic Church and its activities. The Majlis al-Milli was established as a parallel institution to the Coptic Orthodox Church with a mandate to oversee Coptic endowments (*awqaf*), the management of Coptic schools and institutions, and the running of Copts' personal status courts. From its establishment and up to the 1950s, there was a power struggle between the Coptic Orthodox Church and the Majlis al-Milli over the latter's mandate, with the Church often refusing to cooperate or to allow the Majlis to exert any influence over the regulation of the financial resources or the management of the internal matters of the Church. Nevertheless, the Majlis al-Milli continued to play an extremely important role in the lives of Copts and the Church by virtue of its influential representatives, who often had access to those in positions of power within the government, and by virtue of its relentless struggle to reform the Coptic Orthodox Church. It emerged as another legitimate voice representing Copts, thereby undermining the hegemony of the Coptic Orthodox Church as the sole mediator and representative of Copts vis-à-vis the state. Hassan notes that "the fierce competition between the clergy and the lay upper class also played itself out around the issue of who was to represent the community before the state—a prerogative that for centuries had been the church's" (Hassan 2003: 58). Other than influencing key governmental decisions and policies affecting Copts, the Majlis al-Milli also exerted its influence with respect to the selection of the patriarch, the leader of the Coptic Orthodox Church (el Masri 1982).

The authoritarian nature of Nasser's regime led to an inhibition of political pluralism and civil society activism, which greatly affected the participation of Copts in both arenas and in Church reform as well. Nasser's government adopted policies that sought deliberately to curb the powers of the Majlis al-Milli and by default expand the power of the Church leadership. In 1957, a presidential decree regarding the new by-laws for the election of the patriarch reflected all of the demands made by the conservative ecclesiastical ranks within the Church and dismissed all the concerns and propositions of the Majlis al-Milli. For example, the new election by-laws stipulated that the candidate must be at least forty years of age and must have been ordained as a monk for at least fifteen years (al-Bishri 1981: 457). The latter would mean that the highly educated reform-minded men who had joined monasteries only recently were excluded from the nomination process. The pro-reform movement within the clergy had hoped that the nominated candidate would be selected based on winning the largest number of votes. In contrast, the conservative members of the clergy wanted a draw between the candidates with the largest number of votes. The government approved the selection of the candidate through the draw system.

Other policies adopted by Nasser's regime also curbed the powers of the Majlis al-Milli. First, in 1955, the unified court system came into being and personal status courts for Copts were annulled, thus canceling one of the sources of power for the Majlis. Second, the *awqaf* belonging to Copts were removed from the authority of the Majlis al-Milli and assigned to the Coptic Orthodox Waqf Organization, whose members were to be chosen by the pope, "thereby depriving the Communal Council of its financial control" (Hassan 2003: 103). Moreover, the sequestration of both Islamic and Coptic *awqaf* and the restrictions laid on property ownership by the churches and monasteries to two hundred feddans also impacted the Majlis al-Milli (al-Bishri 1981: 456).

The state's imposition of restrictions on civil society in general inhibited virtually all forms of civic life, including Coptic civic engagement, whether with respect to Church reform or to national politics. Coptic nongovernmental organizations (NGOs) were coopted by the government and in some cases their property sequestrated (as in the case of the Coptic Hospital in Cairo). Further, Coptic members of the aristocracy, as with other members of the same social class, became politically marginalized once their principal asset, land, was taken from them as a consequence of the land reform measures adopted by the new government. The weakening of the Coptic laity was accompanied by the strengthening of the political and social role of the Church. As Hassan notes, "ironically, President Nasser's authoritarian regime unwittingly schooled the church for a political role by weakening the Christian secular aristocracy as well as the liberal institutions like Parliament and the Communal Council in which they played an important role" (Hassan 2003: 103). First, the Church's role as the religious and political representative of Copts was deepened. Second, Copts had been engaged in the public life of the nation as citizens with different ideological, political, and cultural affiliations, but as the role of the Church as spokesman of the Copts was strengthened, their religious affiliation became their main marker, not their citizenship. Third, the weakened Majlis al-Milli was not substituted by any other institution that pressed the Church for greater accountability, transparency, and reform.

Many commentators (al-Bishri 1981; Kamal 2006; al-Bahr 1984) have pointed to the importance of the personal relationship that developed between President Gamal 'Abd al-Nasser and Pope Kyrollos VI in resolving sectarian issues. This personal relationship was critical to the emergence of an informal entente between the Church and the state, one which entailed the state offering the Church leadership a set of concessions in return for its political support. For example, some of the concessions that Nasser granted included the approval of and financial support for the construction of St. Mark's Cathedral. Nasser dispensed half a million pounds from the government's budget for the construction of the cathedral and participated in the festivities that were held on the occasion of its inauguration (Heikal 1983; Gouda 1981).[3] Moreover, since permits for building churches were granted by the security apparatus and were by no means easy to obtain, Nasser's intervention facilitated the process of at least obtaining the official permit required for the construction of churches. Heikal recounts that

> it was understandably humiliating for the Patriarch to find that any applications for building permits he made got lost in the labyrinth of the Ministry of Interior. So he approached Nasser on the subject. Nasser was sympathetic, and asked how many new churches the Patriarch thought he needed. The answer was between twenty and thirty a year. Right, said Nasser, and immediately gave him permission to build twenty-five new churches a year. (Heikal 1983: 158)

Moreover, since the patriarch was elevated to the position of *the* representative of the Copts, he was granted some important political concessions regarding Coptic representation in public life. Soraya Hassan notes that "it was an open secret that anyone wishing to get into the single party electoral body he [the president] had set up, the Liberation Rally, had to get the Pope's blessing, because Nasser submitted the list of his electoral appointments to the pope for scrutiny" (Hassan 2003: 104).

In return, Pope Kyrollos gave Nasser consistent and unlimited political support, not only as an individual but on behalf of Copts in general. In 1967, when Nasser announced his resignation after the defeat of the 1967 war, Pope Kyrollos visited the president in his home to announce the Copts' insistence on his leadership (Gouda 1981:82). The personal friendship between the two became a symbolic signifier of the forces binding the Egyptian state with the Coptic citizenry. No longer were individuals voicing their demands, aspirations, and agendas via conventional channels of civic engagement with the state, such as civil society organizations and political parties. The Church assumed the position of mediator between Copts and the state (Kamal 2006). Where Copts were appointed to the government, the Church assumed, by extension, that it could play the role of mediator between them and the state. However, the mobilization of these candidates was much more difficult, as Heikal argues:

> after a time the revolutionary leaders tried to make amends by appointing Copts as ministers, but the men chosen, though admirably qualified for the posts they were to fill, were in all cases technocrats, without any particular standing among their fellow-religionists. The Patriarch and other community leaders tried to use these new men as a channel of communication with the government, but they were very conscious that it would not be like the old days. (Heikal 1983: 155)

Obstruction of the President–Patriarch Pathway

The death of Nasser in 1970, followed closely by Kyrollos' death in 1971, brought two new actors onto the national scene—President Anwar al-Sadat and Pope Shenouda III. At the outset, a similar kind of entente to that which had existed between Nasser and Pope Kyrollos was forged between the two leaders. Pope Shenouda III made several statements and gestures aimed at indicating his support for the new president, and the latter was also willing to grant certain concessions to the new patriarch. According to Moussa Sabry, a close confidant of the president,[4] the kinds of concessions that Sadat bestowed upon Shenouda included the following: "when the Majlis al-Milli was established, the government gave ear to the pope in the selection of the members and the prime minister asked the pope for a list of nominated candidates as members of the People's Assembly so that the government can choose from among them" (Sabry 1985: 133). Both Sabry and Heikal also recount how President Sadat met with Pope Shenouda III and the bishops and conceded that if the wishes of the pope were for the construction of thirty churches, well, he approved the construction of fifty churches. Later, the bishops would complain that the minister of interior, al-Nabawy Ismail, was showing great reluctance to implement the president's approval of the construction of the fifty churches and that none of the bureaucratic obstacles encountered was removed. It would seem that bureaucracy, red tape, and resistance from the state security apparatus meant that having a presidential decree was one thing and its implementation was entirely another (Sabry 1985; Heikal 1983).

A series of factors contributed to the heightening of political tensions between Sadat and the pope, including the rise of Islamist groups, increased sectarian incidents, and the growing role of Coptic immigrants as a lobby group in the United States against Sadat's policies.[5] Sadat's growing representation of himself as "the believer president" and support for the Islamization of society as well as the nation's laws (amendment of the constitution) were all interpreted as attacks on the fundamental principle of citizenship, which is founded on the notion of a national rather than religious identity. Moreover, none of the recommendations made by the truth commission headed by Gamal al-Oteify in the famous al-Oteify Report of 1972 was implemented by the government.[6] One of the most important recommendations made by the report was the reconsideration of the legal framework governing the construction and repair of churches, which required a presidential permit on a case-by-case basis.[7]

For his part, Sadat was greatly provoked by Shenouda's revolutionary style of politics, far different from his predecessor's non-confrontational low-key manner. In March 1980, Pope Shenouda responded in words and deeds to what he perceived to be President Sadat's government's passivity and inaction toward acts of violence waged by militant Islamist groups against Christians as well as the proposed *ridda* law, which stipulated that a person who converts from Islam will face the death penalty. Pope Shenouda canceled Christian Orthodox Easter celebrations and withdrew to the monastery. The cancellation of Easter celebrations[8] (mass) was an oppositional tactic with far-reaching political ramifications. Shenouda's act was not only a message of protest to the government but also one that was relayed to the entire world, including the U.S. administration and Copts in the diaspora. Moreover, Pope Shenouda's retreat to the monastery was an equally important oppositional tactic that came to signify his disengagement from his role in public Egyptian life, conveying a clear message of discontent and anger.

The unwritten agreement between the president and the pope was beginning to crumble, culminating in the president's decree announcing the annulment of the previous presidential decision of 1971 that pronounced the appointment of Shenouda as pope. The government mouthpiece, the *Mayu* newspaper, published the practicalities of his house arrest, the invalidation of the pope's signature on all official documents, his confinement to his monastery in Wadi al-Natrun, and the prohibition of his meeting with the public.[9] The entente was over. According to Heikal, the real cause of the intensification of conflict between the president and the patriarch was the fact that the latter refused to promote Coptic pilgrimages to Jerusalem, which would have enhanced the position of the president in meeting the Camp David accords with tourism promotion (Heikal 1983: 221). Sabry argues that Pope Shenouda's refusal to support Sadat's policies led to the tension in their relations. He suggests that the public attack on the pope in Sadat's famous speech of 14 May 1980 was a reaction to news that the pope had called upon Copts not to participate in the referendum that was to be held on the change to article 2 of the constitution. In 1971 Sadat had amended Egypt's constitution to refer to shari'a as *a* source of legislation. In 1979, Sadat proposed a referendum to amend article 2 yet further to stipulate that "Islam is the religion of the state and Arabic its official language. Islamic shari'a is *the* principal source of legislation."[10] This rewording meant that shari'a held precedence over all other sources of legislation in the constitution, and effectively meant that judges could dismiss civil law that was deemed incompatible with the shari'a. Pope Shenouda expressed his rejection of the proposed amendment both before and after it was passed. On 17 January 1977, Pope Shenouda convened a meeting with the Holy Synod, the thrust of which was that since shari'a involves the application of the Qur'an and the Sunna, then it is only reasonable that its application be restricted to Muslims. He suggested that its application nationwide would signal a flagrant violation of the principle of freedom of religious belief enshrined in the constitution ('Abd al-Fattah 1984: 101).[11] Writes Heikal, on 26 March 1980, "Pope Shenouda delivered a speech in which he angrily attacked the idea that the shari'a law should be the basis for legislation and claimed that Islam was being made the new form of nationalism" (Heikal 1983: 219; 'Abd al-Fattah 1984: 227). Further, Shenouda's insistence on greater representation of Copts in decision-making positions and public trials for those who attacked Copts in sectarian incidents was not welcomed by Sadat. Sabry also argues that protests organized by immigrant Copts who met Sadat in the U.S., which he found to be a great embarrassment, were pivotal in escalating the crisis, and that it was shortly afterward that Sadat decided not to meet with Shenouda (Sabry 1985: 150).

The *Mayu* announcement also declared that a papal committee comprising five bishops would be responsible for overseeing the papal duties. While the escalation of events could be attributed to the rising animosity between Sadat and Shenouda, there were in fact several other players whose actions were to have important bearings on the crisis. First was the state security apparatus, which reported directly to the president. It was under Sadat that the State Security Investigations apparatus (SSI) emerged as the mediator of sectarian relations in response to the growing number of assaults by militant Islamists on Coptic places of worship, homes, and private property, which threatened to escalate into large-scale massacres if not contained. The "sectarian question" became identified as a threat to "national security" and was hence relegated to the SSI to "manage." The SSI believed that the weekly meeting the pope held for the Coptic congregation should be canceled because it sparked intense sentiments among the youth—a step with which Pope Shenouda refused to comply. The state security apparatus advised that the bishop in Alexandria be relocated as, it alleged, he was responsible for fomenting sectarian strife. Shenouda did not budge. Moreover, it is upon the recommendations of the reports prepared by the SSI, detailing a list of bishops allegedly fomenting sectarianism and fanaticism, that the decision to imprison them, in the now famous arrests of September 1981, was taken (Sabry 1985: 160).

Moreover, despite the pope's attempt to continue to play the role of dominant spokesman (or statesman) of the Copts, it is clear that there were varied reactions among different Coptic power bases to the pope's heightened tensions with President Sadat. The Majlis al-Milli of Alexandria and the Synod of Bishops of Alexandria supported the pope's stance. Other local councils chose to take a more conciliatory stance, especially after witnessing heightened sectarian tensions in their own dioceses.[12] The divergence among bishops was also quite conspicuous. According to Guirgis Gouda, Bishop Samuel urged Coptic members of the People's Assembly to vote in favor of the proposed reform of article 2 of the constitution, despite the fact that Pope Shenouda urged them to vote against it (Gouda 1981: 245–46). Another power to contend with, which had yet to mobilize its resources at the time of Pope Kyrollos, was Copts of the diaspora. The position of several Coptic immigrant lobbyists was that the pro-government position taken by Bishop Samuel, Bishop Athanasious, and other bishops made it seem as though it was Pope Shenouda III who was being difficult and uncooperative and taking a hard-line position. Their adoption of positions that were different from that of the pope made it seem that more compliant allies could be found within the Church (Gouda 1981: 253). Some members of the Coptic diaspora in the

US, for example, refused to recognize the papal committee established by Sadat, lobbied against the bishops who accepted such roles, and continued to protest against the Egyptian government's handling of sectarian issues. The Coptic associations established in the diaspora continued to grow in strength and to represent an autonomous voice, often incongruent with policies adopted by the Church.

The Emergence of a New Entente between Shenouda and the State

It took more than four years after his appointment as president for Mubarak to terminate Pope Shenouda's house arrest in 1985. There is a paucity of historical material on the circumstances leading to the decision to end the pope's house arrest and open new lines of communication between the Church and the state. However, there is substantial evidence to suggest that, at least on the part of the patriarch, there was a new commitment to abandoning his earlier confrontational style of politics. Pope Shenouda's tone and discourse vis-à-vis the government changed radically after his release in 1985.[13] This could not be solely attributed to the change in the country's leadership. There had no doubt been a personal element to the level of animosity that prevailed between him and Sadat, but historical accounts of the relationship between the pope and Hosni Mubarak when the latter was vice president suggest that there was also a high level of enmity between Mubarak and Shenouda.[14] The government's changed policy toward Islamists also served to improve relations between the regime and the Church. 'Abd al-Fattah argues that as a consequence of the growing threat of Islamist militancy to the government, it abandoned its policy of engagement in favor of a more confrontational tone, suggesting that now the Church and the state shared a common enemy ('Abd al-Fattah 1984). Yet Pope Shenouda's rapprochement with the government came earlier than the latter's crackdown on Islamists, thus refuting the theory of a causal relation between growing Islamist militancy and Shenouda's change of tone.

Similarly, Shenouda's new, non-confrontational approach could not be attributed to a change in the level of sectarian tensions between Copts and Muslims. Sectarian strife continued unabated through the 1980s.[15] It has been suggested that Shenouda's approach could have been affected by the loss of fervor and enthusiasm for pushing for peace with Israel at all costs on the part of the Egyptian government and new efforts on the part of Pope Shenouda to limit the influence of the Coptic diaspora as pressure tools ('Abd al-Fattah 1995: 94). However, the Church leadership could not silence or control voices of protest among Coptic emigrants, either during previous decades or after the termination of Shenouda's house arrest. They remained a force that acted independently of the Church. *Al-Hala al-diniya fi Misr* (The Religious Situation in Egypt)[16] described the relationship between the government and the pope after his release as involving a "tactical agreement" ('Abd al-Fattah 1995: 94). The report argued that some of the elements of the tactical agreement that existed in the Kyrollos–Nasser entente were restored. An examination of the nature of the relationship between the two would suggest that this entente may have resulted in Pope Shenouda pursuing a non-confrontational policy toward the government in return for the termination of his house arrest and for reestablishing a channel of communication between the patriarch and the president. The tactical agreement may also have included the greater collaboration that arose between the SSI and the Church, since many of the issues on pending sectarian issues involved state security intervention in matters such as the construction and repair of churches.

In addition to adopting a non-confrontation policy toward sectarian incidents, the pope also pursued a policy of open support for the Mubarak regime and its policies, very much in line with his previous support for Sadat in the earlier years and with his predecessor's policy in the 1950s and 1960s. The political function of the patriarch as a supporter of the president and representative of the Copts was enforced from the time of his release from house arrest until the referendum over the constitutional amendments in March 2007, although, as is evident below, this support was not consistently extended to all the regime's power bases.

Pope Shenouda not only expressed his personal support for the president and his party but also institutionalized this policy across the Church hierarchy. For example, during the presidential elections of 2005, in which Mubarak was campaigning for a fifth term in office, the pope openly expressed his support for Mubarak's re-nomination and called upon Coptic Christians to vote for him. Moreover, he officially ordered all bishops to vote positively in the referendum for Mubarak's fifth term. The Holy Synod, led by Pope Shenouda, issued an official statement in the lead-up to the referendum openly supporting Mubarak's presidency. The implications of this action were far reaching. It signified a political stand rather than the expression of a personal opinion. It was a political stand institutionalized on all levels of the Church hierarchy and officially reflecting the Church's will, represented by the Holy Synod. It also sent out a message to Copts that their religious leaders, the models whose examples are to be followed, should support Mubarak as opposed to other candidates.[17] The Coptic Orthodox Church also capitalized on its religious power to make other politically significant gestures in support of Mubarak's regime. For example, the Holy Synod decided to celebrate Mubarak's victory in the presidential referendum by having all churches nationwide ring their bells. This gesture was highly significant, given that church bells, in accordance with Orthodox doctrine, are only to be rung on the commencement of mass and other religious rites.[18] The use of a purely religious practice for an overtly political function raises questions over the blurring of lines between the realm of the religious and realm of the political.[19]

Pope Shenouda's enforcement of punitive measures against members of the ecclesiastical order who dared choose a presidential candidate other than Mubarak showed the extent of his willingness to eliminate any political opposition to Mubarak in the Coptic Church. Father Philopateer Gameel, a priest working in one of Cairo's poor suburbs, was a member of al-Ghad Party,[20] whose leader, Ayman Nour, ran against Mubarak. Pope Shenouda froze Father Philopateer's service for a period of a year (that is, he inactivated his duties as a priest). While the decision was made in the name of the Holy Synod, it was not preceded by a trial, in violation of church laws.[21]

Further, in the run-up to the People's Assembly elections of 2005, the Coptic Church leadership called upon its followers to vote unilaterally for candidates of the National Democratic Party (NDP), Egypt's de facto ruling party, which remained the country's dominant party until Mubarak's ouster in 2011. In some dioceses, priests were openly calling upon parishioners to render support to NDP candidates (all Muslim) even if competing candidates were Christian. For example, in the Upper Egyptian governorate of Minya, the Church gave instructions to parishioners to vote in favor of the NDP as opposed to the Tagammu' (leftist party) candidate, who happened to be a Christian. This scenario was reenacted in several electoral constituencies around the country.

Pope Shenouda's position on the debates that ensued regarding the amendment of the constitution also showed a clear bias toward supporting the NDP line. In 2007, President Mubarak proposed amending the constitution on the premise that some of its articles were outdated. Opposition parties argued that some of the amendments aimed at restricting political freedoms and undermining the prospects of any other party that tried to contest the NDP. Consequently members of parliament (MPs) from opposition parties decided to boycott the parliamentary session in which the vote on the constitutional amendment was to be cast. Opposition parties and other political forces also led a nationwide campaign to urge Egyptian citizens not to go to the polls on 26 March 2007 as an act of protest. The NDP desperately needed to have citizens participate in the referendum in order to give some semblance of the changes having been passed democratically with the majority of Egyptians supporting them.[22] It is in this context that Pope Shenouda's request to all Copts to participate in the referendum must be understood. All bishops were instructed to inform parish priests in their dioceses to mobilize parishioners to participate in the referendum. This involved making announcements during church services on a sustained basis in all parishes, and, to set an example, Pope Shenouda cast his vote at the polling station, where he made a statement about the importance of Egyptians positively participating in the elections for "the sake of achieving freedom, stability, democracy and development for all."[23]

Moreover, one of the controversies sparked by the debates that took place in the months before the constitutional referendum was the revision of article 2 of the constitution, one of the articles that the government insisted should be kept intact. Those in favor of amending article 2 argued that since Egypt is characterized by religious pluralism and is a secular country, any reference to shari'a being the principal source of legislation should be removed, especially since neither the Egyptian constitution of 1923 nor that of 1953 made any such reference.[24] Pope Shenouda's embracing of the government's viewpoint was significant as it carried political weight against the secularists and offered a striking contrast to the fierce opposition he had expressed to the very same article some thirty years earlier during the Sadat era. In support of the government, Pope Shenouda said that the problem lay not in the actual text (nass) of the article but in its application, and that since the majority of Egyptians are Muslim, it is their right to have Islam as the formal religion of the country and source of legislation, but that Islam secured rights between citizens and guaranteed the rights of non-Muslims. What is pertinent is Shenouda's reference to the rights of non-Muslims in Islam rather than the rights of citizens in a nation-state. The statements he made about the political role of the clergy in supporting the government further attest to the fact that his position was geared toward legitimizing the government's stand. He explained that officials need the support of "men of religion" since they have credibility as being truthful with the people.[25]

Hany Labib, a writer on Coptic issues, interpreted the above gestures as evidence of the pope's patriotism and commitment to the nation rather than undue meddling in politics. He argued that there was a distinction between "patriotic loyalty" and "political activity or activism," the former being a position that represents the nation as a whole, irrespective of differences in political, class, and religious affiliation, and the latter representing, for example, the clergy's adoption of a political role, which would be an entirely different and unacceptable scenario. Based on this distinction, Labib argued that Pope Shenouda's support for the constitutional amendments and his calls to Copts to participate in the referendum were examples of his patriotism. Similarly, his position against the revision of article 2 was another "patriotic stand."[26] This argument is a weak one, however, because by supporting the government's stand, Pope Shenouda adopted a highly partisan position that privileged the NDP over other political parties and movements, and later served to undermine the positioning of the Church in post-Mubarak Egypt. It also suggests that all those who do not follow the government's policy positions would be unpatriotic. Based on Labib's argument, all political parties that boycotted the referendum would be unpatriotic. Similarly, calls to remove reference to shari'a in the constitution were elicited by activists, intellectuals, and human rights advocates with diverse political affiliations. If Labib's argument regarding the pope's position were to apply, it would suggest that their support for secularism is also unpatriotic.[27] However, other Copts, both members of the ecclesiastical order (for example, Father Marcos Aziz) and the laity (for example, renowned Coptic activist Magdi Khalil) also publicly called for the article to be revised, along the lines prescribed by Bishop Morcos.[28]

Pope Shenouda's politics of engagement with the government in general has also been the subject of much criticism from different Coptic groups. One criticism came from members of a lay movement composed of Coptic writers, thinkers, and activists from different ideological positions (leftist, liberal, pro-government, anti-government) who held two conferences on reforming the Coptic Orthodox Church.[29] During those conferences, many speakers expressed their concern over the increasingly political role of the Church and its impact on citizenship, namely that Copts would engage with the state according to the directions or guidance of the Church as opposed to behaving as independent citizens. More outspoken criticism has been voiced by some Coptic groups in the diaspora, which have accused Pope Shenouda of selling out to the government. For example, U.S.-based organization the Coptic-American Union, a lobby group for Coptic rights in Egypt, accused the pope in one of its statements of

> having done nothing to protect his flock. He has, instead, aligned himself with despicable actions perpetrated by the Egyptian government by cooperating in the cover up of numerous crimes against the Copts. He has also flagrantly compromised the safety and future security of the Copts by shamelessly aiding and abetting the Egyptian government in its forward movement to destabilize and eradicate the Coptic culture in Egypt, through continued persecution, fear and infiltration.[30]

Pope Shenouda himself conceded in an interview that he chooses not to reply to the "allegations of discrimination" made by Copts in the diaspora because when he does, they accuse him of having come under the authority of the state.[31] While these voices were a minority within the laity, nevertheless they indicate that it could not be taken for granted that the political views of the pope represented those of all Copts. They also suggest that there were Copts who were prepared to publicly contest the Church leadership's policy without leaving the Coptic Orthodox Church. In other words, the voices of protest came from within the Church's own constituency and not from without.

The pertinent question is the nature of the 'rewards' bestowed upon the Church hierarchy in return for their political alignment with Mubarak's policies. Based on the rules of the entente set in the 1950s, it would be expected, first, that the government would grant the pope special privileges (that is, through nomination and appointment of Copts in government, responding to his personal requests on political matters, and granting permission for the construction of churches.). Second, it would be expected that the SSI would be cooperative in handling the 'sectarian file,' which ranges from obfuscating any internal dissent against the pope, to preventing the escalation of sectarian violence against Copts and handling the process of church construction and renovation properly. In a bid to show goodwill on the part of the government, a presidential decree delegated to governors the responsibility for approving applications for the construction or renovation of churches. However, there continued to be Church complaints about obstacles to obtaining such permits. One interpretation of this was that the political support was only a window-dressing measure aimed at giving the impression of religious and political harmony—one devoid of any genuine intention to achieve structural change. Another interpretation was that the SSI had become so vast and powerful that it is impossible to assume that their agenda was always in harmony with that of other agents in the government. It also follows that the Coptic Orthodox Church had to negotiate the terms of the entente on several fronts: the president, the political policy-making arena, and the state security apparatus. Having to negotiate with more than one party increased the prospect of failure to reach agreement and hence compli-cated the rules and terms of the entente. Indeed, as Paul Sedra argues, Pope Shenouda may have hoped to revive the old entente between Pope Kyrollos and Nasser (Sedra 1999), but by the 1990s there were several nodes of power involved in mediating the relationship within both gov-ernment and state security that required negotiation on several fronts, which in reality was not always possible.

The Wafaa Saga: An Open Wound

The tensions that emerged in the entente between the Coptic Ortho-dox Church and the state following the Wafaa Constantine crisis in 2004 are a consequence of various power-holders being involved in mediat-ing the relationship between the Church and the state. These tensions also suggest that the terms of the entente (the Coptic Church rendering political support in exchange for particular government concessions for the Church leadership) were being challenged by the policies pursued on both sides. The rupture in the relationship between the SSI and the Church was triggered by the Wafaa Constantine saga. The then forty-seven-year-old Wafaa Constantine, an agricultural engineer, worked at one of the government offices in the Delta town of Beheira. Her husband was a priest who had been disabled for many years after his feet were amputated as a result of diabetes. In 2004, Wafaa Constantine left her marital home, where she was subject to domestic violence, and went to a police station, where she expressed her desire to convert to Islam. She was reported missing on 27 November 2004.

According to press accounts, on 3 December, the police station in Cairo, in coordination with the state security apparatus of Beheira, informed Bishop Bachomious, the metropolitan for Beheira, of Constantine's desire to convert. Bachomious asked for some time to look into the matter and choose an appropriate time and place for a meeting with Constantine. During this period, Constantine's exact whereabouts were unknown, although it is presumed she was being held at the state security premises. The exact details of what happened during those days when she was missing are unknown. Did Wafaa Constantine insist that she be protected from exposure to the Church hierarchy for fear of being convicted? Did she change her mind and not want to convert to Islam, but was not given a chance to retract by the SSI? Any theory can only be based on speculation.

The absence of any knowledge regarding her case created an atmosphere conducive to rumor and speculation among Coptic parishioners in her hometown, centered on her potential abduction and forced conversion. On 6 December 2004, hundreds of Coptic youth protested, calling for the return of the priest's wife. The protests continued for two consecutive days and culminated in clashes between the police stationed outside the Abbasiya Cathedral and demonstrators, some of whom were detained on charges of thuggery, obstructing traffic, resisting authority, and throwing stones at the police, which led to the injury of sixty-two members of the police force and some of the youth.[32]

The sequence of events in the days that followed is extremely important for understanding the escalation of tensions between the state security apparatus and Pope Shenouda personally. On the evening of 8 December, while the protesters were still demonstrating at the cathedral, Pope Shenouda left the papal premises, canceled his weekly meeting with the Coptic congregation, and withdrew to the monastery. He said he would not return until issues affecting Copts had been resolved, one of the most important of which was related to the state's handling of conversion cases. The matter was settled later that same night when state security agents allowed some bishops to meet with Constantine, presumably under direct orders from President Mubarak, since the pope later expressed his gratitude for the president's intervention to end the Constantine saga.[33] The state security apparatus was forced to allow the Church access to Constantine, who subsequently expressed her desire on 14 December to remain a Christian by proclaiming this in front of the prosecutor general.

According to Luke Bebawy (2006), an agreement was reached between her and the bishops in which she would remain a Christian but be separated from her husband. It was also agreed that she would reside at one of the monasteries at Wadi al-Natrun.

What is significant in this crisis is the pope's decision to adopt a series of highly confrontational measures: cancellation of his weekly meeting, retreat to the monastery, and public statements of reproach of the government. His retreat to the monastery only ended two weeks after the Constantine crisis had been defused.[34] This was not the first time that the pope had adopted a position of open confrontation on an issue affecting the Coptic community. For example, in 2001, when *al-Naba'*, a tabloid newspaper, published pictures of a defrocked monk having sexual liaisons with women, Pope Shenouda asked the government to intervene and take measures against the newspaper. However, in the case of the Wafaa Constantine saga, the pope was expressing his opposition to the government *itself*, and specifically blaming the state security apparatus for its handling of the crisis. High-ranking Coptic sources claim that three different appointments were made with him by the government for returning the priest's wife and none of them was respected. During the protests, one of the cathedral's officials announced the return of Wafaa Constantine, but when demonstrators asked to see her in person, this did not materialize since state security promises had not been kept.[35] The crisis reflected that there was no singular, unified government will with a harmonized agenda. Rather, there was a multiplicity of wills, including that of the security apparatus, the president, and others.

The Coptic Church's attack on the SSI was shared by others, but for very different reasons. A deluge of books and press articles on the subject appeared during and after the Constantine saga reprimanding the SSI for bowing to the Church and for showing weakness in face of what was regarded as illegitimate coercion and disrespect for freedom of belief, as well as for operating outside the law. The state, and the SSI in particular, were attacked for their handling of the crisis from predictable sources—Islamists and Nasserists. Prominent Islamist writer and former judge Tarek al-Bishri insisted that the practice of reporting to a police station that then arranges for a consultation session with the clergy, after which the person formally registers their conversion at al-Azhar, was illegal.[36] He agreed that conversion to Islam is acceptable without any of these steps, and that all that is required is the announcement of the *shahada* and a belief in Islam. Al-Bishri said that the request that Constantine be delivered to the Church was "bewildering and more so since she was delivered through the security source and I believe it was built on a political decision; therefore this handing her [over] is not legal and there is no law in Egypt that allows the authority to hand in a person to a specific authority because of his belief."[37] He accused the government of allowing the Church to become a political group separate from the national community and noted that this was unacceptable. Al-Bishri said that the only fault of the SSI was that it had delivered Constantine to the Church.

Renowned Islamist thinker and writer Muhammad Emara also rebuked the government for delivering Constantine to the Church and raised questions as to whether she had converted back to Christianity of her own free will.[38] Radical Islamist preacher Sheikh Yusuf al-Badri, along with nine lawyers, filed suit against the Ministry of Interior for handing Constantine over to the Church. He argued that no proof was provided to the public to the effect that she converted back to Christianity after embracing Islam.[39] Mustafa Bakri, then an MP and former editor-in-chief of *al-Usbu'*, speculated as to whether Wafaa Constantine returned to Christianity of her own free will and whether after being 'delivered' to the Church she was free to return to her family. He wondered what kind of guarantees exist against the Church possibly terrorizing her and denying her freedom of choice. He also accused the state of inciting sectarianism by bowing to the conditions laid down by the Church (insistence on returning Constantine). He wondered why the Egyptian government treated the Church as though it were above the law while simultaneously increasing its repression of Islamist expressions of dissent.[40]

In analyzing the role of the Church in this incident, these sources questioned if the Church was assuming that it was above public law, and whether it had assumed leadership of a political, not just spiritual, nature vis-à-vis the Copts.[41] Fahmy Howeidy, for example, in analyzing the role of the Church, questioned whether "it represents spiritual leadership or political leadership and these questions also extend to include the nature of the church with the state and the limits of its abidance with law and the public order."[42]

In the absence of Wafaa Constantine's voice in this saga, it is difficult to establish how the configuration of different powers (Church, the SSI, political leaders, and others) influenced her agency. What became conspicuously clear was that she was being used as a pawn by all. For the Church, she, as the wife of a priest, represented the standing of the Church within the wider community. For Islamists, her case was one of the violation of a Muslim's right to freedom of religion by a belligerent Church flexing its muscles. Certainly, when the crisis erupted in 2004, no one would have predicted that it would resonate for years to come, as it continues to this day. Perhaps if the Coptic Orthodox Church leadership had compelled Wafaa Constantine to make a public appearance (as it did with Camillia Shehata seven years later; see chapter 7), this would have assuaged a public that was turning increasingly against it. One can only speculate as to why the Church did not pursue this path. There are a number of possible explanations. One is that Pope Shenouda's wounded pride prevented him from taking a step that would be interpreted as giving in to public opinion, and that in his political calculations, it had not occurred to him that the matter would linger as long as it has. Another possible explanation is that the SSI gave the Church instructions to prevent an interview in case sensitive security information was released. A third is that Wafaa Constantine was unsure of her choice, and it was therefore deemed unwise that she should make a public appearance. In any event, it is likely that she had very little say in the whole matter and would have waited for instructions from the Church. What is argued here is that in retrospect the decision not to allow Constantine to make a public appearance was one that had severe consequences for the Church's image, making it appear like an institution that locks Muslim women behind its doors.

The Constantine incident challenged the terms upon which the Church–state entente were established in the 1950s. For its part, the Coptic Orthodox Church leadership felt that the government had failed to provide it with the type of political concessions that were expected as part of the tacit bargain that existed between them, because after promising Pope Shenouda that Constantine would be returned at a particular hour on a particular day, the SSI missed this appointment.[43] Pope Shenouda's image with his constituency was compromised and his pride wounded. On the other hand, the SSI felt that the Coptic Orthodox Church's position on the matter failed to conform to its own responsibilities under the entente. Breaking ranks with its support for the Egyptian government, the Church openly accused the SSI of mismanaging the crisis during a press conference. Further embarrassment to the SSI was caused by Pope Shenouda's direct appeal over their heads to the president. The SSI being forced to yield to Pope Shenouda's will meant that it emerged as the defeated party, a fact that it was not to forget easily. In fact, the whole affair became the basis of a vendetta between the SSI and the Church leadership, one that was subsequently to affect the way in which SSI–Church relations developed, as will be discussed in the next chapter.

In conclusion, this chapter has argued that from the 1950s, an entente was forged between the Egyptian government and the Coptic Orthodox Church, embodied in the personal relationship between President Nasser and Pope Kyrollos. This informal entente demanded the Church's political support for the regime in return for the government granting the Church certain concessions. Despite the fact that, historically, the Church leadership had rendered its political support to the status quo, what was distinct about the entente was that the Church emerged as the undisputed political voice representing all Copts, in a context where other voices, such as that of the Majlis al-Milli, were constrained. While the historical personal relationship between president and pope was ruptured in the later stages of the Sadat presidency, another entente was forged between the regime and the Church after Pope Shenouda's release from house arrest under Mubarak. Such an entente became increasingly difficult to manage as the players on both sides multiplied and the SSI's power to control and manage relations with the Church grew while the Church's access to political (as opposed to security) channels weakened. The Constantine affair represents a critical juncture in the history of SSI–Church relations and became the basis for a vendetta between the two, as will be discussed in the next chapter.

4 | The Politics of Backroom Vendettas: The State Security Investigations Apparatus versus the Coptic Church Leadership

In *al-Karama* newspaper's edition of 2 August 2010 is a highly revealing article that encapsulates the nature of Church–state–Coptic citizenry relations toward the end of Mubarak's regime.[1] The article describes how then Minister of Interior Habib al-Adli presented a memorandum to Ahmad Nazif, then prime minister, on the rise in the number of Coptic protests driven by "petty reasons" and insisted that the persistence of such a trend could lead to heightened sectarian incidents and strife—a situation that the state could not tolerate.

The memorandum, which was prepared by the SSI, highlighted that "most recently, a number of Coptic clerical leaders have deliberately sought to provoke Coptic citizens to protest and stage sit-ins for the pettiest" reasons "as though it were a flexing of Coptic muscles." Al-Adli pointed out in his memorandum that "a number of priests and major [lay] figures in the Church" in a number of governorates were bent on inciting citizens against the public order and encouraging them to go on riotous demonstrations and stage angry sit-ins without purpose. Al-Adli cited the names of these men, the details of each of these incidents, and the role of each leader or religious personality in each case. At the end of his memorandum, al-Adli requested that Nazif intervene with the Church immediately upon the return of Pope Shenouda from his medical treatment trip to the United States, to convince the clergy and leaders in the Church to step back from such actions that harm the state. He argued that these *mushaghabat* (agitations) will only lead to increased tension, the loss of rights, and the appearance of Copts as a sect operating outside the law, and that "*any Coptic demands will not be achieved except through formal and legitimate channels through Pope Shenouda*" (author's emphasis).

This memorandum perfectly encapsulates the power dynamics between Church and state as represented by the most influential players. It is the story in a nutshell: it is the SSI—presided over by the minister of interior—that manages sectarian matters. The SSI was annoyed by Coptic protests, which it deemed to be driven by petty reasons. It called upon the prime minister to relay a stern warning to the pope to the effect that such protests should cease. Other than the obvious power-over inferences of such a warning, what is evident is the assumption that the protests, instigated by either the clergy or lay leaders, can be controlled by the Church leadership. It also makes it clear that the only legitimate channel open to Copts for making their claims as citizens is not through direct appeal to the state in the form of public protest but by mediation through Pope Shenouda, whom the state recognized as the only legitimate political spokesman for ten percent of the country's citizens. It is also evident that Copts are neither restricting their agency to appealing to the pope nor desisting from making their claims through engagement in unruly politics.

The Politics of Containment: Security Rebuff of Shenouda

If the Wafaa Constantine saga highlighted the tensions in the entente between the SSI and the Coptic Church leadership, the Maximos crisis that followed suggested not only an unwillingness on the part of the SSI to support Pope Shenouda but also a reluctance on the part of the president to stand by him. The approval of the Ministry of Interior for the establishment and expansion of a rival church leadership in Muqattam, Cairo, with its own archbishop, sent a harsh political message to Pope Shenouda personally. It is significant that the Ministry of Interior's decision to allow this church (outside the authority of Pope Shenouda) to thrive came less than two years after the conclusion of the Constantine saga, raising questions as to whether this was a form of revenge from the SSI for the loss of face it suffered as a result of having bowed down to the Church. The St. Athanassios Church was allowed to thrive and grow for two years until the Administrative Court—and not the government—ruled that its leader Anba Maximos was acting in violation of Egyptian law, thus leaving the status of the church in limbo.[2]

Max Michel became Maximos the First, the founder of the St. Athanassios Church in Muqattam, and archbishop of the Holy Synod for the Orthodox Church in Egypt and the Middle East—a title that Pope

Shenouda would claim that he alone had the right to bear. Max Michel began his career as a student in the Coptic Orthodox Seminary, from which he graduated and where he was ordained a consecrated deacon[3] to serve in the city of Tanta.[4] In 1976, Pope Shenouda decided to terminate his service in the Church, although he was never excommunicated or charged in a Church trial by the Holy Synod.

There are two different accounts of why the pope turned against Michel. The official Church account is that Max Michel was responsible for spreading erroneous doctrines inconsistent with Church teachings. He, meanwhile, claims to have been banished from the Church for his admiration for the teachings of the late Father Matta al-Miskin, a renowned Coptic scholar, monk, and spiritual father of the monks of Anba Makkar Monastery, who have had a long-term rift with Pope Shenouda.[5] After his expulsion, Max Michel established the St. Athanassios Association, in accordance with the law that allows citizens to establish organizations for the purpose of religious education. He was able to recruit some members and supporters, but later left Egypt to pursue a doctorate in theology at Saint Elias College in Nebraska in the United States, where according to Maximos, he joined their Holy Synod. The Holy Synod of the American Diaspora of True Orthodox Christians are Old Calendarists (Christians, mainly of Greek Orthodox origin, who follow the old Julian calendar as opposed to the Gregorian one). The Holy Synod ordained him assistant bishop, then bishop, and finally archbishop, thus enabling him to establish a synod for Egypt and the Middle East and ordain bishops and priests.

Egyptian law allows citizens to establish branches of organizations based abroad as long as they receive the approval of the Ministry of Foreign Affairs. The Foreign Affairs Ministry granted Maximos this permission (although there were rumors that it was granted at the personal request of Condoleezza Rice).[6] Maximos' followers were mainly disgruntled members of the Coptic Orthodox Church or Copts who stood to benefit from Maximos' more lenient standing on divorce and remarriage. (Unlike the Coptic Orthodox Church, Maximos' church recognizes the eight conditions for divorce set by the Majlis al-Milli in 1948, which were rescinded by Pope Shenouda. Maximos' church also allows the remarriage of divorced Copts.)

In July 2006, Maximos announced the establishment of a Holy Synod for the Orthodox in Egypt and the Middle East and ordained two bishops and placed them in charge of archdioceses across the country. It is that initiative that heightened the opposition of the Coptic Orthodox Church leadership to the establishment of Maximos' church. The fact that the Ministry of Interior did not take any measures against this (despite the fact that all churches require an official permit) was interpreted by the Church hierarchy as a deliberate policy of undermining the authority and status of Pope Shenouda as the sole head and representative of the Ortho- dox Church in Egypt. While the Ministry of Interior did not officially issue Maximos a permit for the establishment of his church, it nonethe- less issued his identity card with his new name and with the title "Head of the Synod of the Church of St. Athanassios," in clear recognition of him and his status. Surprisingly, the date of issuance is May 2005, well before Maximos declared himself archbishop.[7]

Maximos was an embarrassment to the Coptic Orthodox Church, which made a series of pleas to the government aimed at repressing Maximos' church. An *Al-Masry Al-Youm* article quotes Bishop Morcos as saying, "Yes, I hold the government responsible for his existence because up till now he [his church] is functioning on an illegal basis. . . . I appeal to President Mubarak to put an end to this farce because we will not accept this."[8] A point can be made about freedom of belief and association, how- ever, in the Egyptian context at the time, for it is significant that while the government continuously violated many basic rights, it opted not to take action against Maximos.

Pope Shenouda made several requests to the government to have the Coptic Orthodox Church uniform (ecclesiastical attire) registered so that only accredited members of the clergy would be authorized to wear it.[9] This move would prevent Maximos from dressing almost exactly like Pope Shenouda and prevent the bishops he ordained from wearing attire identical to that worn by Coptic Orthodox bishops. Pope Shenouda indicated that the lack of response to the Church's appeal for the registra- tion of Church attire could not be attributed to the absence of a higher political will, making clear allusions to the role of the security apparatus: "I have previously spoken to Mubarak about the registration of monks' attire and he gave his orders for implementation but we do not know who is responsible for delaying [implementation of] his orders."[10] And yet the official statement made by Mubarak indicates an unwillingness to sup- port Pope Shenouda against Maximos. When asked in a press conference about the attempt to split the Church with the ordination of a pope other than Pope Shenouda, and the possibility of his intervention to resolve the issue, President Mubarak commented, "I congratulated Pope Shenouda on his return to Egypt after his recovery [from sickness]," adding, "I do not intervene in religious affairs just as I did not intervene in the affairs of the judiciary before, and the Copts are able to resolve their problems on their own without intervention from anyone."[11] Although the statement is crafted in such as a way as to give the impression of respect for the autonomy of each institution, it is in effect a rejection of the appeals made by the pope and other members of the Church leadership. Such appeals had not only come from Church quarters but also from MPs and intellectuals. For example, twenty members of the Shura Council (upper house of parliament) made a request to the prime minister demanding clarification of the government's position on the division in the Orthodox denomination for the first time in the Church's history.[12]

Finally, Pope Shenouda warned in a television interview that "if the state supports Maximos, the Copts will revolt"—an indication of his willingness to adopt more confrontational tactics in his engagement with the state. It was an important signal to the state that its endorsement of the Church as mediator on behalf of the Copts could backfire. The Church could give its constituency political direction, but it could not be taken for granted that the Church would consistently support the government.

What is noteworthy about the Maximos saga is that it suggests that the Church–government entente was being strained on all levels. The crisis was a political one as much as it was a security one. Mubarak's refusal to respond to the Church's appeal to put an end to the Maximos saga suggests that he did not want to grant Pope Shenouda more prestige, legitimacy, and power than was seen fit or was desirable. One of the central elements of the smooth functioning of the entente was recognition of Pope Shenouda's standing, and, certainly, the Maximos saga wounded his pride terribly. It is arguable that Pope Shenouda interpreted this government stance as a failure to maintain the informal pact that existed between him and the state and that it therefore later drove him to alternate between acquiescent and confrontational stances in his dealings with the regime, as opposed to remaining consistently conciliatory.

Shenouda's Reprisal: Partial Withdrawal of Political Support for the Government

The Pope's response to the sectarian incident that erupted in May 2007 in the village of Ayat, Giza, attests to his abandonment of a quietist, behind-the-scenes approach to dealing with the government. Pope Shenouda responded by issuing an open letter addressed to the president and signed by the Majlis al-Milli in which he accused the SSI of failing to avert the crisis. The statement categorically blamed state security for not preventing sectarian strife and made reference to the SSI's knowledge of the activities leading up to the attack on the Copts and its complacency in taking any measures to stop them. The letter, which was widely published in the Egyptian press, was an embarrassment for the Egyptian government and in particular for state security, which had become the target of the Church's open and public condemnation.

Pope Shenouda's departure from his role in the entente manifested itself in another important political incident: his withdrawal of political support for NDP candidates in the Shura Council elections of 2006. While the Shura Council elections are far less important politically than presidential or parliamentary elections, this nonetheless represented the first time he failed to pledge his categorical support for the ruling party since his release from house arrest. Unlike in previous elections, Pope Shenouda did not give instructions to bishops to mobilize parishioners to vote for NDP candidates. This was possibly the first time in the history of the Church since the time of Nasser that its patriarch did not ask Copts to vote in favor of the candidates of the ruling party. Instead, Copts were urged to cast their vote for whomever represented their interests, regardless of whether they were NDP members or not.[13]

The political message of refraining from supporting the NDP relayed by the Coptic Church leadership can be seen as a reprisal for what must have been perceived as the state's undermining of the pope (through tolerance for Maximos' church) as well as its marginalization of Copts in the Shura Council. The very small number of Copts nominated by the NDP in the Shura Council elections was by default an indicator that the Church was marginalized in the political process itself. This further testifies to the growing tension between the pope and the regime and suggests that the rules of the entente—political support for the regime in return for certain political concessions for the Church leadership—were being contested by both parties.

The Rise of Coptic Civil Activism, the Demise of Church Hegemony, and the SSI Strikes Back

Two major challenges emerged during the late 2000s that were to test the Church's authority, the first associated with a number of Copts opposing the Church leadership's stance on family matters, and the second associated with Copts defying the Church's passive stance toward sectarian incidents. They were led by very different actors with different agendas, but they were both manifestations of an autonomous agency unwilling to yield to the Church.

On 29 May 2010, the Supreme Administrative Court, the court of highest appeal on administrative matters, ruled that the Coptic Church was obliged to allow two divorced Coptic men, Hani Wasfi and Magdi Ayyub, to remarry. The men had been granted civil divorces but, in accordance with Church regulations, were prohibited from marrying again. Pope Shenouda held a press conference and insisted that the Church was entitled to abide by biblical teachings that outlaw divorce, regardless of what the state said. Hundreds of Copts protested on the premises of the Abbasiya Cathedral against the court decision. The pope appealed to the president and, shortly thereafter, the Supreme Constitutional Court overruled the verdict, closing the case but not the file.

Popular reactions were divided. On the one hand, there were those who attacked the pope for his contempt for the rule of law. They argued that the refusal to accept civil divorce is only one indication of the Church's unchecked powers as a state within a state. Advocates of this stance were Islamists, human rights activists, and a few Copts known for their pro-government stance. On the other hand, there were those who maintained that the lower court's ruling was an affront to the principle of respect for the autonomy of each religious group in mediating personal status matters—marriage, divorce, child custody—in accordance with its own religious precepts. Supporters of this position were other Islamists, who spoke of the rights of non-Muslims in Muslim jurisprudence, and Coptic advocacy groups in the diaspora.

Pope Shenouda may have emerged triumphant in the eyes of his followers after the Supreme Constitutional Court ruled in his favor, but public opinion was split, with many wondering about the proper limits of the papal sphere of influence. The crisis also revealed the extent to which all parties were deploying a human rights discourse to advance non-democratic ends. Islamists, intellectuals, and high-profile, pro-government Copts who had long played down or even denied religious discrimination against Copts by state and society were suddenly eager to defend the rights of Copts against the Church. The Church, which had conventionally resisted the Islamization of politics, was suddenly making reference to the rights of non-Muslims under Islamic law. Women's rights organizations, which had never defended the rights of non-Muslim women in Muslim family law (despite the serious compromises of gender equity therein) (Tadros 2010b), were suddenly excited about saving Coptic women from the patriarchal Coptic leadership.

The second internal challenge came from Copts who chose to protest openly acts of sectarian violence even if this necessarily ran against the Church's stance on the same issues. The participation of thousands of Copts in protests after the attack in Nag' Hammadi on 6 January 2010 on Christians leaving a church after Christmas Eve mass, sustained over several weeks, was emphatically not Church-led. On 7 January, over one thousand Copts congregated in front of the hospital where the bodies of the deceased were to be delivered to their families. In an impromptu protest, they demanded the resignation of the governor, Magdi Ayyub, for failing to provide security in the governorate.[14] Another three thousand Copts assembled in the Abassiya Cathedral on 13 January 2010. They called again for Ayyub's resignation, applauded Georgette Qallini, MP, for her stand in parliament, and showed little sympathy for Kirollos, bishop of Nag' Hammadi. The bishop's position had shifted radically from the immediate aftermath of the events, when he had said, "This is a religious war about how they can finish off the Christians in Egypt." Kyrollos subsequently changed his tone and heaped praise on the government for doing everything possible to improve conditions for Copts. Rumor had it that his change of views transpired after he met a high-level delegation from Cairo led by business tycoon and then MP Ahmad Ezz, who had considerable clout within the ruling NDP party.

Protesters also called upon Pope Shenouda to take action but his response was to make an appearance on a balcony accompanied by a few bishops, who tried, to no avail, to calm the crowd. The pope's non-confrontational stance on the attacks accentuated the emerging disconnect between the religious hierarchy and the Coptic citizenry. No sign of this disconnect was clearer than during the events of 17 February in Abbasiya Cathedral, where the pope resides. An estimated five thousand Copts convened at the cathedral by candlelight to mark the passage of forty days since the attacks in Nag' Hammadi and demand a more concerted effort in addressing sectarianism. Commemorations forty days after a person's death are a tradition upheld by both Christians and Muslims, dating back to the time of the pharaohs. All protests stopped at seven o'clock, in time for participants to attend the pope's weekly sermon, which was open to all members of the Coptic Orthodox Church. Yet the pope ignored what was happening in his cathedral, using the occasion to emphasize the prohibition of marriage between Coptic Orthodox and Catholics, and between a widower and his bereaved sister-in-law.

The gap between the Coptic Church leadership and the laity undermined the bargaining power of the Church with the state. The Church leadership banked on its ability to mobilize parishioners in support of its political stances in its engagement with the regime. In return for mobilizing its constituency in favor of ruling party candidates in elections, for example, the regime was expected to grant certain concessions to the Church. These concessions did not necessarily trickle down to the flock. Now, disillusionment with the Church hierarchy, added to distrust of the government's willingness to protect Copts as citizens, weakened popular responsiveness to calls from the pope or other Church officials to support the government. Indeed, on 24 February, demonstrators stood before the High Court of Justice to demand the release of those held by the police in Nag' Hammadi for denouncing police complicity in the sectarian incidents. What was slowly emerging was a Coptic citizenry no longer willing to be directed by the Church in its exercise of political and civil rights. The implications were that citizen engagement was emerging in new spaces (such as the group of Copts who chose to protest in Tahrir Square rather than in the cathedral), with new agendas (that touched on day-to-day forms of discrimination) and new protagonists (such as politically marginalized youth).

The string of peaceful protests led by Copts dispelled the pervasive myths that Copts were no longer active citizens and that they had succumbed to the "creeping Islamization" of society by taking refuge within Church walls and immersing themselves in religiosity. The fact that thousands occupied public and Church spaces to demand their rights as citizens pointed to a high degree of political engagement. However, neither the intelligentsia nor Islamists nor the SSI saw the Coptic protests as independent of the Coptic Orthodox Church leadership, whether at a headquarters or a diocese level. As is evident from the article quoted at the beginning of the chapter, the SSI firmly believed that Coptic Church priests and bishops were the movers and shakers behind the protests. The Islamists, including prominent thinkers like Muhammad Selim al-'Awa, firmly believed that this was part of a strategy by the Church to flex its muscles further.

The SSI sought to 'punish' Pope Shenouda for his perceived unwillingness to contain the protests against the Egyptian regime through the Wafaa Constantine conundrum (see pages 76–81), which categorically turned public opinion against him. The Salafis (extreme ultra-orthodox Muslims), who had long had an entente with the SSI against the Muslim Brotherhood (Tadros 2012c) and who had thus far refused to participate formally in politics, waged a campaign against Pope Shenouda himself, the Coptic Orthodox Church leadership, and the Coptic minority. It seemed logical that state security would leave the pope to suffer the full force of unruly popular sentiment, in the form of sustained demonstrations and other open calls for his removal. But in this particular instance, security forces were complacent to the point of complicity in creating an enabling environment for Salafis to intensify their campaign against the pope in a context in which most protests and demonstrations by non-state actors were banned and met with police brutality. State security clearly emerged victorious in the interim, leaving Pope Shenouda with minimal room for maneuver. According to one press report, fourteen separate Salafi protests demanding the 'release' of Camillia Shehata, one of the Coptic women said to have converted to Islam, came from mosques in 2010.[15] Since protests could not occur without police consent, with 'illegal' gatherings being rapidly ringed in and dispersed, it goes without saying that state security allowed the anti-Christian slogans and speeches to be made out in the open on these occasions.

One of the demands of the Islamist protesters was that Camillia Shehata appear in public, since they argued that she was locked up against her will like Wafaa Constantine. The reasons behind Pope Shenouda's delay in having Camillia Shehata make a public appearance are unknown. Is it that he did not have the permission of the SSI to do so? When Camillia Shehata made a public appearance, she accused the SSI of confiscating her personal papers and hinted at their misuse of them. The pope may have assumed that the issue would eventually blow over, at the same time underestimating the extent to which the SSI would contribute to the enabling environment for the Salafis to sustain their attack. He may also have underestimated the extent to which the Camillia Shehata saga was generating communal hostilities toward Copts. Certainly, when Camillia Shehata appeared many months later on television (see chapter 7), there were many who wondered if an earlier appearance could have defused the situation. Pope Shenouda's handling of the Shehata saga left a great deal to be desired. The Church's policy of silence was interpreted as evidence that the accusations that Shehata had converted and was being held against her will probably held some truth. By 2011, the situation had become so explosive on the ground for Christians, who were routinely subjected to accusations on the street that their Church was locking up Muslim women, that a Coptic activist who spoke on condition of anonymity confided that she and others sought a meeting with the pope during one of his Wednesday sermons to convey the urgent necessity of a Church response to the Camillia saga. The pope's gatekeepers sought to prevent her from conveying the message so that in the end she handed the pope a handwritten note. She believes that Camillia Shehata's appearance a few days later was a response to that.

In the middle of this saga, in a 15 September 2010 interview with widely read newspaper *Al-Masry Al-Youm*, Bishop Bishoy added fuel to the fire. Asked if monasteries and other Church properties should come under the management of the state, as many of the protesters wanted, he replied, with considerable annoyance, "That's incredible! The people who demand such things are forgetting that the Copts are the original inhabitants of Egypt. We are interacting lovingly with guests who descended upon us." A few lines earlier, Bishoy had referred to the *jizya*—the poll tax formerly imposed upon non-Muslims, which the Copts paid until 1856—so the reader was left in no doubt that the 'guests' were Egypt's seventh-century Arab conquerors and their Muslim descendants.

On the same day, an enraged Muhammad Selim al-'Awa took to Al Jazeera's airwaves to excoriate Bishoy for his remarks. He emphasized that, in the case of Camillia Shehata, an authoritarian regime was allied with a Church that was refusing to comply with the constitution, the rule of law, and the sovereignty of the Egyptian state. He then accused the diocese of Port Said of importing weapons from Israel by sea, presumably in preparation for armed action against Muslims. It was the first time, he concluded, that there was an organized separatist plan for the establishment of a Coptic state. This incendiary allegation, emanating from a figure of such political weight, was enough to spark sectarian attacks across the country, as demonstrators outside mosques exclaimed, "We are not guests!" The police, meanwhile, leaked to the press that the Port Said shipment in question was from China, not Israel, and that it contained toys, not weaponry. Public opinion was beginning to favor the notion that the Church was acting as though it were a state within a state. Yet it is striking that there should be such resemblance between the content of the complaint of the Ministry of Interior as exemplified in the memorandum from Habib al-Adli to Ahmad Nazif mentioned at the beginning of this chapter and that of the Islamists' and the opposition's response to the Shehata saga. While this is not to suggest that the SSI manufactured the response in its entirety, it is to suggest that there is at the very least a convergence of agendas. The political space of the Coptic Orthodox Church may have narrowed, but 'alley space' was being claimed by independent Coptic movements, a theme to which I return in chapters 5 and 6.

Conclusion

The situation toward the last days of Mubarak's regime suggests that the entente between Church and state was under intense strain. For the Church's part, Pope Shenouda III resorted to the same measures and tactics of open protest and dissent that he used in the 1970s. These included retreating to his monastery, protesting against government policies in public letters, making open appeals to the authorities calling for action against injustice, and finally, and perhaps most importantly, withdrawing the full and unconditional political support he had rendered to the regime and the ruling party. For the president, his tolerance of the existence and indeed expansion of a parallel church whose leader claimed to be the patriarch of the Coptic Orthodox people cannot be interpreted in any other way except as an attempt to undermine Shenouda as the uncontested leader of the Copts.

One can only speculate as to the causes behind the cracks in the entente. No doubt, the personal political commitment of the president and the pope (even if they could be assured, which is again questionable) had become insufficent to sustain an entente of the kind that existed in the 1950s. There were too many important players on both sides with diverse and changing agendas and that had enormous impact on the potential for the entente's preservation. For example, besides the 'will' of Pope Shenouda, there were the agendas of a diverse, pluralistic, and active Coptic diaspora. Some of them had begun openly to contest the authority of the pope to speak on behalf of all Copts and were using their own power base to mediate requests, which radically challenged the way in which the Egyptian state chose or preferred to handle the 'Coptic question' in Egypt. Moreover, there was also dissidence within the ranks of the ecclesiastical order, so it became very difficult to guarantee obedience to the will of the pope across all the bishoprics and parishes. Different bishops also had different arrangements and alliances with individuals and power bases within the Mubarak's regime. For the government's part, while Pope Shenouda continuously made appeals to President Mubarak personally, this did not necessarily always translate into a 'government' response to a situation or criris. There was also the will of the SSI to contend with, since it had almost become a parallel state within a state in its own right. It is difficult to know whether the government's political will was expressing itself through the state security apparatus or if the latter had become sufficiently autonomous to be able to pursue its own agendas vis-à-vis the Church.

The pope continued to extend and withdraw support to and from the government depending on the nature of concessions being secured at any particular moment. Pope Shenouda was aware that a rupture in relations would lead to his complete political marginalization and an opportunity for his enemies or contenders within and outside the Church to fill his place. On the other hand, President Mubarak was aware that there was much at stake in alienating the pope, especially with respect to his public image internationally.

Toward the very last days of Mubarak's rule, the tacit agreement between pope and president continued to survive, albeit hanging by a weak thread. It was usually left to Zakariya Azmi, head of the Presidential Office, to convey messages from the president to the pope, but toward the end of the Mubarak era, it became increasingly difficult to get the ear of the president via his counsellors, and communication between Pope Shenouda and President Mubarak became less frequent. The entente between the state security apparatus and the Coptic Orthodox Church leadership had evaporated by the end of Mubarak's era and Pope Shenouda's bargaining power and access to policy-influencing arenas had become weak. Bishop Moussa's reflections on Pope Shenouda's maneuvering space in the last phase of Mubarak's reign are telling. He said that toward the end, the only channel open to the Coptic Church for expressing grievances was through the president—if they could get through to him. Neither parliament nor political parties were open to listening and there were no Copts in parliament with whom to engage. "When we used to cry out to the President through Zakariya Azmi and Mustapha al-Fiqi, the President would intervene in the issues we raised only, for example, when the Shubra al-Khayma building was demolished, or when the governor of the

Red Sea was harassing us," said Bishop Moussa,[16] but explained that the Coptic leadership's room for maneuver was becoming steadily slimmer.

The 25 January Revolution showed not only that the SSI's quest to prevent Copts from protesting would be thwarted once again, but also that the Church leadership would have very little power over the Copts who chose to participate in the uprisings. The revolution challenged the notion that Pope Shenouda was the sole legitimate representative of the Coptic citizenry's political demands. Citizenship via the pope's proxy had been eroding bit by bit, challenged from more quarters than one, a theme to which I return in chapters 5 and 6.

5 | Mitigation, Management, and Resolution of Sectarianism under Mubarak

This chapter examines the escalation of violence against the Christian minority in particular during the last decade of the Mubarak era. It examines the causes of conflict between Muslims and Christians, what precipitates hostilities, how incidents are managed, and how they are settled. The first part of the chapter presents three case studies of sectarian assault, all occurring in 2010–2011. These are presented in the chronological order of their unfolding: first, the Nag' Hammadi incident, which points to collective assault on Copts specifically on the basis of their religious affiliation; second, the Camillia Shehata saga, which points to the use of women as pawns for religious mobilization; and, third, the crisis erupting over the building belonging to what became known as the "'Umraniya Church clashes." These three incidents are reflective to a large extent of main areas of sectarian violence. The second part of the chapter analyzes the micro-dynamics of conflict in Mubarak's Egypt, highlighting emerging patterns of the precipitation of sectarian assault on Copts, how these are managed, and the ways in which 'closure' is played out.

The nature of the assaults on Copts witnessed under Mubarak's rule was qualitatively different from the communal violence the country witnessed during Sadat's era in the 1970s, when violent assaults reached their apex. In the 1970s, sectarian violence largely took the form of attacks on churches and other places of Coptic worship, as well private businesses (goldsmiths, pharmacies, and so on). The attacks were often launched by members of militant Islamist groups, who would initiate attacks in areas other than the ones they originally came from and, in that sense, were seen as 'alien' to the communities in which they erupted.

Mufid Shihab, the former minister of state for legal and parliamentary affairs and the regime's point man for human rights matters, dismissed the incidents witnessed in Mubarak's Egypt, reiterating the usual discourse of isolated incidents and complete religious harmony: "All I can say is that Egypt is free from sectarian strife, though there are isolated sectarian clashes from time to time between extremist Muslims and Copts."[1] Yet the sectarian attacks of the 2000s in particular were directed not only at places of worship but also at individual citizens and communities. They were instigated not by outsiders or Islamist radical groups but often by ordinary people. However, as indicated in chapter 2, religious intolerance had become internally bred and diffused, not externally induced, which implies that social relations between citizens had, to a very large extent, in certain parts, become defined by religious polarization. This is due in no small measure to the role of the government, in particular the SSI, as well as the pervasive cumulative impact of the Islamization of society from below.

The Nag' Hammadi Incident
and the Collective Punishment of a Community

A murderous nighttime attack on Coptic worshipers as they left a church on 6 January 2010, the Coptic Orthodox Christmas Eve, in the Upper Egyptian town of Nag' Hammadi left six Copts and one Muslim guard dead, as well as many more wounded. As with all previous incidents when violence broke out between Egypt's Muslim majority and its Coptic Christian minority, the Egyptian government was quick to deny that the motive could be sectarian. Spokesmen pointed to "foreign fingers" that were supposedly stirring up sedition, in hopes that the file on the incident could be closed as quickly as possible and the state could resume displaying an image of Egypt as typified by 'national unity.'

In this incident, the government adopted another conventional response to sectarian clashes—deployment of a heavy security presence—and this time, too, this backfired. Immediately after the shootings, the state sent contingents of riot police to Nag' Hammadi and its environs in the province of Qena to enforce peace and block entry to and exit from the town. Neither mission succeeded. The burning of houses and shops, mostly owned by Christians but also some owned by Muslims, continued in several sites in Qena. The security cordon, rather than detracting attention from the killings, caused the government major embarrassment, as the news media protested the blockade but continued reporting all the same. When the security apparatus arrested members of human rights groups who had come to investigate the incident, the news was widely circulated by the organizations, sparking an international outcry.

Premeditated murder

The security forces in Qena moved fast to make arrests in the case, detaining three local men on charges of premeditated murder on 8 January. The three, allegedly led by Muhammad Hasan al-Kamuni, were said to have committed the crime in retaliation for the rape of a twelve-year-old Muslim girl by a Christian youth in the vicinity of Nagʻ Hammadi on 19 November 2009.

There had already been vigilante retribution for this alleged assault, though police detained a Coptic street vendor the same day and charged him with rape. On 22 November, in the village of Farshut, a number of shops, pharmacies, and houses belonging to Copts were set on fire by unidentified young men shouting, "We are avenging the honor of our daughter." Shortly afterward, local authorities told the Copts of al-Kom al-Ahmar, the home village of the alleged rapist, that the state feared for their safety and thought it best if they temporarily left. Many Muslims protected their Christian neighbors' property, but there were still attacks on homes and shops, raising questions of police complicity.

As Christmas drew near, according to Bishop Kirollos of the Nagʻ Hammadi diocese, the atmosphere grew tense. He reported getting the message, "It is your turn," on his cell phone. "My faithful were also receiving threats in the streets," he told the Associated Press after the Nagʻ Hammadi shootings. "Some were shouting at them, 'We will not let you have festivities.'"

It appeared, therefore, that the Nagʻ Hammadi murders were part of a pattern of sectarian incidents characterized by two important features. First, a crime attributed to a Christian was answered with collective punishment of all Coptic citizens in the area and, second, state security was lax in containing vigilantism, which implies that the possibility of the SSI's involvement in catalyzing the tensions cannot be overlooked. In October 2009, there was another illustrative series of events in Dayrut, a town in the province of Asyut, north of Qena. A Christian man was accused of disseminating racy photos of a young Muslim woman via cell phone, leading her family to kill his father. There is a long tradition in Upper Egypt of vendettas *(tha'r)* in response to murder or crimes related to 'family honor'—usually referring to sexual assaults on women—prompting the killing of the person responsible for the crime or a member of his family. Yet the Dayrut events escalated beyond the bounds of a predictable honor killing. Shortly after the incident, the local al-Azhar Institute, a branch of the storied mosque-university in Cairo, was the site of incitement against Christians, which culminated in sporadic burning and looting of Coptic-owned properties.

No isolated act

The Nag' Hammadi attack rapidly proved difficult to contain on the political front as well, as opposition and civil society actors were unexpectedly harsh in their criticism of the government's handling of sectarian crises and persistent in their articulation of demands for change. On 9 January, senior leaders of political parties, human rights activists, and members of civil society organizations gathered in front of the Egyptian High Court of Justice to protest. Representatives of the protesters submitted an appeal to the prosecutor general to examine the laxity of state security in dealing with the incidents in Nag' Hammadi, Farshut, and Dayrut.

Independent human rights groups like the Egyptian Organization for Human Rights had vigorously investigated past episodes of sectarian violence, such as the 1998 killing of two Copts in the Upper Egyptian village of al-Kushh. However, since then, most human rights organizations have been silent on the matter of the rising number of sectarian incidents, with just a few exceptions. But the official account of Nag' Hammadi was subjected to scrutiny from a much wider portion of the political spectrum, including quasi-official bodies that had scarcely before acknowledged a problem with religious discrimination in Egypt. On 3 February 2010, some two hundred public figures and activists rallied before the People's Assembly to call for action against the increasing occurrence of sectarian attacks in Egypt. Among the participants were members of the National Committee against Sectarian Violence, a civil society initiative formed only days before the Nag' Hammadi attacks. The protesters presented to Fathi Surur, the speaker of parliament, a list of demands, including changes to the common law on places of worship, which had been awaiting parliamentary debate since 2005, as well as issuance of legislation against discrimination and for equal opportunity and religious freedoms.[2]

Tensions over Nag' Hammadi were heightened after the release of a highly critical report produced by the government-controlled National Council for Human Rights (NCHR). The council sent its own fact-finding mission to the scene, including former Coptic MP Georgette Qallini, but critics were disappointed by the lack of follow-through. Despite its hard-hitting contents, the report closed with a diluted statement merely condemning the incident without recommending further action. A parliamentary session chaired by Fathi Surur ended in stormy confrontations between Qallini and the governor of Qena, Magdi Ayyub al-Masri, as well as Surur and other members of the ruling party. Qallini was appointed to parliament by the president, rather than elected, but she was an outspoken critic of the conduct of the executive branch in Nag' Hammadi. In the parliamentary session, the Qena governor repeated police claims that al-Kamuni was driven by his anger over the rape of the Muslim child by the Christian man in Farshut. Surur asked if there were sectarian underpinnings to his rage. The governor said no, that al-Kamuni was a "registered criminal" whose motives were "criminal and not political." He added that calm had returned to Nag' Hammadi. A heated debate ensued in which Qallini accused the governor of lying, noting that while he claimed all was quiet, the town of Bahgura, close to Farshut, was burning. The then members of the ruling party defending the government drowned out her voice by jeering.[3]

The argument that the Nag' Hammadi attack was an 'isolated' act of anger had already been debunked by independent commentators. Ibrahim Eissa, editor-in-chief of the newspaper *al-Dustur*, was scathing: "The representation of the crime as though it were a vendetta is no less a crime than the original murders. Since when have Upper Egyptians pursued a vendetta by killing at random? The vendetta has rules; it is carried out against the actual violator or his family, not randomly." In words reiterated by other critics, Eissa continued: "The choice of day and place—the feast day of Copts and the church where they celebrate it—shows that the shooting was aimed at the Coptic faith and community, not against a Coptic rapist or his family. Let's not beat around the bush: This was an act of extremism and fanaticism, and all this talk about an isolated, individual act is nonsense."[4]

While the incident propelled many to decry openly the performance of the SSI in its handling of sectarian incidents, calls to "de-securitize" the management of such matters were easier said than done. There are fundamental challenges to engaging with sectarianism in Egypt through appropriate political channels rather than through the prism of a 'security file.' The government lacks the political will to acknowledge the deep-seated sectarianism in Egypt, the kind that is not instigated by foreign powers or Islamist extremists and not 'exaggerated' by troublemakers seeking to tarnish Egypt's image. Mufid Shihab, in Geneva to defend Egypt's record before the U.N. Human Rights Council, not only denied the existence of sectarianism but also promised that the government would "do more to correct reports made by some organizations in this respect." There was speculation that the persistence of sectarian strife gave the regime an excuse to keep extending the state of emergency first imposed in 1981, which allowed it all manner of extraconstitutional leeway.

But it was not only the absence of political will that was obstructing the process of addressing the homegrown roots of sectarian tension. With the exception of select political party leaders, human rights activists, and intellectuals who had come out against an ineffective, piecemeal approach to the growing violence, society was still, by and large, in a state of denial. The Nag' Hammadi attacks are a case in point. The difficulty in engaging communities on sectarianism by making them look at the issues and talk about them arose from the fact that the concept of citizenship had become politically and socially bankrupt, so that people tended to cling ever-defensively to their religious identities.

'Gendering' religious strife and religionizing gender struggles

A few months after the Nag' Hammadi incident, from July 2010 and up to April 2011, another sectarian crisis erupted, this time of a very different nature and reflective of the centrality of how gender relations on a micro level had come to bear on the wider political arena. The moral panic came to a head with the case of Camillia Shehata, twenty-seven years of age, known in the media and on protesters' placards simply as "Camillia." At the end of July 2010, she was reported missing by her husband, the priest of an Upper Egyptian parish. Hundreds of Copts demonstrated at the local diocese amid suspicions that she had been abducted and forcibly converted to Islam.[5] Shortly afterward, the SSI revealed that Camillia was in Cairo and was not being held hostage. The police placed her in the custody of her husband and father, in keeping with deeply patriarchal (and bicommunal) norms of treating women as minors in need of guardianship.[6] Her family said she was residing at an undisclosed location belonging to the Coptic Church. On the street, however, the story became that she had been 'handed over' to the Church. Rumor had it that Camillia had willingly converted to Islam and taken up the *niqab* (full face veil), and that she was being detained against her will by the Church, along with another wife of a priest. Mosques packed for prayers at the end of Ramadan became rally sites where banners were lifted for "freeing sister Camillia" and taking disciplinary action against Pope Shenouda.[7]

It is important to note that the campaign to release Camillia Shehata from her supposed bondage at the hands of the Church was also championed by human rights and women's rights organizations. The Arab Network for Human Rights Information held a press conference on missing persons at which it called upon the Coptic leadership to allow Camillia to speak freely to the "outside world." Women's rights figures stood up to demand the emancipation of Camillia from an oppressive Church. A women's rights organization, the Center for Egyptian Women's Legal Aid, intended to file a lawsuit against the Church to compel disclosure of Camillia's whereabouts.[8]

Camillia then appeared in a videoclip posted on YouTube. She confirmed the state security's tale that she had left her home of her own volition and had not been abducted. She continued that she was not being held against her will by the Church, but was in seclusion to escape the media and its intrusion into her personal life. According to interviews with family members, she had left home because of a protracted marital dispute, a situation to which her husband, the priest, later admitted. The prominent Islamist thinker Muhammad Selim al-'Awa stated on the air that Camillia had not converted to Islam and had been 'handed over' to her family.

But the matter was far from over. State security said the video was authentic, but doubtful protesters claimed that the woman on screen was not Camillia, but a lookalike. Dozens of Muslim women dressed in *niqab* entered the streets to demand that "sister Camillia" be allowed to practice her religion, Islam. The demonstrators held aloft pictures of a woman, said to be Camillia, wearing a *niqab*. They raised slogans against the head of al-Azhar for his silence on the case. Most significantly, they openly accused Pope Shenouda III of keeping Muslim women in Christian custody against their will and accordingly demanded that he be removed as head of the Church.[9]

Given the great sensitivity of Muslim–Christian relations in Egypt, the fact that the SSI allowed the protests to build up and to spread meant that they bore the stamp of the SSI's blessings on them. It is not difficult to understand why the SSI consented to these protests: its long-time vendetta with Pope Shenouda over the Wafaa Constantine affair was still simmering, and this provided it with an opportunity to put him in his place. On 3 September, demonstrations took place near the giant al-Fath Mosque in downtown Cairo. The ensuing week, after the Eid al-Fitr prayers that mark the close of Ramadan, protests occurred at the 'Amr ibn al-'As Mosque in Old Cairo,[10] calling upon President Hosni Mubarak to "recover" Camillia from Church custody. On 24 September, thousands joined a gathering outside the al-Qa'id Ibrahim mosque in Egypt's second city of Alexandria to reiterate the plea for presidential intervention.[11] On 1 October, thousands more, including members of the Islamist-led lawyers' syndicate and numerous cadres of the Salafi movement, took to the streets around al-Fath. The next week, an esti-mated two thousand people demonstrated in Alexandria, repeating the chants about Camillia and denouncing Pope Shenouda and other Church hierarchs.[12]

There were sporadic demonstrations by Copts, including a handful in the diaspora, as Egyptian Christians living in the United States and Great Britain went out to protest against the anti-Church rallies taking place in their home country. Coptic protesters in Egypt usually assemble at the Coptic Patriarchate in the central Cairo district of Abbasiya, where Pope Shenouda resides. In this crisis, however, he strictly prohibited any such actions on the premises.

Lost honor of lost women

The hubbub over Camillia Shehata is a clear case of how sectarian sentiment can be fomented and directed by individuals sharing notions of imagined communities, as famously conceived by Benedict Anderson (1991). There will never be a shortage of women to serve as pawns in the battle over what is often constructed as a threat to religion. Almost every actor of political significance—human rights advocates, intellectuals, writers, political figures—has had something to say about Camillia. Interestingly, and to their credit, the Muslim Brothers have not. However, renowned members of the Muslim Brotherhood were seen at the demonstration in Alexandria. The Brothers' official abstention notwithstanding, there has been a strong sense among many Muslims that a recalcitrant Coptic leadership is willfully provoking the Muslim majority.

Copts, on the other hand, have perceived a predetermined agenda to portray Camillia as a Muslim, irrespective of the measures taken to show her free agency. They have been alarmed, as well, that many demonstrations have moved on from the specific matter of Camillia to shout out another message: "Down with Pope Shenouda."

In Egypt, however, there is no freedom of religion in the first place. Egyptian citizens who are not Sunni Muslims do not enjoy equal rights to practice their religion freely. In the Camillia saga, it is important to remember that while the majority of Sunni Muslims are subject to severe restrictions, and possible persecution, if they wish to convert to Christianity, Christians are permitted to embrace Islam as a matter of course. The imbalance in the right to freedom of religion was further accentuated with the abolition by state security of the *ligan al-nush wa-li-irshad* (guidance committees) in 2003. These committees allowed the Church or Coptic families to verify whether members who wished to convert were doing so of their own free will. This move only intensified the conviction of Copts that they must rely on the Church's bargaining power, rather than citizenship rights, to negotiate with the state.

It is a truism of study of patriarchal societies that concepts of honor are tied to women. The Coptic demonstrations in Upper Egypt upon the 'disappearance' of Camillia Shehata were driven by a sense of having lost a priest's wife to a predatory state, one representing the interests of the majority rather than being the state of all its citizens. The phenomenon of abduction is thoroughly gendered in Egypt, since it is always a woman, and never a man, who is thought to have been abducted for the purposes of conversion. When rallies later took place in every part of Egypt, they were driven by a desire to emancipate the Camillia who had ostensibly donned the *niqab* from the clutches of the Church. The gatherings were about defending the honor of Muslims in claiming what is rightfully theirs—a sister in Islam. At no time in memory had such a large number of women wearing the *niqab* engaged, week after week, in collective protest.

Certainly, there have been fierce sectarian clashes over land, places of worship, and the commentary of religious leaders, but none has so fired the imagination of both Muslims and Christians like cases involving women in what is an intensely patriarchal society. At the same time, some women's rights activists also took sides, assuming that Camillia was being held against her will, which suggests that they, too, had fallen into the trap of objectifying the woman under scrutiny. Tellingly, none of the women's rights activists who spoke out had any kind of constituency of Coptic women behind her. The stand of these women, side by side with staunchly anti-feminist Islamists demanding Camillia's 'release,' shows that the crisis of inter-communal relations is underpinned by highly dubious power games.

The Egyptian regime was practiced at deflecting the public's attention from grave political and economic crises with the religion/gender card. One case in point is the vehement debate in 2006 over Culture Minister Farouk Hosni's negative public statements on veiling, at a time when the regime was busily designing fixes to the electoral system that had, much to their chagrin, brought eighty-eight Muslim Brotherhood members to parliament the preceding year. At that particular political moment, in the summer and autumn of 2011, the regime again desperately needed a diversion. There was growing dissent surrounding the transparency of the November parliamentary elections, which put increasing stress on the regime while tarnishing its external image. Further, with official sources stating that the prices of vegetables and fruit (not to mention meat) had risen by 300 percent, the government was particularly wary of issues that could unite the population across various dividing lines. Ibrahim Eissa brilliantly captured this dynamic in an article titled "al-Aqbat al-Muslimun wa-l-lahma" (Copts, Muslims, and Meat).[13] Eissa was fired on 5 October 2011 from his position as editor of *al-Dustur* newspaper after he insisted on publishing a short piece by the independent opposition figure and former director of the International Atomic Energy Agency Mohamed ElBaradei. It is no secret that the termination order came from al-Sayyid al-Badawi, who had purchased the paper the previous month and is the leader of Wafd, a then regime-friendly opposition party. The firing of Eissa, as well as other critical writers, may be seen as part of a clampdown on the press, which served the same purpose for state security as the sectarian demonstrations, guaranteeing minimal attention to the parliamentary elections.

The Art of Not Being Governed
In November 2010, in the informal settlement of 'Umraniya in the governorate of Giza, the central security forces attacked a church on the basis of its violation of the law of construction and renovation of churches. The church had been offering informal accommodation to an increasing

number of parishioners by converting part of an adjacent building into a prayer room.[14] The security forces arrived on the premises, intending to tear down the building for being in violation of the law, specifically its stipulation that permission must be obtained before any structure is used as a place of worship. This security move provoked the congregation to mount a protest at the site. Police waded into the crowd, leading to the death of two parishioners and the injury of many others. Over 150 Copts were incarcerated, and released only in early January 2011. The press blasted the protesters for failure to respect the rule of the law, mostly neglecting to mention the discriminatory strictures in the law against the construction of places of worship by Christians. It is a fact that hundreds of buildings used as mosques do not have permits yet are supplied by the government with water and electricity, and certainly not threatened with demolition by the police.

What followed was highly critical in revealing the extent to which an organic Coptic lay protest movement was emerging independently of the Church—and indeed in direct contestation with the Church authorities. Rather than protesting within the confines of the church courtyard, Coptic youth took to the streets.[15] The significance of this public act cannot be emphasized enough. It suggested that they had gone beyond seeing the Church as the mediator between them and the state in addressing their demands and rights as citizens and had gone to claim such rights for themselves. When Copts protested behind the church fences, they were appealing to the Church leadership authorities to relay their anger to the policymakers. When they took to the streets, they were claiming rights for themselves. By default, it means that they had refused the patronage of the Church over them politically, even if the Church continued to be the base for fulfilling their spirituality and practice of faith.

The Coptic youth-led public protests, which were widely discredited in most of the press outlets as being full of anger and seeking *masalih fi'awiya* (narrow interests), mobilized dozens of people. They publicly attacked President Hosni Mubarak, the Ministry of Interior, the governor of Giza, and the regime itself.

Among the Copts interviewed who participated in the 25 January uprisings, many said that they believed the Copts' protests from 'Umraniya were the real precursor to the revolution because they were an instance of average citizens, not the political elites belonging to Kefaya and other movements, protesting against the state. The intensity of their assault on the government, captured in their attacks with stones and bricks on the Mudiriyat Amn al-Giza (Giza Security Directorate), was alarming. It indicated that an important barrier of fear had been broken. Concurrently, it showed the extent to which the Coptic Orthodox Church was unable either to contain or to control the Coptic lay citizenry, which had chosen to exercise its agency in a highly contentious way, irrespective of what the Church told them to do.

An analysis of a series of attacks on Copts[16] suggests that there is a number of recurring factors that amounts to a disconcerting pattern of failure to prevent their occurrence, poor handling of the situations themselves, and ineffective resolution of the conflicts. A number of important recurring patterns of engagement are analyzed here. First, some incidents were premeditated, and the SSI was alerted to the possibility of their occurrence but no action was taken to mitigate the simmering crisis or take the precautionary security measures to prevent their escalation into clashes. Often there is material evidence to suggest that an attack was imminent, such as the distribution of highly inflammatory flyers and handouts. On 10 February 2002 in the village of Bani Walams, affiliated to the municipality of al-Adwa in the Upper Egyptian governorate of Minya, a mob attacked the local church (St. Mary's) while the congregation was saying celebratory prayers following its refurbishment. They burned thirteen homes and several cars, while the church exterior was damaged as a result of stone throwing. According to Bishop Agathon, who was present in the church at the time, the SSI was informed of the possibility of an assault happening on that day forty-eight hours before, and the priest had reported the threats received, warning of an assault on the congregation that worshiped in the church.

On Friday, 9 January 2008, the SSI was made aware that the residents of the village of al-Nazla, in Fayoum intended to undertake an assault on the Copts in the village that same day and did nothing to prevent the looting and burning of private property and the church premises. When a Coptic woman who had converted to Islam and married in the village left her home and fled with her child to her parents in Cairo, the villagers were insulted, and rumors spread that she was kidnapped. The villagers sought revenge for the woman's escape by systematically burning homes and twenty private businesses belonging to Copts and attacking the church.[17]

In Alexandria, when rumors spread that a play derogatory to Islam called "I Was Blind but Now I See" had been performed two years previously in a local church, on 21 October 2005 thousands of demonstrators from the nearby mosque gathered in front of the church in question following Friday prayers, shouting anti-government, anti-church slogans and holding high copies of the Qur'an. When protesters tried to force their way into the church, security forces responded by using rubber bullets and tear gas. The events did not stop there, but spread into nearby suburbs, leading to attacks on nearby churches, the destruction of a hospital and several shops belonging to Christians, as well as the burning of several cars. During demonstrations, eyewitnesses reported that Bibles were burned and people condemned the government for turning against the Muslims and protecting the Christian traitors. There were also calls for a formal apology from Pope Shenouda, as head of the Coptic Orthodox Church, for offending Muslims and demands that he take action against those responsible. The police, despite knowing that there had been calls made throughout the preceding week for worshipers to congregate after prayers on that day at the nearby mosque, just stood and watched as the number of people in front of the church increased, only finally intervening when attempts were made to storm the church.

In the village of Bamha where two thousand people had mobilized on the 11 May 2007 to attack Christian property after rumors spread that a Copt intended to convert his home into a church, flyers were distributed the night before inciting Muslims to take action. The matter came to the attention of Coptic citizens, who had alerted the security forces on Friday morning, but no action was taken (Shoukry 2009; Andrawous 2007).

A second recurring pattern is that attacks often occur on Fridays, following morning prayers. The local mosque is often a space used for the incitement and mobilization of members of the community to violence. The local sheikh, or someone given the floor, often makes inflammatory speeches during the Friday sermon, using religious idiom and rhetoric to incite the faithful to attack the non-Muslim population.

In the case of the assault on the church in the village of Bani Walams (see above), the rhetoric emanating from the local mosque (which was heard by all via loudspeaker) was highly inflammatory and directly called upon believers to take action against unbelievers.

In the case of Bamha above, the assault occurred on Friday, 11 May 2007, and was soon followed by calls to jihad. According to witnesses, the local mosque's imam was responsible for inciting the people to go out and attack Copts during the Friday prayers. In fact, the Copt whose home was allegedly going to be converted into a church was building an extension for a place for his soon-to-be married son. The assault involved the burning of thirty-five homes and property, the looting of agricultural produce, and the injury of ten persons, with two left in serious condition.

On Friday, 7 November 2003, in the village of Gerza, affiliated to the municipality of al-Ayat in the governorate of Giza, thirteen homes were burned and looted and no fewer than five Copts were injured. The Copts of the village, having failed to obtain an official permit to build a local parish church, had congregated for prayers in one of the local residents' homes.

It is likely that a significant proportion, if not most, of the incidents mentioned here occurred on a Friday, following prayers, after delivery of an inflammatory sermon, through the use of the mosque space for the mobilization of collective action, urging people to go out on a jihad, to defend their Muslim brothers, and so on.

A third recurring factor is that the escalation of violence sometimes takes the form of collective punishment of members of the Coptic community, in reprisal for the occurrence of a dispute between two individuals, a Muslim and a Copt. When villagers heard that the wife of a Muslim man, Muhammad al-Sayyid Zaki, who was a convert to Islam, had fled her home, they sought revenge by burning the houses of the Copts in the village despite the fact that they had nothing to do with the case.

Following the discovery of an illegitimate relationship between a Christian man and a married Muslim woman, people leaving a mosque after prayers on Friday, 20 June 2008, in the village of Tamya, Fayoum, called upon residents to join them for a protest on the Friday after against the Copts of the village. This was despite the fact that the two families had already resolved the matter. Some of the villagers still sought to take revenge by haphazardly burning property belonging to the Copts in the village.[18]

Moreover, when a fight erupted between a Muslim and a Coptic man, and the former was hit on the head and died in December 2005 in the municipality of Kafr Salama, in the governorate of Sharqiya, the call from the mosque was to "go save your Muslim brothers." The villagers took revenge by burning and looting the property of Copts systematically, even if they had nothing to do with the incident itself or were in no way related to the person or persons involved.

A fourth factor is that the SSI, the ambulance corps, and the fire brigade were usually alerted to the escalation of violence, but no action was taken for several hours, during which the number of casualties increased.

Following the tensions in Nagʻ Hammadi in January 2010 (see page 98), assaults were carried out on the private businesses and homes of Copts living in the nearby village of Bahgura. It took more than five hours for the fire truck and ambulance to arrive, despite being promptly informed of what had happened.[19]

In the case of the Bamha incident (see page 109), despite the fact that they had been alerted to the planned assault, the security forces and firefighters arrived two hours after the escalation of violence involving the mobilization of two thousand people. By then the property was completely burned down.

A fifth factor is that a curfew was imposed on the residents of the area in question and there was a purposeful policy of preventing journalists and human rights activists from entering the area or talking to the people involved. This was often followed by the state-sponsored media's emphasis on national unity, social harmony, and the values of citizenship.

A sixth factor is that, in terms of the means of resolving conflict, almost every incident of assault was followed by SSI-organized *ligan al-sulh* (reconciliation committees), which in effect prevented the application of the rule of law. Nabil ʻAbd al-Fattah argued that these reconciliation committees directly undermined the notion that Egypt is a country where the rule of law is mediated by the courts, in effect reducing the role of the judiciary in areas that were supposed to be under its prerogative, therefore undermining the very notion of Egypt as a modern state.

Historically, the process of modernization required a shift from a reliance on informal mechanisms of addressing disputes to one involving the development of state institutions to which citizens could resort when needed (ʻAbd al-Fattah 2010). The SSI engineered the reconciliation committees, brokered by itself, and forced the outcome upon all parties in a village, prohibiting victims from seeking justice through legal recourse. The idea of informal committees for administering justice is not a new one. They exist in many countries, and in some, such as Bangladesh, have assumed international repute. In Egypt, there is a long tradition of resorting to informal committees. Nader Shoukry highlights the fact that in the *ʻurfi* (informal) justice system, the head of a tribe who is reputed for being just and wise, and whose verdicts are considered morally binding, is called upon to arbitrate after hearing the accounts of both parties. Since the process is governed by the principles of shari'a, there are specific conditions to be met with respect to the selection of the judge, the presence of witnesses, the presence of the defense, the process of issuing a decree, and so on. However, notes Shoukry (2009), what has occurred is the distortion of how *'urfi* courts are administered. They are used as channels with which to force victims to relinquish their rights, for, absent the conditions of free choice, victims are blackmailed with the threat of further distress if they do not agree to the terms imposed upon them. Simultaneously, the perpetrators of violence or injustice escape punishment. Regrettably, even in incidents where the filing of a lawsuit is legally required because of public harm incurred (cases of terrorism, burning of public property, and so on), cases are closed on the pretext that an *'urfi* court has arbitrated in the matter.

There is one significant difference, perhaps, between *'urfi* courts as they would have been administered in tribes and Bedouin communities and as they were administered in cases of sectarian violence: namely, that the arbitrator was the SSI, which was able to exercise soft power (coercion) and hard power (incarceration and threats of torture) should citizens fail to comply. Its power did, in many instances in Mubarak's Egypt, surpass that of the Office of the National Prosecutor and, hence, it was empowered to usurp the course of justice through the administration of an *'urfi* ruling. Ironically, it is a case in which the arbitrator of justice was an accomplice in the very act of violence that was instigated in the first place.

In the 2002 incident mentioned above, in the village of Bani Wallams, the SSI propped up a reconciliation committee that forced Christian residents to commit to not filing a lawsuit against the perpetrators of violence. The imam who incited the violence was similarly not held to account. In the case of Gerza in 2003, Coptic residents were forced to attend a reconciliation session on the governorate's premises, which again involved pressure being placed on the victims to drop all charges against the perpetrators, who were released without charge. The session was characterized by the usual rhetoric of social harmony and national unity but no talk of justice.

A seventh recurring factor is that reconciliation committees institutionalized the collective subjugation of a religious minority to the majority. Perhaps one of the worst incidents of the administration of injustice through the SSI's reconciliation committees was in Kafr Salama in 2005. The likely legal recourse in this instance would have been to arrest the citizen who had entered into a fight with the victim (who died in the fight) and bring him to justice. Instead, a reconciliation session was initiated that imposed an LE500,000 *deya* (compensation fee) to be paid by *all* the Christians in the village for the deceased, who was Muslim. In addition, the family of the person who had entered into the fight was to be expelled from the village. No compensation was offered for the families in the village whose property had been looted and burned to the ground. The verdict of this reconciliation session served to deepen and institutionalize the notion of collective penalization of citizens on the basis of their affiliation to the religion of the individual who perpetrated a crime.

In the case of Bamha, the reconciliation committee ruled that the house in question could be used for Sunday School classes but its owner-ship deferred to the diocese. All legal charges filed by Christians whose property was destroyed were to be immediately dropped and the perpe-trators released. No compensation for the damage incurred was offered. Despite the fact that the house in question was not going to be used for worship, the long-standing issue of the Christians' desire to have a parish church in which to pray was raised during the reconciliation committee session.

An eighth factor is that reconciliation sessions involved the manipula-tion and blackmailing of victims into dropping all legal charges. Perhaps one of the most infamous cases of a forced reconciliation session took place in 2009 after the assault on the Abu Fana monastery, which per-turbed the National Council for Human Rights as well as a number of local human rights organizations. On 14 April 2006, a reconciliation ses-sion was convened between the monks of Abu Fana and the Bedouins living in the surrounding areas. The Bedouins acknowledged the monas-tery's entitlement to the land upon which the premises are built, agreed that the monastery was entitled to build a protective fence around its premises, and promised not to attack the monastery again. In the recon-ciliation session that followed in 2009, after an assault by Bedouins on the monastery, the monks dropped all charges and it was agreed that any contravention of this agreement would incur a fine of LE500,000.

In January 2008, the monastery of Abu Fana in Upper Egypt was attacked again by the same group of Bedouins. The monks identified the persons but no action was taken by the police to arrest them. In May 2008, sixty members of the Urban tribe attacked the monastery and bullets were fired, leading to the injury of seven monks, of whom three were kidnapped and tortured over a period of nine hours. The attack on the monastery involved the destruction of several properties and agricultural land. In the shootout, one Muslim was killed. The authorities arrested a Coptic contractor and his son despite the fact that they were not on the premises. The subsequent forensic investigation and the court ruled that there was no evidence to suggest that they were implicated and requested their immediate release, but the police did not enact the court ruling. After months of incarceration, the security forces pressured the monks to retract their lawsuit against the people of Urban in return for setting the detained Coptic contractor and his son free. On 12 September 2008, a reconciliation session was convened in which the monks agreed to drop all charges and the Urban agreed to drop charges against the contractor and his son. In return for reconciliation between the Urban and the monks, the security forces agreed to release all those detained from the Urban, plus the contractor and his son.

A ninth factor is that reconciliation sessions often encouraged more violence and assaults, whether in the same village or in adjoining ones, rather than deterring them. If one of the purposes of the reconciliation committee sessions was to foster community cohesion and tolerance by encouraging all parties to commit to a contract of no assault, they failed. The experiences of Abu Fana and 'Izbit Bushra, 'Izbit Guirgis, and 'Izbit al-Fuqa'i are clear cases in point. This is not surprising since not only were the perpetrators released without charge, but the outcomes of the reconciliation sessions also served only to send the signal that violence and assault were effective means of preventing the construction of a church in the village.

On 20 and 21 June 2009, residents of the village of 'Izbit Bushra in Beni Suef launched several attacks on the agricultural land and property of Coptic residents, angered by news that a church was to be built in their village (Shoukry 2009). The police convened a reconciliation committee in which they asked the Coptic residents to drop the charges and their Muslim counterparts not to attack the church premises and Coptic residents. Soon after, residents of the village attacked the priest's residence and citizens were attacked. The police responded by arresting nineteen Copts and eight Muslims. The response was to hold another reconciliation session, this time involving the bishop of Beni Suef, the governor of Beni Suef, officials from the Ministry of Endowments, members of parliament, and, of course, the SSI. Long speeches about national unity were made and all parties requested to live in harmony and peace. The right of Coptic citizens to have a place of worship was sidelined, and the matter more or less closed. The police followed this by releasing all those who had been detained (Shoukry 2009).

Since there are strong links between a village and its surrounding areas, the signals emanating from these reconciliation sessions (that the government would intervene to endorse the villagers' will to prevent Coptic residents from religious practice if the former rose up and made demands) encouraged other villagers to adopt similar strategies of opposition. One week after the reconciliation session in 'Izbit Bushra on Friday, 3 July 2009, members of the community of 'Izbit Guirgis, also a village in the municipality of Fashn, Beni Suef, set afire a house that was intended to be used as a church and destroyed the homes of Copts, with the knowledge of the SSI.[20] A reconciliation session soon followed in which all charges against the perpetrators were dropped and they were instantly released. The SSI decided that the premises could not be used as a church because of their proximity to a mosque and that other premises needed to be found. In a context where there is a mosque on almost every corner of any village, the SSI's condition can only be interpreted as prohibitive. Two weeks later, a repeat of the assault on the local house used as a place of worship occurred in 'Izbit al-Fuqa'i. Christians had been using the house for worship for no fewer than twenty years, with the knowledge of both the residents and the SSI. However, rumors spread that the Christians intended to add a cross and a bell and other structures that would make its function as a place of worship visible. On 17 July 2009, following the Friday prayers in the municipality of Beba, governorate of Beni Suef, approximately two thousand members of the community attacked homes and property belonging to Christians while stirring others to join in the jihad against the unbelievers.[21] Again, Copts were forced to attend a reconciliation session in which they were pressured to drop charges against the perpetrators and those who had incited them to violence.

What Lies behind Volcanic Eruptions of Violence?

Against the increasing securitization of relations between Muslims and Christians through the central role played by the SSI, and the Islamization from below sponsored by Islamists, it is fair to say that what emerged in rural Egypt were not cases of individual discriminatory practices but patterns of systematic persecution. This has become manifest in a number of ways: incidents where the security apparatus was aware of the planning of assaults and failed to take measures to prevent the escalation of violence; the mobilizing role of mosques in inciting hatred through the use of religious rhetoric, such as declaring jihad against unbelievers; the systematic assault on Coptic citizens' residence and property, which often occurs under the eyes of the authorities, which only intervened at the point when significant damage occurred; the collective punishment of Coptic citizens by members of the community for individual incidents; and the collective punishment of Coptic citizens in the reconciliation sessions convened by the SSI. A systematic policy by the SSI of using soft and hard power to prevent Copts from seeking legal recourse served not only to institutionalize a state policy of communal subjugation but also sent out a clear signal to other communities not only that perpetrators of violence would not be held accountable, but also that mounting collective assaults was an effective means of imposing their will on the government.

This leaves us with a question: What explains the dynamics of inciting religious hatred and lies behind these volcanic eruptions of collective acts of violence against citizens of a different faith?

As with any conflictual situation, there is always a complex constellation of factors whose interplay at any particular historical moment leads to the escalation of violence. As indicated above, the SSI played a central role in failing to prevent the escalation of violence, in managing crises in such a way as to increase casualties, both human and material, and in resolving conflicts in a manner that fed a long-standing sense of injustice on the part of Copts and a sense of vindication on the part of perpetrators. There are instances that reflect an exception to this rule, for example, when SSI officers intervened to warn sheikhs in local mosques to desist from using hate speech or when they took the necessary security measures (by cordoning off an area where assault was expected). However, the persistence of incidents involving clashes that were premeditated and that could have been avoided suggests that there were grave shortcomings in the SSI's responses to sectarian incidents.

What is argued here is that the SSI not only *reacted* in a way that exacerbated sectarian assaults against Christian minorities but also actually *manufactured* sectarian violence *in some instances*. The SSI played a leading role in giving the signals in rural communities that they could force a religious minority not to exercise its right to a place of worship by going out en masse to assault it because, after all, the reconciliation session would side with the majority and would not accuse or blame the perpetrators.

According to Nabil 'Abd al-Fattah, the SSI resorted to reconciliation committees in order quickly to contain an incident before it spread to nearby areas and became too difficult to control and also to avoid being held accountable if another state actor became involved and questioned its handling of the situation ('Abd al-Fattah 2010: 57).

The SSI played an instrumental role in engineering the Camillia She-hata crisis by withholding from the public information that she had not converted to Islam and by giving the green light to Salafis, joined by other Islamists, to launch a systematic campaign against Christians to "demand sister Camillia." Perhaps the greatest charge laid against the SSI was its role in orchestrating the bombing of the Two Saints Church in Alexandria (see chapter 7).

The motivations behind the SSI's role in inciting sectarian hatred against the Coptic minority were many. First, there was clearly a state policy of divide and rule, designed to divert attention from its corrupt political governance and economic mismanagement, both of which led to the impoverishment of the majority of Egyptians, increased levels of deprivation, and resulted in various forms of social and political exclusion. Second, there was a vendetta between the Coptic Orthodox Church leadership and the SSI. As mentioned in chapter 3, the Church leadership had been neither compliant nor submissive in relation to the SSI, and one might argue that this is a battle of political wills that has lingered on well after the demise of Mubarak's presidency. Third, it is impossible to overlook the possibility that members of the SSI may themselves harbor religious prejudices against the Christian minority and believe that strategically the only reason to engage with it is to keep it in its place. It is noteworthy that while Coptic citizens are allowed in small numbers to join the police force, they are completely prohibited from joining the SSI. The SSI is considered an exclusive corps within the Ministry of Interior and its powers increased dramatically after Habib al-Adli took over the Ministry in 2000 (Tadros 2011c). Fourth, by combining soft power (granting the Church leadership the ability to build a church and pray in it, but denying it an official permit) with hard power (mediation of reconciliation committees, use of threats of incarceration), the SSI is able to exercise political control, by putting the Coptic minority in a highly vulnerable position, by making it constantly subject to the mercy of the security apparatus, and by playing on Copts' fears that the Muslim majority may turn against them without the SSI to regulate matters.

However, the state of communal tensions is not only a product of the SSI's agency. Why would people respond to calls stirring them to jihad against fellow community members? Why would the presence of a church be considered offensive to the point of mobilizing people to organize collectively to punish and attack those who worship in it?

There are many possible explanations. Robeir el Fares suggests that the impoverishment of the Egyptian people and their sense of powerlessness vis-à-vis the state, which has failed to provide them with a bare modicum of social, economic, and political rights, lies behind the increased assaults on Christians. He suggests that the only way they are able to vent their anger is through attacking the weaker party. El Fares substantiates his hypothesis by pointing to the fact that all the sectarian assaults that have occurred against Copts have been committed in economically marginalized areas of Egypt, whether in villages or urban informal settlements.

It seems that the increased deprivation of the Egyptian people is a factor, but taken alone it has limited explanatory power. Incidents of sectarian strife occur in impoverished areas not only due to class factors but also because these are the areas where human security is at its weakest and where radical Islamist ideology is most widely diffused. They appear to arise out of a combination of impoverishment, the absence of an effective and responsive police that can swiftly take charge (without the exercise of brutality), and Islamist forces that deepen religious divides and play an instrumental role in mobilizing people along those lines.

Islamization from below, through a combination of Islamist activism and a state-sponsored policy of privileging Islamic identity over all others, has contributed to an intense need to affirm one's religious identity by undermining that of others ('Abd al-Fattah 2010). It is significant that crowds are driven to launch attacks after their incitation in local mosques to go on a jihad or defend fellow Muslims. Collective assaults on Copts where a Coptic citizen was involved in a dispute suggests that people interpret and mediate relations through religion.

What the state (and the SSI) may have underestimated is the extent to which its policy of containment and repression would lead to the emergence of a Coptic resistance movement that would act independently of the Coptic Church and yet still have the ability to mobilize a Coptic constituency, a theme to which I return in chapter 8.

6 Against All Odds: The Copts in the 25 January Revolution

This chapter examines the nature of Copts' participation in the uprisings that led to the ousting of President Mubarak. Generalizations about Coptic citizens are avoided in view of the diversity of their political orientations and socio-economic backgrounds. However, this chapter seeks to identify some underlying patterns of engagement, recurring issues, and perspectives and interpretations of how the agency of Coptic citizens was exercised. I argue that while there were many precursors to the 25 January uprisings, political, social, and economic, the Coptic-led protests that followed the bombing of the Two Saints Church in Alexandria on New Year's Day in 2011 served, together with the success of the Tunisian revolution, as an important precursor to the opening of the floodgates. Copts participated in the organization of and mobilization for the 25 January uprisings in spite of the opposition of the Coptic Church, in spite of fears that the Islamists might ride the revolutionary wave, and in spite of the inevitable security crackdown as well as the objections of their families. Driven by the same grievances and demands for bread, freedom, and social justice as their Muslim compatriots, Copts participated in the revolution first and foremost as Egyptians. Unified by a common goal to rid the country of Mubarak, Egyptians were able—for eighteen days—to put aside religious prejudice and construct a socio-political culture that was inclusive and pluralistic. The fact that Copts participated in large numbers in these protests can be attributed to agential and structural factors. Agentially, many Copts who participated in the eighteen days of the uprising related to their Egyptian identity without having to eliminate or forgo their Coptic identity. The fact that the young revolutionaries' discourse and leadership structure was inclusive and premised on the civility and peacefulness of their struggle appealed to many Copts.

While the Coptic Orthodox Church leadership was absent from the uprisings, the Qasr al-Dubbara Church, affiliated to the Evangelical Church, played a prominent role in supporting the uprisings in Tahrir Square. After the ousting of Mubarak, the Islamists sought to retell the story of the uprisings, minus the Copts, the liberals, and the youth revolutionary groups, setting themselves as the guardians of the uprisings. The narrative of the Copts who participated is therefore critically important in countering this particular discourse.

The Precursors

Following more than five years of sustained protests on just about everything—from shortages of cooking gas, bread, and basic commodities, to criticism of workers' low pay, corruption, and hereditary power—2011 started off on a bad note for the regime. The bombing of the Two Saints Church in Alexandria on New Year's Eve radicalized large numbers of Copts, who were joined by Muslims in nationwide protests against the Ministry of Interior and the regime itself. This represented a significant rupture in relations between Copts and the Mubarak regime. For many decades, Mubarak's regime had presented itself as the guardian of the civic state against the Islamist threat and, by default, the Copts' last line of defense against Islamist tyranny. This rhetoric was debunked by Copts following the bombing of the Two Saints Church, which turned them squarely against the regime's security apparatus, the Ministry of Interior, the political leadership, and the ruling party.

Bloody New Year's Eve

About one thousand worshipers were attending midnight prayers on 31 December 2010 when a bomb tore through the church of al-Qiddisin (Two Saints) in the Sidi Bishr district of the Mediterranean port city of Alexandria. The attack left twenty-five people dead and over two hundred injured. The Ministry of Interior first announced that the explosion had come from a car bomb and then dismissed the possibility, saying it was the act of a suicide bomber and later announcing that a Palestinian group was responsible for the attack. Prior to the Maspero Massacre of 9 October 2011, the attack in Alexandria was the worst on the country's Christian minority since the shootings in Nag' Hammadi on 6 January 2010, the Coptic Christmas Eve, which left eight people dead and several injured.

The initial reaction to the bombing was a highly emotional one. A wide range of state and non-state actors sharply condemned the attack and called upon all Egyptians—and not just Copts—to observe a period of mourning. Quick to express their anger and grief, for example, were leading politicians of the government and opposition, including the Muslim Brotherhood, the Sheikh of al-Azhar, and other prominent members of the state-sponsored and independent Muslim clergy. In the immediate aftermath of the bombing, there was also a clear impetus by the media to deny that the perpetrators and planners could possibly be Egyptian. On 1 January 2011, President Mubarak appeared on state television to describe the attack as a "terrorist operation that carries, within itself, the hallmark of foreign hands which want to turn Egypt into another scene of terrorism like elsewhere in the region and the wider world." For their part, the Copts of Alexandria and other parts of the country held sustained protests, the tenor of which was heavily anti-government, as they blamed the state for failing to provide adequate security for the Christian minority's major public gatherings.

Probably to dampen political tensions amid these protests, Pope Shenouda III did not cancel the Christmas Eve mass on 6 January, and the next day accepted the holiday good wishes of visiting dignitaries, as it was customary for him to do so. Yet the mood among Copts was anything but celebratory, with many churches removing Christmas decorations, women wearing black in solidarity with the families in mourning, and police enforcing tight security around the churches. On Christmas Eve, the government-controlled media broadcast nationalist songs and programs whose hosts and guests testified to Egypt's interreligious cohesion. There were numerous reports of Muslims attending church, also in solidarity.

Despite these outpourings of sympathy and shows of national unity, the bloody events marking the New Year did not prompt systemic change in the handling of inter-sectarian relations in Egypt. The reactions from officials, intellectuals, and the press conformed to the usual, standard pattern characterizing their engagement with attacks on Christians. Taken together, the reactions comprised an almost entirely coherent narrative: it is not sectarianism but random terrorism that threatens Egypt; foreigners are behind it; and what is needed to combat the problem is merely more solemn affirmation of the equal citizenship of all Egyptians. The cyclical nature of this narrative helps to explain the impasse in Egypt's sectarian question.

'De-religionizing' the Incident

Following the first reports of the killings at the Two Saints Church, from Mubarak downward, the Egyptian establishment seemed keen to refute the notion that the incident was sectarian, in the sense of Muslim-on-Copt violence. As political commentator Karima Kamal pointed out, the denial reached the extent that some figures close to the regime argued that both Muslims and Christians had in fact been the intended targets, since a mosque was situated across the street from the church. A few hours after the bombing, Fathi Surur, the long-time speaker of parliament, completed the story, intoning that Egypt does not have a sectarian problem and that no Egyptian could have committed such an act.[1] Writing in the quasi-official *al-Ahram*, veteran columnist Salah Muntasir also attributed the attack to foreign actors. While he did not deny that Egypt had witnessed attacks on Copts in its recent past, he averred that the Alexandria bombing had targeted all Egyptians and could not be linked to previous, sectarian incidents.[2] The implication of these interpretations, at times baldly stated, was that anyone saying that the attack targeted Copts had a political agenda, perhaps to embarrass the state, perhaps to sully Egypt's image abroad. According to an inside source in *al-Ahram*, the newspaper's writers were given strict instructions to toe the government line, with the threat of serious consequences for any departure from it. In retort to the likes of Muntasir, Ahmad Yusuf Ahmad, professor of political science at Cairo University, pointed out the political motivations behind the urge to deny that Copts were the specific targets of the attack. The reactions to Alexandria, he suggested, fell in line with the initial, emphatic portrayals of the Nag' Hammadi shootings as a case of *tha'r*, the kind of vendetta practiced by some Upper Egyptians with strong tribal ties, rather than the targeting of Christians leaving midnight mass. Ahmad recalled the confidence with which these statements had been made, despite evidence that the victims had nothing to do with the incident that had allegedly sparked the vendetta.[3]

For many, conspiracy theories offered an easy way out of thinking seriously about what had precipitated the violence. Some fingered the Mossad, the Israeli national intelligence service. Some writers with a

reputation as political thinkers, such as Hasan Nafaʻ, a retired professor of political science at Cairo University and former spokesman for
the National Assembly for Change led by Nobel laureate and opposition figure Mohammed ElBaradei, put forward conspiracy theories. Nafaʻ
wrote that "from a purely rational perspective" he could not exclude the
possibility that Coptic organizations in the diaspora were behind the
Alexandria bombing.[4] "Since Islamist extremists have blown up mosques
in several places around us to incite sectarianism that they believe serves
their interests, it is not inconceivable that Coptic extremists might have
participated, directly or indirectly, in the bombing of the church to insti-
gate sectarianism," he argued. The aim of such a devious plot, Nafaʻ
continued, would be to "give the United States and Israel the opportunity
to leap to the Copts' defense, enabling the Copts to expel the conquering
Muslims from Egypt at last."

Many were also quick to claim decisively that al-Qaeda was behind the
attack. Slightly beforehand, an al-Qaeda affiliate in Iraq, the Islamic State
of Iraq, had issued a threat of further attacks on Christians across the
Middle East following an assault upon a church in Baghdad that left fifty-
eight people dead. In a communiqué, the group warned Christians that
"the killing sword will not be lifted" from their necks. The Islamic State
of Iraq justified the Baghdad slaughter with the fact that it had previously
announced the expiration of a deadline it had set for the Coptic Orthodox Church in Egypt to "release" two women who it (and many Egyptian
Muslims) believed were converts to Islam. But al-Qaeda did not claim
responsibility for the Alexandria church bombing, as is its conventional
practice, while it was quick to do so in the case of the Baghdad church.
There are therefore serious questions as to whether the attack in Egypt
was al-Qaeda's doing.

The Egyptian population was congratulated for its commendable display of national unity and its refusal to bow to the outside conspirators
who wished to divide the country and undermine its political stability.

One of the most disconcerting aspects of the state of denial surrounding the Alexandria bombing was the attempt to assign equal
responsibility all around for the climate of deepened sectarianism that
followed the bombing. The most extreme instance was the aforementioned column by Hasan Nafaʻ, in which he argued that analysts of the
sectarian question in Egypt had focused excessively on Islamic funda-
mentalism while neglecting its Christian counterpart. "Like thousands

and maybe millions of others," Nafa' wrote, "I regularly receive letters from numerous Coptic organizations who have no concern other than to ignite the flames of sectarianism in Egypt." What is suggested by the likes of Nafa', however, is an approach to understanding incidents of sectarian violence that distributes half the blame to each side in the sectarian equation. Such an analysis misrepresents not only the course of history but also major underlying power dynamics.

Unseen Divide

The nationwide protests that erupted in the aftermath of the bombing of the Two Saints Church in Alexandria were the second time Copts (joined by Muslims) took to the street to express their opposition to the regime, its policies, and its practices. They called for the resignation of the minister of interior, openly decried the performance of the security sector in Egypt, and indirectly attacked President Hosni Mubarak and his son Gamal for their complacency. The press was engaged in a bid to prove that equal peril emanates from fundamentalists among both Christians and Muslims. Reports and opinion pieces appearing in *al-Ahram* over the 2–6 January 2011 period, in particular, presented the protests as evidence of the extremism and violent tendencies gripping a portion of the Coptic citizenry. In the days leading up to Coptic Christmas, demonstrations took place across the country, usually led by Coptic youth, although Muslim sympathizers also joined some of the rallies. The protests were mostly peaceful, although there were rare instances where protesters threw stones or glass at the police. These gatherings were countered, however, by a high level of police brutality, including the use of tear gas, all of it captured on television. The forms of state repression were no different from those used against most non-violent protesters from 2005, including members of the Kefaya movement for political reform, striking workers, and many others. However, unlike protests led by Kefaya and other anti-establishment movements, which were never attacked by citizens, attacks on these peaceful protests were also the object of communal assault. A group of Muslim residents responded to peaceful Coptic protests in Qalyubiya, just north of Cairo, on 4 January by attacking the local church of St. Mina and Kyrollos, causing serious damage to the building.[5]

In the opposition press, however, previous waves of demonstrations were rarely termed extremist; on the contrary, they were often praised. These Coptic protests, on the other hand, were castigated in many state-run and opposition press outlets as evidence of religious extremism, serving the narrative, in conformity with that of the government, that there were fundamentalists everywhere and that everyone's fundamentalists were equally to be feared.[6] Wahid 'Abd al-Magid and 'Amr al-Shubaki are notable examples of prominent intellectuals who condemned the protests instigated by Coptic youth as sectarian.[7] Their stance was perplexing. Coptic youths were consistently reproached in the writings of many intellectuals for living in a cocoon, reacting to the rise of political Islam by turning to the Church for refuge, and inwardly adopting an apolitical posture. In view of this scathing critique, which at times accused Copts of mortgaging their agency to the Church, it would seem logical for intellectuals like these two writers to applaud the post-Alexandria protesters for airing their complaints peacefully in public spaces. That demonstrations took place completely independently of (and, in some cases, against) the Church's will might have been welcomed as evidence of a newfound determination on the part of youth to participate in politics. Yet to attack these acts of civic engagement by labeling them 'sectarian' showed the extent to which armchair activists in Egypt had become disconnected from the experiences of the masses. It showed an inclination to theorize rather than understand people's agency by listening to their life experiences and political deliberations as they were being expressed on the street.

Countdown to the Uprisings

Some authors such as Samir Morcos and Samer Fawzi (2012) suggest that in the immediate lead-up[8] to the 25 January uprisings, the Tunisian revolution and the Alexandria bombing were the two key precursors to the mobilization of the masses. The protests following the Alexandria church massacre were seen as a precursor on several counts: they broke the fear barrier for a group that was conventionally assumed not to enter into open confrontation with the regime; they involved large numbers of Christians and Muslims who were united against the regime; the slogans and calls for protest were highly contentious (calling for the removal of the minister of interior, openly criticizing the Mubarak regime, and so on); and they occupied strategic places (such as public squares). What is certain is that at least for a significant proportion of Copts—perhaps not for the country at large—the Alexandria incident was very much alive at the back of their minds as epitomizing regime brutality to the extreme.

The reasons for their participation in the revolution, however, are rather more complex and need to be seen in a broader context.

The 25 January uprisings happened against the backdrop of almost daily eruptions, which are worth documenting here (see Rabi' 2011).

2 January 2011: Nationwide protests against lax security, the Ministry of Interior, and the regime.

4 January 2011: Protests following the bombing continue, leading to clashes between the demonstrators and security forces in Cairo and Qalyubiya. The Nubians organize a protest in front of the Cabinet office building demanding their right to their land around Lake Nasser and refusing resettlement elsewhere.

5 January 2011: The death of a young Salafi, Sayyid Bilal, after being tortured to death in association with his questioning about the church bombing.

9 January 2011: The opposition, including the Muslim Brotherhood, organizes a number of protests nationwide against the bombing of the Two Saints Church in Alexandria.

10 January 2011: The residents of the village of Rayda in Minya block the main road to prevent the governor of Minya from passing and to express their anger at the closure of the local bakery selling subsidized bread.

17 January 2011: A young Egyptian man sets himself on fire in emulation of Muhammad Bouazizi, the Tunisian street vendor whose self-immolation sparked off the December 2011 Tunisian revolution, shouting out to the SSI that his rights had been violated. Activists stage a protest in Cairo, Mansura, and Daqahliya against state policies.

18 January 2011: There are four more attempted suicides via self-immolation, with one person dead. Clashes erupt between hundreds of Egyptian and South Asian workers after a factory lays off the Egyptians in order to hire South Asians. Seven hundred workers from the Ministry of Agriculture hold a protest calling for permanent employment contracts. Workers in the textile industry in Alexandria began an open demonstration against corruption. Textile workers in Minufiya hold a demonstration for the disbursement of the payments due to them and threaten to burn themselves.

20 January 2011: Eleven more people attempt suicide via self-immolation and five of them die. Housing-tax civil servants stage a protest in Alexandria demanding the disbursement of the monies due to them. Thousands of public school students stage a protest and clash with state security.

24 January 2011: The residents of the village of Qatur in Qalyubiya governorate stage a protest and block the roads during a visit by then Minister of Housing Ahmad al-Maghrabi in protest against the imposition of additional fees for the extension of sewage services to their houses. Housing-tax civil servants stage a protest in Cairo against the failure of the government to deliver on its promises to them. Six hundred physicians go on strike in al-Minshawi public hospital in Tanta in protest for monies still owed to them.

25 January 2011: The uprisings that culminate in a revolution begin, with bloody clashes taking place between protesters and security forces in the afternoon.

The purpose of this record of events leading up to the 25 January uprising is to show that levels of discontent and anger were already simmering beneath the surface across professions (workers and doctors), across geographical locations (rural and urban), and within and outside government (civil servants and activists campaigning against a hereditary presidency). Self-immolation was by no means a new phenomenon in Egypt—men and women had been burning themselves in despair for a long time, often by dousing themselves in gasoline and setting themselves afire. However, this phenomenon gained a new significance following the Tunisian uprising. The incidents were also occurring on a repeated basis since the mid-2000s (see Ali 2012).

Against this backdrop, a number of political forces and groups openly called for a nationwide uprising on 25 January, which marked Police Force Day (see Ezzabawy 2012). Ironically, this was the first time that the government had ever decided to celebrate 25 January by making it a public holiday. What had supposedly been an attempt to mollify an angry population became an opportunity for many people to spend the day off in public protest against the status quo. In the days leading up to the 25 January uprisings, religious leaders, both Christian and Muslim, openly advocated against participation in the protests. Major political forces such as the Muslim Brotherhood, Salafis, and some leading political parties such as the leftist Tagammu' Party all categorically rejected the call for participation in the uprisings.

Leaders of all three Christian denominations denounced the participation of their followers in the planned 25 January protests. Speaking in a press interview, Bishop Morcos, the spokesman for the Coptic Orthodox

Church, said, "We do not know the goal of these demonstrations, its details, or who stands behind them." He added that the Coptic Orthodox Church had called upon its youth not to follow the calls for participation in demonstrations that promote destruction. A similar stance was taken by Reverend Andrea Zaki, deputy head of the Evangelical Church in Egypt, and Bishop Antonious Aziz, representing the Coptic Catholic Church.[9] On 25 January, the pro-government *Rose al-Yusuf* magazine published public statements by Pope Shenouda III in which he called upon all bishops to raise awareness among Copts not to participate in the planned 25 January protests. These instructions were widely disseminated across all the parishes in the Sunday morning mass, attended by large numbers of the laity. They were also circulated on the websites belonging to the Coptic Orthodox Church. The pope warned against following groups that wish to undermine the country's stability and cause chaos and destruction.[10] It is very clear from the public statements made by the Coptic Orthodox Church leadership that it was not only taking a position as a Church against the protest but was also actively ordering its laity not to participate. Such a conspicuously overt usurping of the rights of citizens of Christian denomination to engage politically as they see fit would backfire miserably against the Coptic Church, both internally and, to a much larger extent, externally in terms of its own positioning in the post-Mubarak political order. Bishop Moussa, who was part of the pope's close entourage, later sought to explain the pope's position by claiming that it had emanated from a lack of clarity regarding the nature of the protests and that the pope had assumed that the planned demonstrations were a call for destruction and vandalism, or at best, a protest under the tutelage of a single political force (Ayad 2011: 200–201).

Given the widely held view of the Coptic Orthodox Church as exercising hegemonic power over Christians (perhaps more so than the Catholic and the Protestant Churches), it was assumed that Copts would act in a sheep-like manner and comply with the pope's orders. In fact, hundreds, and later thousands, of Copts defied the Church and joined the protests. Given that a significant proportion of them were practicing Christians, how did they reconcile their commitment to participate in the protests with the knowledge that they were defying their Church's leadership? The explanations are many and highly revealing.

The first and foremost explanation is that many of the protesters felt very strongly that while the Church can and should exercise spiritual leadership, it does not have the right to assume political leadership of its followers. For many of the participants, the notion of rendering unto God what is God's and unto Caesar what is Caesar's provided the moral justification for why they should not comply with the Church's order. Rania Abd al-Shahid, a twenty-five-year-old Coptic woman who participated in the uprisings from 28 January onward, was highly critical of the role of the Church in mobilizing support for Mubarak during the presidential election and for the ruling National Democratic Party in the parliamentary elections: "It would have been better if the Church had undertaken a role in raising [political] awareness only and leaving it up to the people to choose. Hence it was natural for the Church to warn Copts against going out to the uprisings but I was against these statements and I encouraged people to go."

The second explanation is that there were Copts who could find explanations for the Church's position that would render it understandable to them but not necessarily morally binding. Several participants said they understood why Church leaders feared greatly for the lives of members of their congregations but that this was not sufficient a reason to convince them to follow instructions against participation. Nasser Sobhy, a photojournalist who participated in the eighteen-day uprising, argued that the Church leadership should not be so fearful for its 'children,' and that it had cocooned them inside the Church, transforming them into a passive people: "Therefore I was against the decisions that were declared by the clergy and and the senior ecclesiastical order." Many young Copts who participated in the uprising also interpreted the Church's position as reflective of its fears that the uprisings would be Islamist-led and populated and, hence, serve to counter the interests of the Copts' quest for civilian rule.

The third explanation is more in line with James Scott's "hidden script": namely that in view of the immense political and security pressures that have conventionally been placed on the Church leadership to comply with the regime, the Church had little space to object. In reality, however, there is a hidden script, namely that Copts are free to choose how to engage in politics as they see fit. Prominent leader of the Coptic lay movement Kamal Zakhir, who has been active in advocating for internal church reform, argued that the pope's statements deterring Copts from participating must be read in light of the kind of pressures that he and other religious leaders in similar positions were under from Mubarak's dictatorial regime. Zakhir argued that the pope's statement bore great resemblance to the statement issued by the Grand Sheikh of Al-Azhar almost to the point of being identical. "This is the nature of institutions that fall under the pressure of dictatorial rule," he argued, adding that the Church would have had no leeway in challenging the head of state.

The fourth explanation, conveyed by some participants, who represent a more radical stance with respect to the Church's position, is that the quest for stability at all costs reflects the advanced age of many public leaders, who are therefore disconnected from the youth they ostensibly represent. Hany Hanna Aziz, who became known as the orator of Tahrir Square and one of the key leaders of the revolutionary coalition who resided in the square over the course of the 25 January uprising, emphasized that one of the most salient statements made during the eighteen days was "we are the young who will not listen to the seniors." He explained that the youth emerged as a distinct group, rising against their elders, whether they be Muslim Brotherhood youth defying the Brotherhood's Supreme Guidance Bureau, Christian youth battling the Church leadership, or young members of the Wafd Party challenging their leaders. He said, "Although some of the older people had a role in the revolution which we cannot deny, it was a case of the youth against the elders."

Regardless, Copts found sufficient moral ground with which to defy the Church leadership's position without having to feel that this was somehow a denial of their Coptic identity or religious allegiances. Moreover, as mentioned earlier, for many Copts, this was not the first time that they had defied Church orders not to protest—the 'Umraniya and Alexandria incidents were the predecessors.

So why did the Copts join in the protests? The overwhelming answer emerging from interviews with Copts of different socio-economic and political backgrounds was that they participated for the same reasons that other Egyptians went out to protest. Some interviewees objected to being asked why they are participating as Copts and insisted that they were participating as Egyptians and therefore sharing the same grievances and concerns that drove everyone else to protest. However, many of the Copts who participated in the uprisings mentioned in the interviews that although they participated primarily as Egyptians, this was not to deny that their exposure to religious-inspired forms of persecution at the hands of Mubarak's regime had stirred up their desire to take to the street. This sentiment was eloquently expressed by Tharwat Samuel, the managing editor of *al-Tariq wa-l-haqq* (The Way and the Truth), a Coptic newspaper that encouraged Copts to participate in the uprisings. He argued that Coptic youth went out to the uprisings like other youth, yet "I cannot say that there were Coptic motives [behind their participation] but as part of Egyptian society they felt the injustice afflicting them. It is true that they felt exposure to more injustice and persecution but as part of society."

Faced with a common enemy—Mubarak's regime—the Copts' patriotic identity assumed precedence over their religious identity, even though they were required neither to forgo their religious identity nor to sideline it in order to partake in the uprisings. Hence, the factors motivating many Copts to participate were both agential, in the sense of choosing to participate as part of a wider polity, and structural, in the sense that the political discourse and organization of the uprising at the outset was ideologically and logistically inclusive of Copts. In other words, the youth coalitions' leadership's appeal lay in the fact that it was free from any religious underpinnings and involved representation from both Muslims and Christians. This speaks to Barth's (1969) emphasis that social identities are to a certain extent constructed and maintained through shifting boundaries. The demarcation of identity boundaries is negotiable. A situational analysis would suggest that in the event of the uprisings against Mubarak, Copts chose to engage through their allegiance to an Egyptian identity that is shared with all Egyptian citizens who care about the territorially bound nation-state. However, this choice was also influenced by the contextual dynamics that favored the delineation of identity based on citizenship and not religious affiliation. In this sense, similar dynamics influenced the desire of Copts to participate in the 1919 revolution and the 2011 uprisings. In both instances, Copts and Muslims engaged as citizens bound together by a common identity (allegiance to Egypt, the nation-state) and by a common enemy (British colonial power in 1919, the Mubarak dictatorship in 2011). What was critically important to their participation in both instances was their ability to attach themselves to an overarching identity where they were not 'the other.' The fact that many Copts, as others, had concerns as to whether the uprising was Islamist-led or not before participating indicates the extent to which their participation was contingent upon the nature of the identity (and political project) of the organizers. In instances where identity is mediated by religion (Islamists), Copts' demarcation of their religious distinctiveness is emphasized. This is driven by their sense of being seen as 'the religious other' in relation to the framing of the Islamists' identity (see Introduction for further discussion).

The Copts Take to the Streets

Since the uprisings from 25 January onward involved hundreds of thousands of people, with numbers in some instances believed to surpass one million, it is very difficult to determine the scope or level of participation of Coptic citizens within the larger crowds. This is especially true in this instance since they neither organized nor amassed into a bloc that can easily be identified as 'Coptic.' Since they were undifferentiated from the masses in Tahrir Square and other public squares across the country, it was impossible to distinguish between them and other Egyptians. This stands in contrast, for example, with the workers' movement, which made its identity explicit in some of the protests through banners and slogans. The one exception to this rule perhaps is the participation of priests in the protests, who could be identified by their dress, and were often seen at the podium of the makeshift stage in Tahrir Square addressing the crowds side by side with Muslim religious leaders. However, although not conspicuous, the participation of Coptic citizens was evident from the names of the people who participated in the youth coalitions and the testimony of those in Tahrir Square.

The participation of Copts, as for Egyptians more generally, varied depending on geography. Hence, the highest level of participation by Copts was in Cairo's Tahrir Square, followed by Alexandria. In Minya, where citizen participation in the protests was generally low, the Copts' involvement was also quite limited. In Suez, one of the sites of the bloodiest confrontations between protesters and security forces, which left hundreds dead and seriously injured, Coptic youth and lay members joined in the protests, as did all other youth. Adel Shendy, a thirty-nine-year-old teacher who participated in the uprisings, recounted that he heard about the uprisings on 25 January through acquaintances and friends, both Copts and Muslims, and decided to participate in the protests that were held in Suez. He pointed out that the local church urged them not to participate for fear that the protests would be anti-Christian, in view of Suez's reputation for being a stronghold of the Muslim Brotherhood and Salafis. "Before the revolution we tried to have a vigil to protest what was happening to the Copts but the priests and church servants prevented us, saying, 'Hold the vigil inside the church,' and we would object, saying, 'If we do it inside the church, who will hear us? It should be outside the church so that the people see us,'" said Shendy. Shendy was one of the activists who called upon the people of Suez to take to the street.

The manifestations of national unity were widely publicized in both the western and Middle Eastern media (such as Al Jazeera). The most popular slogan chanted in Tahrir Square that related to religious unity was "Muslim, Christian one hand!" Other slogans, all of which rhyme in Arabic, included "Not Mubarak, not al-Adli, the Crescent [stands with] the Cross" and "They tried to divide us, our sheikh stands beside our priest" ('Abd al-Sadek 2011: 190). These slogans speak to the idea that it was the government that sought to create rifts between Muslims and Christians and that without the oppressive regime there would be social harmony and even the prospect of a prosperous Egypt. One slogan reads *"Ya Muhammad 'ul li-Hanna Masr bukra ha-tib'a ganna"* ("O Muhammad, tell Hanna tomorrow Egypt will be paradise"), with Muhammad being an obviously Muslim name and Hanna meaning John in Arabic, representing a Christian. Other slogans included "Not religious, not sectarian; we want a civil state." The word *madaniya* (civil) became widely circulated in Tahrir Square. Attempts to infuse or replace slogans with Islamic ones were often drowned out by louder shouts of *"madaniya, madaniya!"*

There were particular images that caught the imagination of the foreign media and came to symbolize the unity of Muslims and Christians. The most memorable was one of Muslims praying with Christians surrounding them to protect them from security force attacks. The other is the image of Christians praying and singing hymns (wrongly reported in the media as the performance of mass) surrounded by Muslims. The image of a sheikh and priest holding hands, both carried aloft on people's shoulders, as well as images of Bibles and Qur'ans being lifted simultaneously, were all intended to celebrate Egypt's religious pluralism.

Many Christians and Muslims had anecdotes of camaraderie, solidarity, and deep bonds of friendship emerging between strangers during the eighteen days of the Tahrir Square protests. Father Philopateer Gameel (see chapter 3 for background) had initially joined the counterrevolutionary protests that were organized in Mustafa Mahmoud Square because, he was told, these were protests calling for stability rather than the endorsement of the person of Hosni Mubarak. However, when the now infamous Battle of the Camel took place on 2–3 February 2011, he said he realized the regime's deception, turned around, and proceeded to Tahrir Square where he made his apologies to the youth revolutionary groups and offered his condolences for the martyrs. He said he was accepted and witnessed some of the most enduring moments of national unity during the remaining days of the struggle to remove Mubarak: "[Tahrir] Square was full of warm feelings and I often saw veiled women and women in the *niqab* and men in beards come to greet me overflowing with feelings of love and there was this one elderly woman in the *niqab* who said to me, 'We love you. Do not believe what they tell you about us: that we hate you! Do not believe the words of the regime.'"

Such representations are neither fabricated nor exaggerated. They reflect the fact of a singular eighteen-day moment that had a particular culture and unwritten set of rules entirely its own. Tahrir Square became a parallel society with its own values and mores, all bound together by a common purpose—ridding the country of its dictator and its regime. Outside Tahrir Square, with the exception of the solidarity shown among neighbors who set up vigilante groups to fight *baltagiya* (hired thugs or criminals), there were no signs of this heightened level of inter-religious solidarity (at least not more than usual) and certainly after the ousting of Mubarak, the situation changed radically.

The Mornings after Mubarak Stood Down
The position of the Coptic Orthodox Church leadership showed the extent to which it was removed from the pulse of the street, very much like the Muslim Sunni establishment, al-Azhar. Its initial response to the growing power of the revolution was one of silence. The first signs of a shift in political orientation was manifest in Bishop Moussa's two articles, the first published one day before Mubarak's fall and the other one after that. In both articles, published in *Al-Masry Al-Youm*, he lauded the efforts of the Egyptian youth in demanding justice, dignity, and freedom and endorsed their struggle for creating a new Egypt. On the other hand, news was also leaked to the press that Pope Shenouda had called President Hosni Mubarak following his resignation to check on his health. Such a gesture was interpreted as a sign of the Coptic Church leadership's sympathy with Mubarak.

In contrast, although the leadership of the Evangelical Church had also been discredited for supporting Mubarak in the wake of the 25 January revolution, the leading role taken by one evangelical church in support of the revolution saw it emerge as a powerhouse of revolutionary activism. The Qasr al-Dubbara Evangelical Church is situated one street away from Tahrir Square. The pastors of the church, Sameh Hanna and Ihab al-Kharrat, became two of the most prominent Coptic leaders during the revolution and their popularity among many Copts of different Christian denominations grew rapidly. Ihab al-Kharrat recounts that during the days of the uprisings, they gathered lay leaders from three churches and organized prayers for Egypt in Tahrir Square. The prayers and hymns they sang attracted many Muslims, particularly "Lord Bless My Country Egypt," with which, said al-Kharrat, even Brothers and Salafis joined in.

During the days prior to the ousting of Mubarak, when the security force assaults on protesters were at their most intense, Qasr al-Dubbara Church opened its doors to protect the protesters and converted a part of its premises into a makeshift hospital for treating the injured. Its patriotic credentials among the supporters of the revolution became widely publicized. Its revolutionary role did not end with the ousting of Mubarak. The Evangelical Church's leadership and congregation continued to participate in the protests organized by the youth revolutionary groups against SCAF and it continued to play a central role in medical service provision. By default, this meant that it entered into a confrontational relationship with SCAF.

In the eyes of many Coptic Orthodox youth who were deeply involved in the uprisings, the Evangelical Church represented a popular embodiment of what a religious institution should be. Qasr al-Dubbara Church also took the initiative in calling for non-denominational services bringing together all Christians in prayer for Egypt—a move that would have been met with intense opposition from the Coptic Orthodox Church just a few years earlier.

However, the intense interaction between the youth of the Evangelical and Orthodox Churches during the revolution broke many of the barriers that the institutions had built between the two congregations. Against the backdrop of the weakening of the leadership of the Coptic Orthodox Church (not only at the level of the pope but at that of the bishops as well), many members of the Coptic Orthodox Church dared defy (even if sometimes covertly) the strict prohibition on participating in services offered by evangelical churches. This is yet another important direction that can potentially challenge the Coptic Orthodox Church's hold on the youth, as new spaces and relationships are forged outside the Church's walls.

Following the eighteen days that led to the ousting of Mubarak, the mood and power dynamics in Tahrir Square changed in conspicuous ways. The youth coalitions that had led the uprisings no longer had access to the main stage, which had been set up by the Muslim Brotherhood and became exclusively host to those affiliated to or allied with the Brotherhood. The atmosphere in Tahrir Square changed, a change epitomized by what became known as Kandahar Friday, or 29 July 2011, when the slogan "raise your head high, you are an Egyptian" was changed to "Raise your head high, you are a Muslim" and *"madaniya, madaniya"* was replaced by *"Islamiya, Islamiya."* The demise of the ethos of Tahrir Square was tangibly felt. Women who sought to build on the public recognition of their role in the liberation of Egypt from its dictator by going to Tahrir Square to seek their liberation from patriarchy were spat upon and insulted.[11] In another instance, Copts were literally thrown out of Tahrir Square by Islamists. The widely acclaimed position of the army that it would not shoot the people was challenged, as it fired live ammunition on protesters.

The discourse on national unity was challenged: Were the Copts really there? Did they not follow the orders of their pope, who had rushed to the defense of the regime? The contribution of the Copts both in terms of participation and shed blood became a matter for suspicion and doubt, while attempts by parts of the media to inflate the role of the Muslim Brotherhood in the revolution became conspicuous. Prominent activist John Milad Emil, who later became one of the few young revolutionaries to win a seat in the November 2011–January 2012 parliamentary elections, said, "There was a deliberate attempt on the part of the news agencies to downplay the presence of Copts and they tried to convey the idea that the Islamists were the only ones there. This became evident when they changed the photo of the martyr Sally Zahran to a picture of a veiled woman." Emil believed that following Mubarak's resignation, the Islamists sought to alter the narrative of what had happened in Tahrir Square so that they would emerge as the guardians and heroes of the revolution while sidelining or excluding all the other forces that had been in the square, whether they were political parties, liberals, or Copts. Islamists, he argued, tried to assert that they had been the only significant force present in the uprisings by claiming that they were the ones who protected the square and the revolutionaries on the day of the Battle of the Camel. "To the contrary," asserted Emil, "those who protected the revolution were all the people . . . it was also the Ultras [football fans] of Zamalek and Al-Ahly [Sports Club] in large numbers who protected the revolution and the famous image of a person standing in front of a water pumping vehicle is someone from the Ultras and not from the Brothers."

During the first eighteen days of the uprising it was critically important for Islamists to downplay their role to deflect the west's fear that the country would become another Iran. One of the strategic ways to do so, in addition to not raising Islamist slogans or banners, was to emphasize the participation of Copts, who are known for being long-time opponents of Islamists. However, after the revolution, Islamists needed to reclaim their standing as the most legitimate political actors, and to do so it was important for them to sideline Copts, whose anti-Islamic, pro-civil stance would act as an impediment to their quest for power.

The new narrative on Tahrir Square cannot be read independently of the new political configurations of power emerging in post-Mubarak Egypt. It is a context that saw the development of an entente between the army (headed by SCAF) and the Islamists. In return for bestowing upon the Muslim Brotherhood and other Islamist forces the right to form political parties, granting them the legitimacy to engage openly in politics, Islamists were to claim the streets for SCAF at least until the parliamentary elections of November 2011–January 2012 (Tadros 2012c). In this new political landscape, the youth coalitions that had played the critical role of instigating the masses to join the revolution were sidelined by both the ruling authorities and Islamists. The Muslim Brotherhood had during decades of grass-roots work through mosques and welfare services acquired the foundations upon which to build a firm political constituency, a task made easier by their access to immense financial resources and the mobilization of their members through a highly efficient internal organizational structure. The youth coalitions that were the principal champions of a civil polity and non-Islamist government and committed to religious and political pluralism were weakened after Mubarak's ouster by internal divisions and fragmentation and by their lack of access to political constituencies among the masses. This meant the absence of a heavyweight national political actor that could endorse the role of Copts in terms of political representation and power sharing in the post-Mubarak political order.

To conclude, the religiously pluralistic spirit of Tahrir Square faded following the eighteen days that led to Mubarak's resignation. This is partly due to the fact that the social fabric of Egyptian society, which was heavily encumbered by religious prejudice, was not transformed in Tahrir Square. Rather, it was temporarily rejected in favor of a national project that caught the imagination of the people—the removal of Mubarak. Once this was achieved, all unresolved religious tensions resurfaced—after all, there had never been any clear and honest recognition of the existence of the problem in the first place or acknowledgment that injustices had been committed or that reconciliation was in fact necessary. Moreover, for the Islamist political actors in Tahrir Square, downplaying the Islamist project in favor of the notion of a civil state based on equal citizenship for all was a rhetorical device designed to maximize the possibilities of ousting Mubarak. It was merely a means to an end. In other words, the religious pluralistic spirit that dominated Tahrir Square during 25 January–11 February 2011 did not represent a consensus around a vision of a political order shared by all. Finally, the hijacking of the revolution by SCAF and Islamists meant that those who were earnestly committed to a civil, pluralistic state were outmanoeuvred and sidelined.

And yet the story of the unity between Muslims and Christians during the eighteen-day uprising needs to be told and widely publicized, because it serves two important functions. First, it serves as a counter-narrative to Islamists' claim to ownership of the uprisings and their success and prevents them from putting forth a version of events that places their agency at center stage. Second, it is critically important for any future national project that will bind Muslims and Christians together, because it involves a reimagining of the polity along lines that show that it is possible and indeed desirable to make the nation for all, and religion for God.

7 | The Beginning of the End of the Tahrir Spirit

President Mubarak's ouster offered the hope for many Muslims and Christians that sectarian relations would be improved. This sprang from a number of important developments: the power and spirit of Tahrir Square, the leaking of security sources that indicated that the bombing of the Two Saints Church in Alexandria had been the work of the SSI, and the absence of reported assaults against Christian property during the eighteen days of the uprisings. Throughout January–March 2011, public opinion was very much in favor of the argument that Mubarak's regime was sectarianism's main driver and that its removal would lead to religious harmony. Yet the escalating tensions in 2011 following Mubarak's removal indicated that his regime had not been displaced and that sectarian tensions would not suddenly disappear. This chapter argues that a hybrid of new and old power configurations was behind the surge of sectarian assaults on non-Muslims. Three interrelated factors have precipitated sectarian violence in post-Mubarak Egypt. The first is that the removal of the repressive shackles of authoritarianism uncovered the cumulative build-up of social polarization in Egyptian society. In other words, societal faultlines were not an entirely new phenomenon but the outcome of years of beneath-the-surface deepening social hostility. The second important factor is the state-sponsored policy of religious discrimination pursued by SCAF. The third contributing factor to the increased strain on social cohesion is the Salafization of the management of sectarian violence, which substituted the earlier policy of its securitization at the hands of the SSI.

Sectarian Patterns, Old and New, in 2011

Sectarianism increased in Egypt both in terms of number of incidents and levels of violence after Mubarak's ouster. The number of sectarian incidents rose by a third in 2011 compared to 2010 and was double the number of incidents in 2009 and 2008.

Table 3: Causes of sectarian incidents in 2011

Trigger	Number of incidents
Related to Christian places of worship	15
Muslim/Christian gender relations	13
Escalation of small disputes/fights into sectarianism	11
News/rumors of defamation of Islam	1
Reasons related to Coptic converts to Islam	6
Disputes over land	3
Attacks on Christian protesters	4
No identifiable cause	16
Other reasons	1
Total number of incidents in 2011	70

In terms of causes or triggers, the patterns of sectarian incidents follow by and large those of previous years (see Table 2 on page 46) *except for the sudden surge in untriggered assaults.* There had been three untriggered assaults in 2010 and none in 2009 or 2008, and they rose to a total of sixteen in 2011. These are assaults involving violence against Coptic property, places of worship, or homes that do not involve competition over resources, are not a consequence of the escalation of a dispute, and do not spring from a perceived grievance. In other words, these untriggered assaults can be defined as hate crimes generated by a desire to exercise *power over* the victim.

During and after the 25 January revolution, there was a chronic, nation-wide security vacuum from which all Egyptians suffered. However, the cases of assault identified here did not involve general acts of thuggery, but seem to have had a sectarian element to them. In other words, the victims were targeted because of their religious affiliation. This is a disturbing new development associated with the political transition from authoritarianism, and it is unclear whether it will subside once security is tightened more generally across the country or whether the perpetrators will be emboldened by an Islamist-led government to assume that they will be met with clemency and lenience if they happen to be Muslim and the victim a Copt.

In terms of geographical patterns of sectarian violence, the highest incidence of assault was in Cairo, followed by the Upper Egyptian governorates of Asyut, Minya, Qena, and Sohag, and then followed by Alexandria. Yet incidents also occurred across other governorates such as Giza, Helwan, Qalyubiya, and Ismailiya. While incidents of sectarian violence were still predominantly in the conventional hotspots, it seems that a fewer number of governorates were now immune from their occurrence. As usual, most instances of security force intervention were made in response to violent sectarian incidents, with only a minority made to contain a situation before it unfolded into a full-blown crisis.

In the first one hundred days after Mubarak's resignation on 11 February 2011, there were no fewer than ten confirmed attacks on Christian places of worship or property, as well as other incidents of sectarian violence. Of the nineteen church-related incidents that occurred in 2011, eighteen occurred in post-Mubarak Egypt (the only exception being the Alexandria church bombing). These incidents included an army raid on a monastery; arson attacks on churches in Rafah, Sol, Atfih, Dayr Mawas, and Imbaba; the looting and burning of property belonging to Copts in the villages of Badraman and Abu Qurqas; an assault on Christians in al-Qamadir; and the excision of a Coptic citizen's ear in Qena. On 22 February, in the village of al-Shuraniya in the Upper Egyptian province of Sohag, a number of homes were set ablaze and property inside destroyed when rumors spread that the Baha'is who had been expelled from the village in 2009 had returned.[1] There were also repeated attacks by Salafis on tombs of Sufi saints.

The escalation of sectarian attacks contrasted starkly with the spirit of national unity that prevailed in Tahrir Square during the uprising, when Egypt's 25 January Revolution had seemed to bring together Muslim majority and Christian minority.

Yet the spirit of Tahrir Square was bound in space and time. The downtown plaza had a moral economy of its own, a social solidarity across lines of class, gender, and religion that stopped at the impromptu checkpoints. This is not to suggest that the revolutionary youth were schizophrenic. To the contrary, even when they were hospitalized following protests, they sought to counter religious prejudice against Coptic citizens. Many of the youth coalitions and groups were quick to join in solidarity, both prior to and after the revolution, when Copts protested against abuses. However, beyond Tahrir Square, not everyone shared the revolutionaries' spirit. Outside the square, social divides were as concrete as ever, and the joyful days preceding the ouster of Mubarak were not regenerated. The reason is as simple as a cartoon published in *Al-Masry Al-Youm* in which the revolutionary moment is marked by the Egyptian flag, while the phases before and after fly the cross and crescent. The 25 January revolution reinforced a key lesson of the history of Muslim–Christian relations in Egypt: national unity is strongest at times when identity is framed along a common Egyptian identity and weakest when it is framed in religious terms. The emphasis on Egyptian-ness in Tahrir Square was highly effective in uniting rather than dividing. As the previous chapter shows, had the rallying cries been religious in character, Copts would not only have turned away but turned against the revolution itself, if not visibly then inwardly. All this changed radically after Mubarak's ouster.

The growing Islamization of politics in post-Mubarak Egypt badly damaged the democratic credentials of the revolution by mobilizing religion in a highly divisive manner. It was not only that an Egyptian identity was being eclipsed in favor of an Islamic one but also that the level of animosity toward a publicly visible Coptic identity heightened with time. This came against the backdrop of Coptic movements becoming more active in the public arena, more vocal in expressing their condemnation of religious discrimination, and more visible in their display of identity markers (crosses, pictures of Jesus Christ, and so on). In effect, a new political space had opened up and every social and political actor was mobilizing to use it to express his or her voice.

It is debatable as to whether Egyptian-ness was forgone for an Islamically delineated identity after the revolution, or whether the revolution and the new political spaces opened as a result exposed the pulse of the Egyptian street, which had grown increasingly sympathetic to the Islamist message. Focus groups undertaken immediately after the revolution (March–April 2011) revealed that people were talking about "cleansing" their communities of Christians so that God would lift his anger against them and so that they could all live together as Muslims. This did not seem to be a sentiment that arose suddenly after the revolution; it is likely to have been building up for a long time to have come out in the open when the political environment changed.[2]

On 29 July 2011, the largest ever *milyuniya* that year took place in Tahrir Square,[3] with an estimated turnout of two million people. The protestsers called for the establishment of an Islamic state based on shari'a. The most common slogan to be shouted in Tahrir Square on that day was "*Islamiya, Islamiya*" (Islamic, Islamic), referring to the identity and system of governance to which the country must conform. By far, the largest stage was that put up by the Muslim Brotherhood. Atop the Brotherhood's stage were slogans praising the armed forces and people chanting "The people, the army, one hand!" and "Thank you, thank you, to the Field Marshal, a thousand greetings from Tahrir."[4] When the Muslim Brotherhood played a recording of the national anthem, Salafis lashed back "*Islamiya, Islamiya*" in objection.[5]

When members of the April 6 movement appeared on the stage put up by the Muslim Brotherhood in Tahrir Square, they were booed down. On the much smaller stage set up by Kefaya, when three hundred of its members tried to answer back to "*Islamiya, Islamiya*" with "*madaniya, madaniya*," the Islamists took over and, in one instance, empty water bottles were thrown at them (Tadros 2012c). The same demands for the establishment of an Islamic state were voiced across governorates of Egypt, through high-level, efficient coordination between the Muslim Brotherhood, Salafis, and other Islamist groups.

By three o'clock in the afternoon on Friday 29 July 2011, thirty-three political groups had announced their withdrawal from Tahrir and issued a statement explaining that

> while all civil political forces, revolutionary groups, and youth coalitions have abided by the agreement in opposing the military council's divisive plans and keeping away from points of difference, some Islamic forces have violated this agreement and chanted slogans, hung banners, and spread flyers that included our points of difference. Sticking to our principle of always maintaining peacefulness, we have decided to withdraw from this Friday's demonstrations while continuing our sit-in which upholds the revolution's demands.[6]

But some members of the Muslim Brotherhood and the Salafi movements denied ever having reached an agreement with the civil political forces. Safwat Higazi, a leading preacher for the Muslim Brotherhood, told Al Jazeera Mubashir television channel that there had been no agreement to unify demands before the Friday demonstrations. In contrast, leading Muslim Brotherhood youth member Ibrahim El-Houdaiby, who was involved as an intermdiary between the different political groups, emphasized that the Brotherhood had confirmed the stance, together with a number of other Islamist political forces.[7]

The sectarian attacks of March, April, and May 2011 shocked many Egyptians who believed that the country did not have a problem of religious intolerance, only with leaders who whipped up displays of it for their political gain. With Mubarak gone and sectarian incidents on the rise, many offered the explanation that Muslim–Christian tensions were orchestrated by members of the former ruling party in association with disgraced state security officers. Yet analysis suggests the involvement not only of SSI members but others as well in the instigation of sectarian tension: Salafis, the Muslim Brothers, ordinary citizens, and, most of all, the military.

Security became lax after the fall of Mubarak. Egyptians complained of a rise in street crime and the slow response of the authorities to reported muggings and assaults. Disputes escalated into full-blown fights, as the army proved to be an inadequate substitute for a proper police force. Yet there are cases of religiously motivated attacks or criminal activity that took on the form of a targeted attack, that is, specifically singling out Coptic citizens and families. In both instances, the army seemed to practice a policy of studied non-intervention, if not outright complicity, with the attackers. A case in point is the non-action taken toward a local thug with a two-hundred-man militia who took over the villages of al-Badraman and Nazlat al-Badraman in Minya, an Upper Egyptian province. There, some Copts were expelled from their homes and others were kidnapped for a ransom, while the land of still others was expropriated and a levy imposed on Copts for several weeks. The thug in question called the levy *jizya*, the name of the poll tax paid by protected non-Muslims *(ahl al-dhimma)* to Muslim rulers before the mid-nineteenth century. Forty-three human rights organizations wrote to the Supreme Council of the Armed Forces (SCAF) asking for action to be taken against this would-be sultan, but none was forthcoming. Even a year later, in May 2012, the situation remained unchanged.

On other occasions, the army itself was the aggressor. In an under-reported incident on 22 February 2011, soldiers attacked the monastery of St. Pshoi in Wadi al-Natrun with tanks and live ammunition, injuring four people. The army accused the monks of building a fence without a permit (although the land legally belongs to the monks) and later released a statement insisting that only barriers built on state-owned land were razed. Yet, as the blogger Muhammad Mar'i asked, why target the monastery for illegal construction when thousands of unlicensed residential structures are built all the time?

The fifth of March saw the better-documented church blaze in Sol, a village in the vicinity of Helwan, south of the capital. Muslim residents set ablaze the local church, bringing it to the ground, under the gaze of security forces. There were many rumors surrounding the causes behind the sectarian violence. One version of the story is that a Christian man had been in a relationship with a Muslim woman and when the villagers found out, the young man and his family were expelled. Property belonging to Christians was burned and looted. Some of the residents then went to the house of the young woman's father asking that she too be expelled. He appeared in front of his house armed and bullets were shot from both sides, leading to the death of the father and of his cousin. Angry youth then proceeded to burn the church.[8] Other accounts suggest that the youth attacked the church because they believed that magic spells were being cast on its premises in order to win over Muslim women, and that their nightgowns and undergarments were hidden there. As will be argued below, while the army may have rebuilt the church after mass protests ensued, justice was never administered.

The Qena Test and the Wiles of Majoritarian Democracy

Over the course of ten days in mid-April 2011, life in much of Upper Egypt came to a virtual standstill.[9] The crisis began on 14 April, when the government announced that 'Imad Mikha'il, a Copt and a general in Mubarak's security apparatus, was appointed governor of Qena province. Angry Qenawis demanded his immediate resignation, holding rallies and moving to halt railway transport from Qena north to Sohag and south to Aswan.

The protests in Qena only subsided on 26 April when the Cabinet announced a three-month freeze on the governor's term, during which a Muslim official, Maged Abd al-Karim, would undertake his duties. The protesters, however, vowed that they would continue to push for General Mikha'il's resignation. The standoff exposed cracks in state–citizen relations as well as ideological struggles between different forces vying for power.

When the Cabinet had announced its list of governors, there had been immediate opposition to Mikha'il on account of his association with the Mubarak regime. The 25 January Revolution Coalition argued that Mikha'il had been responsible for repression of the uprising in his previous capacity as deputy security head of Giza. In Qena, large protests erupted after Friday prayers on 15 April and continued for several days, preventing civil servants from entering the governorate premises and blocking rail lines. Three days later, the prime minister sent General Mansur al-'Isawi, the then minister of interior (and a Qenawi), and General Muhsin al-Nu'mani, minister of local administration, to hear the people's grievances. The meeting ended in frustration and, shortly afterward, the deputy prime minister refused to accept Mikha'il's letter of resignation. The protesters threatened to shut off the supply of water to the Red Sea governorate and electricity to sugar refineries. Some also threatened the governor with death should he set foot in Qena.

The national press was sympathetic to the Qenawis' stance. Historically, the government has neglected the southern governorates, which have some of the lowest human development profiles nationwide and have been marginalized from the centers of decision-making. Abu al-'Abbas Muhammad, a Qenawi, wrote in the state-run magazine *Rose al-Yusuf* that Prime Minister Essam Sharaf (Egypt's first post-revolution prime minister) should have shown the same regard for Qena that he had shown for protesters in Tahrir Square when he visited the square upon his appointment and told the crowds that his legitimacy derived from them. Muhammad continued: "I say it bluntly: Those who conjured these spirits should release them. The government brought this crisis about and the government should bring an end to it."[10] Indeed, delegating the Qena listening tour to two generals—one of them the interior minister, to boot—was redolent of the old regime's ways, which treated political crises as security matters. Renowned author and long-time regime critic Alaa Al Aswany described the premier's message to Qenawis as follows: "I decide, and whether you like it or not, you will accept my dictates in a state of submission."[11]

But to read the Qena events as a case of citizens confronting authoritarianism would be too simple. Around the same time, demonstrations began in several other Egyptian provinces, including Alexandria, Asyut, Minya, Daqahliya, and Beni Suef, against the appointment of generals from Mubarak's police state as governors. The protests, however, were notably smaller, with participants numbering in the hundreds, while in Qena they numbered in the hundreds of thousands. It was surely not coincidental that Qena was the only province whose appointed governor happened to be a Christian. What happened there involved a constellation of actors: tribal leaders, Salafis, the Muslim Brothers, Sufis, members of the dismantled NDP, and actors in the state security agency, who, according to some reports, helped bring the trains to a standstill. The common objective was not the demand for a civilian governor, but for a Muslim one.

A Christian governor had been appointed to Qena once before. The first Christian governor, Magdi Ayyub, was despised by Coptic Qenawis for being so keen to appear unbiased that he discriminated against Christians. It was during his tenure that Egypt witnessed one of its bloodiest sectarian attacks to date—the shootings of Nag' Hammadi parishioners leaving Christmas Eve mass in 2010. Muslim Qenawis also disliked Ayyub, complaining that he was a weak leader overly afraid of stepping on toes. But there was another complaint as well, namely that he could not participate in Friday prayers.

As for Mikha'il, a group calling themselves "intellectuals of Qena" issued a statement contending that local forces had striven to take opposition to his appointment in a sectarian direction. According to the statement, a Muslim Brotherhood member called 'Abd al-'Aziz had reached an agreement with Qena's director of general security to delay the trains for two hours and was then surprised when protesters permanently occupied the tracks. Muslim Brothers and Salafis led the protests but later more established Islamists retreated. The statement (corroborated by journalistic accounts) highlighted the fact that opponents of Mikha'il put forth an alternative slate consisting of two Salafi sheikhs and a former NDP local councilman to rule Qena. According to several press reports, the town's mosques became platforms for calls to reject the Christian governor because a non-Muslim has no authority *(wilaya)* over a Muslim.[12] Among the popular slogans raised in the protests were: "Islamic, Islamic, not Christian, not Jewish," "Raise your head up, you are Muslim," and "There is no God but God, the Nazarene is the enemy of God." "Nazarene" refers not to Jesus but to Mikha'il, as it is a Muslim designation for Christians, intended as a slur.

Islamist intellectual Fahmi Huwaydi cautioned that Islamists should not be lumped together,[13] but the Qena crisis showed that, in particular political settings, various Islamist factions can and do synchronize their efforts toward a common goal. The Muslim Brotherhood, the Gamaʻa al-Islamiya,[14] and assorted Salafis set up loudspeakers in front of the governorate building, threatening to take up arms if the cabinet did not heed their demand for a Muslim governor. In front of al-Wihda Mosque in the town center, Salafis raised the Saudi flag and called for the establishment of an Islamic emirate. Political activist Hamdi Qandil interpreted this act as one of Saudi Arabia meddling in Egyptian affairs by employing thugs under the cloak of religion,[15] but the flag may not have symbolized counter-revolutionary tactics on the Saudi side so much as the strength of Wahhabi ties to Salafis in Egypt.

Diaa Rashwan, a prominent political analyst and director of one of the country's leading think tanks, Al-Ahram Center for Political and Strategic Studies, argued that since Christians were among the first to oppose Mikhail's appointment, the protests were not motivated by sectarian sentiments.[16] Yet the influence of Salafis and of other Islamists was conspicuous early on. When the two ministers visited Qena, the majority of the forum's attendees were Salafis. "When the minister of interior asked about Copts, he discovered there was no representation and two priests were brought in for a meeting to be held with the minister afterwards," noted one journalist.[17] Also present were the Gamaʻa al-Islamiya, the Muslim Brothers, and "NDP figures." A Salafi sheikh rose and chanted, "We want it Islamic," to which neither minister responded.

The greatest evidence that the primary objection to Mikha'il was his religious identity, not his military rank, came after the government froze his assumption of office. The protesters released a statement saying they had blocked the railways for legitimate reasons, namely that they do not want Qena to fill the "quota" for Copts in government.[18] The Qena crisis is symptomatic of the dilemmas facing post-Mubarak government in Egypt should the Salafis, the Gamaʻa al-Islamiya, the Muslim Brotherhood, and other Islamist forces continue to grow in mobilizing power.

After the interim three-month period ended, Mikha'il was not reinstated in his capacity as governor. Instead, a former governor of Qena, Adel Eid, was made governor once again. The incident represented a victory for the Islamists on many fronts. First, they showed that they could mobilize hundreds of thousands in the name of religion and instrumentalize their constituency to make political gains. Second, they used civil disobedience in a way that brought the country to a standstill (blocking train lines, closing public squares) and for which they were not held accountable. Third, they showed that no constitutional principle—including equality of citizenship—is above the Islamist mantra. While the representation of one Coptic governor among thirty-six would not have changed the power configurations of minority visibility in politics to any great degree, it nevertheless demonstrated clearly the challenges of building an inclusive political community and that there was little or no commitment to even the most basic rules of equal citizenship. In effect, the Qena incident epitomized the effects of democracy conceived of as majoritarian rule. How will the government respond to future incidents of this kind if the majority in a school, village, or local council decide that they no longer wish to have non-Muslims with them?

In effect, the Qena incident was a precursor of the tyranny of the Islamist-led majority once placed in a position of power in parliament (see chapter 11).

Of 'Honor' and Sectarianism

The attacks on the churches in Sol and Imbaba had something in common: both were ignited by perceptions of damaged communal 'honor,' because of the claimed loss of women's virtue. In Sol, Muslims burned the church in retaliation for an alleged relationship between a Christian man and a Muslim woman. The Muslim woman's father had been killed by the Christian man's family because he refused to kill his daughter to cleanse the family's 'honor.' In Imbaba, on 7 May 2011, attacks on two churches in Imbaba, a poor quarter of Cairo, left fifteen dead and over two hundred injured. The crisis began when a crowd of some two thousand Salafis (and unknown others) agitated to "liberate" 'Abir, a Christian woman who they claimed had converted to Islam, been married to a Muslim, and had then been abducted and taken to a building belonging to the Mari Mina Church.

The timing of the 'Abir protests is noteworthy. Islamists had mounted rallies on consecutive Fridays since the summer of 2010 demanding the "release" of Camillia Shehata (see chapter 4).[19] On 29 April, a Salafi-led "Coalition of New Muslims" (I'tilaf al-Muslimin al-Judud) held a large demonstration in front of the cathedral where Pope Shenouda resided, demanding her "release" and the pontiff's removal. On 7 May, Camillia Shehata appeared on television, in the company of her priest, husband, and young son, to emphasize the fact that she had left home after a marital dispute, but had not converted or been held by the church. Mere hours after the broadcast, bearded men believed to belong to the Salafi movement headed to the Mari Mina Church, where 'Abir's husband had informed them that his wife was being held against her will. It was a case of "never mind Camillia, take 'Abir," as Khalid Muntasir later wrote in a scathing column.[20]

At the church, three sheikhs were allowed to inspect the premises, and they confirmed that 'Abir was not present. In the meantime, however, the large crowd outside had stirred fears of an assault on the church, and clashes erupted with neighborhood Copts, including an exchange of gunfire. Property belonging to Copts was burned and looted, and the mob proceeded to set St. Mary's Church ablaze as well. A fact-finding mission from the National Council for Human Rights attributed the violence to the deficient response of security forces and accused remnants of the former ruling NDP of instigating social strife to abort the revolution. The council's report also pointed to extremists trying to reconfigure Egyptian society to ensure that Copts have no rights except as *ahl al-dhimma*.[21]

After the Imbaba incident, Ahmad al-Tayyib, the Sheikh of al-Azhar, admonished Egyptians, saying that sectarian strife could culminate in civil war. Public opinion was quick to pick up on this fear, but thus far remains in overall denial of the dynamics of violence against non-Muslims in Egypt. Sectarianism is blamed on foreign enemies and a "deviant few" Egyptians. How these marginal actors are able to galvanize hundreds of Egyptians to take part in attacks in the name of defending religion is not explained.

There is also a pattern of presenting sectarian attacks as conflicts between two equal parties. An impassioned column by 'Abd al-Fattah 'Abd al-Mun'im, for instance, read:

> We have sacrificed the revolution and Egypt so that the Salafis and the Church can flex their muscles. They are backed up by militias capable of destroying the country in less than ten minutes, and there is no force in Egypt capable of overcoming them, not even the army. They speak in the name of Allah or the Lord. If the case of Camillia is resolved, 'Abir is her substitute. What counts is that the fires of sectarian sedition remain alight.[22]

Of course, neither the Church nor independent groups of Copts have launched an assault on a mosque or property belonging to Muslims during this wave of sectarian unrest. Islamists and some secular nationalists, however, perceive the lobbying of external Coptic groups for international protection of Christians as a religious minority as a provocation and a principal cause of sectarian incidents.

The Coalition of Support for New Muslims, which was active in instigating the protests, has not been held accountable and continues to mobilize followers to take action in incidents where they believe that Coptic women converts to Islam have been held against their will. The same Salafis who were mobilized in their thousands to take to the streets in solidarity with a persecuted Muslim sister vilified the veiled Muslim woman who was stripped of her clothes and dragged across Tahrir by an armed soldier in December 2011. This prompted many women who protested the assault on the woman who became known as the "blue bra woman" to shout out in the Tahrir demonstrations: "Where are you Salafis now, is she not your sister too?"

In the absence of any media campaign to expose the inflammatory discourse and practice of Salafis who follow the Coalition for the Support of New Muslims as hate speech, there are many who find their case convincing, which is that the Church does retain by force girls and women who have converted to Islam and it does so through special concessions made by the state. The fact that Camillia, for example, spoke on television to announce that she never converted and was never retained against her will by the Church has not been found convincing by some because she appeared on a Christian broadcasting station. Camillia said in the television interview that she would not appear on national television and wished that people would respect her privacy. However, the sense of public entitlement to "make sure" that she really had not converted served to perpetuate the rumors that women converts to Islam need intervention to secure their rights against a repressive Church.

The Reconciliation Committees: Subverting Justice

The handling of sectarian crises by SCAF and the transitional government was reminiscent of the SSI's management of the 'sectarian portfolio' during Mubarak's era. The parallels were conspicuous: in both cases, perpetrators for the most part escaped without legal prosecution, reconciliation committees were forced to administer informal injustice, and a standardized discourse of national unity was momentarily adopted to present a selective truth.

As in Mubarak's era, there continued to be no recourse to the court system to litigate in matters of sectarian violence. Only in one singular incident (Imbaba) were the perpetrators of attacks referred to court, but the court acquitted them of all charges on a technicality. The defendants argued and won on the premise that since the Emergency Law had been annulled, they could not be tried in a state security court.

The infamous reconciliation committees that emerged during Mubarak's era (see chapter 5) also became the preferred channel of mediating sectarian matters under SCAF's reign, except that they tended to be qualitatively even more unjust than those of Mubarak's era. In the new configurations of power, it was not the SSI that was mediating the rules, but Salafi sheikhs. In the first week of April, Muslim villagers in al-Qamadir in Minya protested the planned repair of the church of Mari Yuhanna, built with official sanction in 2001 and serving about 2,500 worshipers. The parishioners sought a restoration permit from the army when the building began to collapse. Local Muslims objected, saying they were offended by the church's location in front of their mosque, which was built in 2010. With no intervention from the authorities, another 'reconciliation committee' meeting was convened and the verdict was to move the church premises to a smaller building on the village outskirts, stipulating that it could display no religious markers like a bell or a cross.[23]

Similarly, in the first meeting held in Sol after the church arson, it was agreed (with the army's blessing) that the church should be rebuilt in a different location, preferably on the edge of town, to avoid disturbing majority sensibilities and that the perpetrators (who were caught on camera) would not be tried.[24] Following massive protests led by youth coalitions and Copts at Maspero, the army volunteered to rebuild the church, although the perpetrators were never referred to trial. When the army came under heavy criticism for having called renowned Salafi Sheikh Muhammad Hassan (commonly known as Sheikh Hassan) and many other Salafis and Muslim Brotherhood members to manage the reconciliation committee, they sought to deflect criticism of their continued reliance upon him for managing sectarian strife by explaining that it is "because people listen to him."[25]

The power of Salafis had grown in some parts to the point where citizens stopped bothering to report violations to the police, instead resorting to their local Salafi sheikh. A case in point is the headline of a story in *al-Ahram* on 14 February 2012 (Ibrahim Zaytoun) that reads:

"The Salafis put down sectarian fire in Fayoum." The story is of a Coptic tenant who was harassed by his landlord. When the landlord used a bulldozer to take down part of the apartment, the Copt rushed to the local Salafi leader seeking intervention. A reconciliation committee was set up in which the landowner was asked to repair the damages and pay a hefty compensation fee. The Copt in turn agreed not to file a police complaint. The *al-Ahram* story praises the role of Salafis in mitigating conflict and ends with a note on how social harmony and amicability were restored. The story, which was also reported in *Rose al-Yusuf* ("A Christian Gets Help from Salafis to Reclaim His Apartment," by Hussein Fathi) has a number of important inferences. First, Salafis' authority in the community is recognized. Second, the formal mechanisms for having injustice recognized and redressed are non-existent. Third, Salafis' decisions are binding for all because of the strong community leadership role they assumed after the revolution.

Yet the army's choice of strategic partners is dangerous in view of the vision of majoritarian-based political order that Salafis promote. Islamist-mediated reconciliation sessions were characterized by verdicts that affirmed collective punishment of citizens on account of their membership in a religious minority and awarded a cloak of legitimacy through the participation of the government and SCAF representatives. Regrettably, the mainstream press has by and large tended to represent reconciliation committees as successful in dispelling sectarian strife. Exceptions occur when highly influential political actors speak out. Among the few widely publicized reconciliation committees were those mediated by Muslim Brothers and Salafis in the village of al-Bayada in the town of Amiriya, Alexandria, in January–February 2012. In January 2012, pictures of a local Muslim woman in an indecent posture were circulated by mobile phone among the youth in the village by a young Coptic man. Fearing for his life and the lives of his family, the man in question gave himself up at the local police station but the youth in the village congregated and demanded that he and his family leave the village. This was followed by acts of burning and vandalism on homes and property owned by Copts. In one instance, a member of these families fired bullets into the air for fear of crowd violence. Three reconciliation committee meetings led by Salafis and the Muslim Brotherhood were convened to deal with the matter. The meetings were attended by Lieutenant Khaled Shalaby and Salafi sheikhs, headed by Sheikh al-Sherif al-Hawari, despite the express opposition of the local priest and the Coptic family in question to what was decided in these agreements. In the first reconciliation committee meeting, it was decided that three families would be expelled from the village and that a committee would be formed to sell their property. However, the Muslim youth were displeased with the decision. As a result, a second reconciliation committee meeting was convened and it was agreed that five more Coptic families would be added to the list of those to be expelled.[26] In the third and conclusive reconciliation committee meeting, a contract was drawn up and published in *al-Wafd* stipulating that the '*urfi* agreement reached on 1 February 2012 meant that the 'exit' of the families had been decided for the protection of their lives. One of the striking clauses in the agreement bestows responsibility for selling the properties belonging to the expelled families on the committee and the exact pricing and selling process on Sheikh al-Sherif al-Hawari. The Salafi and Muslim Brotherhood leaders in the reconciliation committee usurped the right of the police to investigate and prosecute, and yet this contract was signed in the presence of the highest security authorities in Alexandria.

The second striking clause holds that the arbitrators will exert efforts to discover the perpetrators and the victims and determine the scope of damage "in accordance with the precepts of shar'ia."[27] The reference to shar'ia is interesting because reconciliation committees have conventionally followed a number of social customs and traditions that have differed from one geographic area to the next. The '*urf*, or custom, in this area was that a man would not be expelled except if there was a case of premeditated murder, and even then, he himself would depart but not his family. As for the punishment for shooting bullets in the air with the intention of frightening people away, custom has it that the person would apologize and compensate any victims injured. The collective punishment of the Copts and their expulsion is anathema to local custom in the village of al-Bayada.[28]

In protest, the Coptic Maspero Youth Movement staged a march to the People's Assembly to express their rejection of the reconciliation committee and the expulsion of Copts from the village.

State-Sponsored Injustice
SCAF and the Essam Sharaf government's position on sectarian matters suggested the adoption of a policy of tolerance toward sectarian assaults

on non-Muslims. First, unjust decisions arrived at through informal reconciliation committees had the blessing of SCAF representatives. Second, in the rare instances when they were tried, none of the perpetrators of sectarian assault was found guilty. Third, under SCAF's direction, victims of assault were arrested, which echoed the handling of sectarian incidents during the Mubarak era when the victims became the accused. Fourth, SCAF and transitional goverments adopted a clear double standard when it came to the matter of the defamation of religion. Fifth, they refused to inculpate the Ministry of Interior for its part in the bombing of the Two Saints Church in Alexandria. Each development will be briefly discussed below.

The ruling powers conveyed signals that had a broader ripple effect at the local level. For example, informants suggested that while religiously prejudiced civil servants who worked in local councils in Minya had refrained from openly showing bias against non-Muslims during the Mubarak era, in the period after the revolution they felt no inhibition about openly displaying their prejudices. For example, for some years now, Christian property owners in particular in rural areas have faced exceptional difficulty in obtaining the necessary permits from local councils to extend or renovate their houses (even if they are two-bedroom village houses). The reason for this is that many Muslims fear that the extended or upgraded house will be secretly converted into a place of worship for Christians. Under Mubarak, civil servants would seek to delay as long as possible the issuance of the permit without offering any kind of justification. In the months that followed the 25 January Revolution, they began to tell applicants that they would not be granted a permit because they did not want more houses to be used for Christian worship (even when residents insisted that the house was going to collapse or that the additional rooms were going to be used as living quarters of a married son or daughter). The fact that the cooperation between Islamist groups and SCAF seemed so strong on the ground also gave the signal that were the Islamists to expand their spheres of influence in the villages (through the Salafi sheikh for example), no one would stand in their way. Consequently, the Islamization of public space that had commenced during Sadat's era and was latent during that of Mubarak came to the surface after the revolution. People were emboldened by the rising power of Islamists to be much more open about expressing their positions on such matters.

SCAF was also held responsible for inaction when the Ministry of Interior stalled the trial relating to the bombing of the Two Saints Church in Alexandria. Shortly after Mubarak's resignation, it was announced that the church bombing had not been the act of a Palestinian Islamist group as was claimed but by the Ministry of Interior's State Security Investigations apparatus. Despite the fact that Habib al-Adli, Mubarak's minister of interior, was tried in 2011 for human rights abuses, in particular for commanding officers to fire on protesters during the 25 January Revolution, he was not tried for orchestrating the bombing of the church in Alexandria.

In March 2011, following the announcement of the dissolution of the SSI, Egyptian protesters stormed the premises of the SSI across the country. Hundreds of thousands of documents were seized by regular citizens. In one of the SSI buildings, documents regarding the orchestration of the bombing of the Two Saints Church in Alexandria were found, leaked to the press, and published in *al-Yawm al-sabi'* newspaper.[29] The documents, which bear the emblem of the Ministry of Interior, suggest that a special corps, named "Number 77," within the SSI was assigned to planning a deadly attack on the church. The motivation was to teach Pope Shenouda a lesson for his hard stance toward the regime and force him to take action to quieten the Copts who were repeatedly holding protests for petty reasons. The SSI had recruited incarcerated prisoners from the Gama'a al-Islamiya, Ahmad Muhammad Khalid, and Abd al-Rahman Ahmad Ali to undertake the bombing. The SSI facilitated their tasks. *Al-Yawm al-sabi'* said that if the documents were fake, the Ministry of Interior should refute their content, which the latter never did. Moreover, the information was corroborated through another source. Omar Suleiman, the former vice president, in his statement to the General Prosecution during investigations into Mubarak's responsibility for the deaths of young people in the 25 January Revolution testified that he had informed the president in a report submitted one week before the Two Saints Church bombing that a major incident would take place in the area and that the SSI and the security men in Alexandria were informed of this. Suleiman noted that forty-eight hours before the bombing the necessary security precautions were not adequately taken in the area "and Suleiman held the SSI responsible for the Two Saints incident," according to his testimony.[30]

Holding leaders from the former regime accountable is an essential aspect of redressing the injustices of Mubarak's regime. In the case of the inquiry into the Two Saints Church bombing, investigations have been especially slow, to the point where Coptic activists have accused the authorities of deliberate footdragging and a reluctance to reveal the truths about who was responsible.[31] In March 2011, St. Mark's Cathedral, with the support of the Majlis al-Milli in Alexandria, submitted a lawsuit on behalf of the families of the victims of the bombing to demand the accountability of the Ministry of Interior. Another lawsuit was filed on 13 December 2011 by St. Mark's Cathedral in Alexandria against the Supreme Commander of the Armed Forces, Field Marshal Muhammad Hussein Tantawi, the prime minister, the minister of interior, and the attorney general for failing to press the Ministry of Interior on the outcome of its investigations into the Two Saints Church case. The Ministry of Interior had until then refused to submit the findings of its investigations to the State Security Court, which prevented the State Security Prosecution from proceeding with the case.[32] Joseph Malak, the lawyer who filed the second lawsuit, said that Khaled Diaa al-Bayoumi, head of the Emergency[33] Supreme State Security Investigations Prosecution, told him that the delay was being caused by the Ministry of Interior's delays and shortcomings. He noted that al-Bayoumi said that even the accused under arrest had not been referred to the Prosecution for questioning and that the latter had sent several requests for the investigations' results but that the Ministry of Interior had not been responsive.[34]

In contrast, the criminal court in Rod al-Farag, in Cairo's Shubra district, was quick to condemn eight revolutionary activists to two years' imprisonment for allegedly attacking police officers and public property while they were protesting in early January 2011. Shortly after the bombing of the Two Saints' Cathedral in Alexandria that took place on 1 January 2011, Copts joined by Muslim sympathizers stood in front of the Rod al-Farag church to protest the Egyptian government's shortcomings with respect to protecting its citizens. The eight activists—all Muslim according to the revolution's Youth Coalition[35]—were all indicted on trumped-up charges, since the protest was peaceful throughout.

A Church on Hold

The strategy of the Coptic Church leadership immediately after Mubarak's resignation was to go completely silent. In view of the level of animosity toward Pope Shenouda for having publicly supported Gamal Mubarak's accession to power after his father, this silence was probably a risk-minimizing strategy. "The Church was on hold," as one leader close to the hierarchy astutely remarked. It could not assume a leading role like the Qasr al-Dubbara Church, nor did it have the political repertoire to assume any active agency in this critical period. Also, on a purely practical level, Pope Shenouda's health had deteriorated considerably by this time, to the point where he was spending more time in the United States for treatment than at home.

The Church leadership's political bargaining power, already on the wane before the revolution (see chapter 3), become almost negligible after the uprisings. For a start, SCAF was not Hosni Mubarak; it did not need the support of the Church to shore up its legitimacy. Whether or not an entente, however fragile, was forged between the Church leadership and SCAF is unknown. Had there been some kind of understanding, it would have involved SCAF giving the Church a say in the appointment of Coptic candidates to parliament and a few other minor concessions in return for the Church's pronouncement of a position against the revolutionary youth and other sources of dissidence against the military. What was certain was that after the first few months of quiet, the Church leadership began to align itself publicly with SCAF. This became conspicuous following the revolutionary youth coalitions' announcement of civil disobedience against SCAF.

Pope Shenouda's silence over the unfolding events in Egypt would not have stirred much opposition had it not pursued once more the position of supporting the ruling regime, both SCAF and the transitional government.

Moreover, the SSI's vendetta with the Church continued to influence the course of events after the revolution, the only difference being that the SSI was now even more opaque and operated in a backstage manner. The role of SSI officers in instigating the anti-Coptic demonstrations in Qena was, for example, alluded to in the press (see page 147).

Moreover, Islamists, who emerged after the revolution as the most powerful organized political force in the country, had long accused the Coptic Church of acting as though it were a state within a state. The Muslim Brotherhood had always been critical of the Coptic Church's leadership for supporting Mubarak and had always argued that the former regime used Islamists as a scare mechanism with which to frighten the Christians. There were rumors that the Muslim Brothers had extended an olive branch to the Coptic Church's leadership and a meeting had been arranged between the Muslim Brotherhood Supreme Guide, Muhammad

Badi', and Pope Shenouda shortly before the latter's death. The content of this meeting is unknown although it is assumed it was a diplomatic courtesy call, as it was brief and the pope was in a very sickly state.

The Church leadership under Pope Shenouda continued to assume a political role on two fronts. First, it sought to mobilize Copts to vote in the 19 March 2011 referendum and parliamentary and presidential elections. Second, it had a say in the Coptic candidates who were appointed to parliament in 2012. However, Bishop Pachomious, who assumed the role of acting head of the Church after Pope Shenouda's death in March 2012, deliberately sought to distance the Church leadership from any overt political role. For example, during the presidential elections, Bishop Pachomious made a public statement to the effect that the Church rests at an arm's length from all candidates and has no voting preferences. This was in stark contrast with Pope Shenouda, who had expressed his preference for a Gamal Mubarak presidency in no uncertain terms.

Hence the Coptic Church's leadership generally adopted a more politically reserved stance toward the rapidly changing power configurations that followed the 25 January Revolution in Egypt by maintaining a low profile. Strategically, given the level of political chaos and insecurity, this may have been the safest route to take.

8 Coptic Protest and Copts in Protest

From the mid-2000s up to the 25 January Revolution and during the transition, a significant proportion of Egyptian citizens engaged in a level of political activism unprecedented in the prior half-century of the country's history. In particular, from 25 January onward, the street gained new significance as people—spontaneously and in organized groups—went out to voice their grievances and demand their rights. It was as if Egyptian society had become highly politicized overnight. This chapter provides insight into some of the dynamics of Copts' mobilization around particular grievances. I choose, however, to differentiate between Coptic protests and Copts in protest. In so doing, I drawn on the work of feminist theorist Sheila Rowbotham (1992), who distinguishes between women's movements that advocate for equality between women and men and "women in movement," which is about the mobilization of women around non-gender-specific causes but which at the same time cannot be delinked in its impact from the work of women's movements since it involves the exercise of people's agency with respect to materialist issues that can have a positive impact on advancing women's equality. Hence there are some Coptic movements whose aim is specifically to fight forms of religious discrimination, such as the Maspero Youth Movement, and there are Coptic Egyptians who participate in social and political movements that protest on a wide array of issues that may not be specific to Coptic rights, such as the Kefaya movement. The lines of demarcation between the two are not definitive. For example, many of the members of the Maspero Youth Movement are also extremely active in youth revolutionary movements. Moreover, members of youth revolutionary movements, such as the late

Mina Daniel, were also active participants in protests specifically related to Coptic issues. However, the protesters are not always the same, the issues around which the two different kinds of protesters, broadly defined, mobilize, sometimes converge and sometimes diverge, and the location of the protests also sometimes differs.

In this chapter, another important distinction is made with respect to protest actions. In some cases, a movement such as Copts for Egypt or the Maspero Youth Movement called for a protest and actively planned for it. In other cases, the protests involved citizens—rather than movements— calling upon each other in the heat of the moment to take to the street or to the church to protest, without direction from a particular movement or leadership. Both forms of protest will be analyzed here.

In terms of the chronological order of the emergence of protesting movements, the first to appear in the Egyptian context in the 2000s was Kefaya. As George Ishak, the movement's co-founder and coordinator recounts, Kefaya brought people to the streets on 7 September 2005 and continued to be active in organizing protests, in particular in 2006. It broke the fear barrier that had previously inhibited people from going to the street, and it broke the silence around a taboo subject: the inheritance of the presidency from Mubarak by his son Gamal. It also took up a number of important political matters, such as privatization, torture, corruption, and the strictures placed on syndicates, non-governmental organizations, and political parties. Ishak identifies the movement as cutting across many different political opinions, bringing together people from different political parties, orientations, and backgrounds, including Islamists, liberals, and leftists (Ishak's introduction in Hussein 2009). He never mentions religious affiliation, most probably because the focus is on Kefaya's nationalist or patriotic character. The fact that Ishak, a Coptic Catholic, was selected through an open system of voting to be the coordinator of the movement is significant. As coordinator, he was the public face of the movement and often acted as its spokesperson. Ishak would probably argue that in the movement's selection of its coordinator, its criteria were religion-blind. In other words, Kefaya did not take religious affiliation into account as much as it did candidates' political competencies, around which there could be a consensus. It is also unclear how many Copts have joined Kefaya and what their backgrounds are. This is probably because their participation within the movement is not expressed in terms of religious identity. Due to limitations of time and space, I restricted my research to Coptic protests rather than Copts in protest, but suffice it to say that Kefaya tore through the shroud surrounding public protest and in effect claimed public space for Egyptian citizenry in a highly visible way. It is impossible, therefore, to talk about Coptic street protests without recognizing the wider political context, since this had an impact on Coptic protests, though in subtle, indirect ways.

This chapter first provides an overview of Coptic protests between 2008 and 2011 and analyzes the nuances behind the numbers. It then specifically focuses on two forms of Coptic protests in the wake of and after the uprisings of 25 January 2011. The first form of Coptic activism examined here is that of protests organized by Coptic movements, their positioning in society and among Copts, their evolution, and their relationship with the authorities and the Coptic Church's leadership. The second is a particular case of sporadic, spontaneous, unorganized protest—what would be considered one-off events. These are important to look at because not all Coptic protests have been organized by Coptic movements.

An in-depth case study of the protests of the *zabbalin* (garbage collectors) of Muqattam will be presented as an example of the more spontaneous form of Coptic protest. I focus on the *zabbalin* in particular because their experience never received the kind of public recognition or publicity that the Maspero Massacre (of October 2011) and the subsequently formed Maspero Youth Movement acquired. On the other hand, the plight of the *zabbalin* at the hands of SCAF is unique: it is an untold story of systematic persecution that is unparalleled within wider Egyptian society, as will be discussed below.

The Rise and Rise of Coptic Protests
Egypt saw a rise in demonstrations in 2011, and Coptic-specific protests fared no differently. In 2010, there were at least six Coptic protests: three on the disappearance of Coptic citizens, one to protest the Nag' Hammadi massacre, one to protest the governorate's demolition of a building on church premises in Minya, and one to protest the demolition of church premises in al-Amiriya. In 2009, there were three protests: one against the demolition of a church in Marsa Matruh, one against the disappearance of a young woman, and one for the murder of a Coptic man in Minya. In 2008, there were three protests: one concerning the murder of a Coptic man, one in Minya against Copts' exposure to violence, and one against

the appropriation of church-owned land by the governor in Qalyubiya. In 2011, there were seventeen protests/demonstrations, two of which occurred in January prior to the 25 January uprising, and the remaining fifteen of which took place from March onward. It would be difficult to account for the full number of protests around which Egyptians mobilized on political, economic, and social matters more broadly as these were occurring on an almost weekly (and in some cases daily) basis, to the extent that the news media stopped reporting on all of them (see Ali 2012). In many of these protests, Copts participated like other Egyptian citizens. Of the seventeen protests that took place in 2011, the majority occurred in Cairo (twelve protests), followed by Alexandria (three), Minya (two), Mallawi (one), and Nag' Hammadi (one). It could well be that the number of protests was much greater, but that they were ignored by the press because they occurred in governorates outside Cairo. It is extremely important to note, however, that just as in the 25 January Revolution when people from different governorates flocked to join the protests in Cairo, so, too, did many of these protests, in particular against the torching of the church in Atfih and the destruction of the church in Marinab, involve the participation of many Coptic citizens who came to Cairo especially to take part.

Almost half the protests that took place in 2011 were organized by the Maspero Youth Movement. Sometimes the call was also made by other movements, such as the Coalition of Copts for Egypt. The other protests were organized by lay Copts from different churches almost spontaneously or with little planning and no visible leadership. In terms of the profile of the protesters, in many cases they were both Copts and Muslims. The Muslims included those who belonged to youth revolutionary movements, those who were active in political parties, and regular middle-class citizens (particularly regarding incidents of sectarian assault in places such as Atfih, Imbaba, and Marinab). Regarding the Copts who participated, some would have been politically active in the uprisings. For others, it would have been the first time they had participated in a protest in their lives. There was a clear cross-class representation, although the majority tended to be from the middle class and petit bourgeoisie.

It is noteworthy that all the protests in 2011 took place outside the premises of the Coptic Orthodox Church (see Table 4 on page 166), which represents a marked shift from earlier years when protests had occurred either on the premises of the Patriarchate in Abbasiya, Cairo, or in the vicinity of a local church. This suggests that Copts were not protesting in order to get their message heard by the Church, which would in turn relay their anger to the authorities. Rather they were making demands on the state directly. It also indicates a slight relaxation of the security clampdown on protests, which had led to an increase in citizen participation in street action in Egypt more broadly.

With respect to the protests in Cairo, some were held in Maspero in front of the state television station. The spatial politics of this is important: if Tahrir came to symbolize revolutionary activism, in particular for more political freedoms and rights, Maspero came to symbolize the area where the rights of Copts were claimed.

Harakat Shabab Maspero: A Coptic Protest Movement

The most notable movement to have emerged, both as a form of resistance inspired by the Coptic cause as well as a youth revolutionary movement with Copts involved in it, is Harakat Shabab Maspero (the Maspero Youth Union). According to Boulos Zaky, one of the founders of the movement, the youth who later came to constitute the leadership of the Maspero Youth Movement had previously led protests following the bombing of the Two Saints Church in Alexandria, the attack on the church in al-Amiriya, and many other occasions. They were active in the 25 January uprisings, although mostly as Egyptians rather than members of a Coptic movement (that is, Copts in resistance rather than Coptic resistance). However, Zaky notes that since many of the youth who later formed the movement were active participants in the revolution, the Maspero Youth Movement came to be seen as emanating from the revolution.

The point of the movement's formation, or its institutionalization so to speak, came in the wake of the burning of the church in Sol. The Maspero Youth Movement organized a large protest in front of the Maspero state television and radio station, within walking distance of Tahrir Square. The spatial dynamics are important: to have held the protests in Tahrir would have been to diffuse the Coptic issue in the wider political struggle for emancipation against military rule. Following the ouster of Mubarak and the capture of Tahrir Square on certain days by Islamists, it may have also put them in a position of direct confrontation, which may have ended in an eruption of violence. Maspero, an area of significant geostrategic importance, became identified with mobilization around demands for equality

Table 4: Summary of protests

Cause of Protest	Location	Date	Who?
Bombing of Two Saints Church, Alexandria	Cairo, Alexandria	5 January 2011	Maspero Youth Movement and others
Shooting of Copts on a train in Minya by police officer	Mallawi, Minya	13 January 2011	Copts in Minya
Demolition of Wadi al-Natrun Monastery wall	Cairo	25 February 2011	Coptic protesters
Violence against Copts and torching of church in Atfih	Cairo	8 March 2011	Maspero Youth Movement
Torching of church in Atfih	Cairo	8 March 2011	*Zabbalin* of Muqattam
Fortieth day since the death of the *zabbalin* protesters	Cairo	15 April 2011	Maspero Youth Movement
Violence of Salafis against Copts and assault on church	Cairo	5 May 2011	Maspero Youth Movement
Discrimination against Copts and exposure to violence	Cairo	9 May 2011	Coptic protesters
Demanding protection of churches	Alexandria	14 May 2011	Coptic protesters
Discrimination	Cairo	15 May 2011	Coptic protesters
Solidarity with the protesters assaulted in Maspero	Alexandria	21 May 2011	Coptic protesters
Disappearance of Coptic girls	Minya	16 June 2011	Coptic protesters
Demolition of church in Marinab, Aswan	Cairo	1 October 2011	Maspero Youth Movement and other movements
Demolition of church in Marinab, Aswan	Cairo	4 October 2011	Maspero Youth Movement and Free Copts
Assault on Coptic protesters and torching of church in Marinab	Cairo	9 October 2011	Maspero Youth Movement and other movements
Violence in Maspero Massacre	Cairo	17 November 2011	Maspero Youth Movement and other movements
Kidnapping of Coptic citizens	Nag' Hammadi, Qena	28 December 2011	Coptic protesters

for Egypt's non-Muslims. Christians and Muslims from within and outside Cairo, from across the whole country, would flock to Maspero, which became the final or first stop for demonstrations. Hundreds of Muslims and Christians congregated over several days demanding that the church in Sol be rebuilt, that an inquiry be announced to investigate the perpetrators, and that those who were accountable be prosecuted. When SCAF wanted representatives from the protesters to negotiate, the movement realized that it had not formed an entity through which to express its will, hence the Maspero Youth Movement took shape. According to Nader Shoukry, a renowned journalist for *Watani* newspaper and one of the founders of the Maspero Youth Movement, the first protest in the post-Mubarak era took place on 5 March 2011 in response to the burning of the church in Sol, and it was in the process of the sustained protests, one day after the next by Copts, that the idea of institutionalizing the movement came to be seen as a political necessity to unite the ever-growing number of Copts who had come to join. At that time, he explains, the movement itself did not have a politically visible face except through a number of statements in the press. However, following the burning of the church in Imbaba, the movement gained political weight as an actor in and of itself "through the negotiations that were undertaken with SCAF and the ministerial cabinet." By then, recounts Shoukry, they had a political office, a media committee, and a coordinating committee and "we led the protests and the sit-ins in an organized fashion and, through the membership forms, our numbers reached 15,000." They hope to have a branch in every governorate across the nation. At the time of writing, the Maspero Youth Movement was not officially registered and had sought legal registration as a coalition with the objective of raising the political awareness of Copts. The movement acts as a pressure group to encourage Copts to engage politically, but is not partisan to any one particular channel. Rather, it works to support Copts' activism in different political parties and associations. The support of Copts' political engagement is, however, also linked with its cause of advancing liberal citizenship. The Maspero Youth Movement had adopted a position against cooperation with the Muslim Brotherhood and a political stance against the cooption of Copts under the Islamist banner.

The Maspero Youth Movement has many of the characteristics of a social movement. Charles Tilly (2004) characterizes a social movement as a collective actor that enjoys "WUNC," that is, they have a *worthy* cause, are *united* in their demands, have *numbers*, and have the *commitment* to persist in their mobilization, so that activism is not a one-off event. The Maspero Youth Movement's cause of raising the status of Copts so that they enjoy the full rights of citizenship is one that has much credibility among most Copts. Therefore, it is seen in the eyes of the Copts as *a worthy cause*. Reservations about the worthiness of the movement's cause came from a few Copts and some Muslims who accuse it of being sectarian. The demand for Coptic rights, the raising of the cross, the slogans of "raise your head high, you are a Copt," and the singing of hymns have been seen as highly sectarian and therefore divisive. Many members of the Maspero Youth Movement acknowledge the fact that during the early months of the movement, the framing of issues in religious terms undermined their ability to engage with the wider populace.

However, both the message and the framing were developed so that their message became expressed in terms of the quest for equal citizenship, with Egypt's flag being raised and the national anthem being sung. The evolution of the framing of the message meant that the Coptic issue became conspicuously framed as a national issue, without losing its appeal to its Coptic constituency. John Milad Emile, a Coptic playright, artist, and activist, said he participated in the protests that the Maspero Youth Movement organized and noticed a transformation in the nature of the demands being made. They shifted from ones specific to the sectarian issue to ones relating to national/patriotic demands, such as those relating to the civic nature of the state and the end to military trials, "and I am really happy with this transformation because they have assumed an Egyptian identity that speaks to all Egyptians," he added.

As with other social movements, the Maspero Youth Movement's identity assumes multiple faces and is shaped by the emerging political context. For that particular movement, the challenge lies in essence in holding on to its iconic representation of Coptic identity—which many felt was being negated and threatened in the new Egypt—while at the time assuming the broader democratic mantra of liberating Egypt to pursue the path of democratic rule.

The Maspero Youth Movement's quest for recognition of religious justice has found a receptive audience among Copts across classes, geographic locations, and political orientations, and therefore gained *unity* across a broad constituency. It has also been able to attract Muslims to its cause, though not in the same numbers. However, embedding the Coptic issue within the wider political transformation taking place in the country meant that the movement also sought to situate itself as one of the revolutionary youth movements that refused to be coopted by the state or other political forces. This latter aspect may not have been as appealing to some of its Coptic followers, but it was certainly critical for gaining the solidarity of other youth revolutionary movements. If the Coptic issue becomes too diluted by the demand for emancipating the country from military rule, the movement will lose its Coptic constituency. If the movement focuses exclusively on the Coptic issue, it will lose its political weight as a movement that is not only advocating for particularistic demands but is a national liberation movement as well.

The Maspero Youth Movement does enjoy numbers that represent a constituency in its own right. The constituency that it has gained is not only due to the worthiness of its cause but also the fact that the two leaders who became associated with the movement, Father Matthias and Father Philopateer, have become symbolic icons of the Maspero Youth. In the Egyptian context, where Copts had become cocooned within the Church's walls, turning civil and political society into arenas of potential mistrust, it would have been difficult for the Maspero Youth Movement to mobilize large numbers without the help of the two priests. This is particularly the case in view of the prominent profiles of both priests, which raised the levels of sustained activism and *commitment.* Father Matthias had become renowned in Coptic circles for his production of *al-Katiba al-qibtiya*, a Coptic newspaper that combined reporting on sectarian assaults and broader incidents of assault with opinion pieces highly critical of the government and its perpetration of injustice. *Al-Katiba al-qibtiya* was widely read among the Coptic middle classes. Father Philopateer had gained prominence for his subjection to imprisonment by the Egyptian authorities for baptizing a Muslim woman who wished to convert to Christianity.

The presence of Coptic priests in leadership roles within the movement is a matter of much deliberation. On the one hand, the Maspero Youth Movement prided itself on being a movement independent of the Coptic Orthodox Church, a movement that is civil and therefore removed from military or ecclesiastical matters. On the other hand, the question arose: should not priests also enjoy the right to exercise their citizenship rights? In a personal interview, Father Philopateer insisted that his participation was in his personal capacity and not as a representative of the Coptic Church. Certainly, the political stances of the Maspero Youth Movement have been independent of the Coptic Orthodox Church hierarchy and, in many instances, have clashed with it. Yet the iconic presence of the two priests has been instrumental in raising the movement's profile among large numbers of Copts. Undoubtedly, they have also played a leadership role and they are aware that if the movement is to be recognized fully as a civil movement, the youth who have participated in its founding need also to assume a political leadership role. The internal challenges are twofold. The first is that the youth may undoubtedly lose most of their constituency if the two priests are not as politically visible. The second challenge is for the priests to recognize that political leadership will emerge organically if spaces are created within the movement. In the interview, Father Philopateer, for example, repeatedly stated that his role is also to deter the youth from responding to provocations that may lead them to drift away from their strategies of engagement. In view of the horizontal nature of many of the youth revolutionary movements that emerged after the revolution, there is an apolitical vacuum that is waiting to be filled by youth leaders.

The *commitment* of the Maspero Youth Movement to the cause of defending the rights of Copts has remained, two years after its formation, intact despite being exposed to some fierce attacks from the government. It is no secret that the Maspero Youth Movement openly defied the Coptic Church leadership's position on several occasions (see chapter 9 on their position on the Maspero Massacre, for example). This was known to the Coptic laity active in Church affairs. Some wanted to keep a safe distance so as not to be seen as being sympathetic to a movement that clashed with the Church authorities, while others saw that out of political necessity the Church leadership could not afford to ally itself to the Coptic Maspero Youth Movement but that the latter had an important political role to play. Various Church leaders made several informal requests to Father Philopateer and Father Matthias to either cancel protests that the movement had announced or reverse its policy positions. In these cases, both priests insisted that they have no power over the movement. However, it is also a social movement that is nascent, and consequently it is dynamic in its evolution, both in terms of how it represents itself and in terms of how it frames its message.

The state also sought to repress the movement, as it did with many oppositional youth movements. The Maspero Youth Movement represents the most vocal, organized political movement holding the state account-able for its religiously discriminatory policies and practices. In view of the state's failure to control the movement via the Church leadership, it sought to break the movement by targeting its iconic figures, Father Matthias and Father Philopateer. In February 2012, both priests were summoned by the judge responsible for investigating the Maspero Massacre and accused of incitement to violence on 9 October 2011, when the massacre took place. Ironically, none of the officers who were responsible for the massacre itself was ever tried. The timing of their summoning is significant, since the movement had joined forces with other political groups in calling upon citizens to participate in a day of nationwide civil disobedience on 10 February 2012 to protest against the poor governance of the country since the 25 January Revolution.

While the attempted containment of the Maspero Youth Movement by the Church and its repression by the government are both understandable, in view of the obvious threat from the movement to their respective power bases, what is perplexing is the reaction of the Egyptian street and public opinion. When images of Maspero Youth protesters appeared on national television, many Egyptians reacted derisively to say that the Copts were getting too big for their boots and engaging in highly inflammatory actions against their Muslim brothers, and that they should watch it. Any expression of Coptic demands, in fact, seems to be regarded by public opinion in Egypt as provocative, even if it is addressed to Egyptian authorities and not the west. The demonstrations were met very negatively, with the arguments that religion-based demands undermine national unity and Egypt's economic recovery. Contrast this response to the general sympathy for the Qenawis who stopped rail traffic to the tourism centers of Luxor and Aswan for ten consecutive days. The Maspero protests, moreover, were organized independently of the Coptic Orthodox Church and in defiance of an order from Pope Shenouda to desist. It is perplexing that the Copts, who have long been criticized in the media for retreating to the Church's 'cocoon,' should in turn be reprimanded for breaking out of it.

Nonetheless, the Coptic Maspero Youth Movement was able to achieve major symbolic as well as substantive policy gains in a very short time. In the case of the burning of the church at Sol in Giza, they were able to revoke the decisions arrived at through the reconciliation committee and pressure SCAF to rebuild the church. In fact, Prime Minister Essam Sharaf went to meet with members of the movement in Maspero himself and invited them to his personal residence to arrive at an agreement. Following the massacre of twenty-seven Coptic civilians and the injury of many more during what later came to be known as the Maspero Massacre, on 9 October 2011, the Maspero Youth were able to collect evidence incriminating the army and insist that if justice were not secured internally, they would seek redress through all possible alternative channels. One significant policy change was the reversal of the Ministry of Education's decision to hold school examinations on 1 and 8 January 2012 in recognition of Coptic Christian pupils' right to celebrate Coptic Orthodox Christmas on 7 January.

Then, on 6 January 2011, on the occasion of Christmas mass, the Maspero Youth held the Church and the army accountable in what proved to be a highly embarrassing situation for the Church leadership, for as Pope Shenouda was thanking and praising SCAF for protecting Egypt, the youth shouted out from the back of the cathedral, "Down, down with military rule." Through sustained protests and sit-ins, they expressed political opposition to religious injustice and therefore forced the political authorities to pay them heed.

The Coptic youth movement's success arose from a combination of agential and structural factors. For one, the political moment following the uprising was ripe for the explosion of political energies and activism. This was the moment when political society was at its most vibrant. Second, the youth revolutionary forces were genuinely interested in supporting the emergence of a civilian, democratic post-Mubarak society and were therefore keen to condemn sectarian violence against Copts, which escalated very quickly and very intensely after Mubarak's downfall. From an agential point of view, the fact that the Maspero Youth Movement was independent of but not against the Coptic Church strategically positioned it in such a way that it was able to gain the sympathy of Coptic citizens without having to sacrifice its independence. This can best be explained by Albert Hirschman's exit, voice, and loyalty thesis, namely that in highly closed institutions (which the Coptic Orthodox Church typifies) where exit is both difficult and costly and where loyalty is prized, the opportunities for reform are best achieved through expressing protest from within, since the ability to influence is substantially lost if the exit option is taken (Hirschman 1970).

For the Maspero Youth Movement to have exited from the Coptic Orthodox Church, that is, for the movement to have declared itself in opposition to the Coptic faith, would have meant the loss of all but a small minority of Copts, since the majority of Copts' loyalties are very strongly tied to the Church. At the same time, for the movement to have worked within the institutional framework of the Coptic Orthodox Church would have risked cooption and the sacrifice of the movement's political agenda.

Hence, it is in the careful balance between being a member of the faithful while concurrently keeping a safe distance from the Church that the Maspero Youth Movement was able to gain legitimacy within the Coptic community and political influence outside it. However, such a balance was not and will not always be easy to maintain. There were incidents where their statements directly contradicted those of Pope Shenouda. Following the burning of the churches in Imbaba (see page 149), the pope publicly appealed to the movement to end the protests in front of the state television station in Maspero. The movement did not obey and the protests continued for another four days. According to one press report, in early February 2012, the pope sent one of his bishops to ask the Maspero Youth Movement not to protest in front of the Ministry of Interior and reminded them that the Church ends up paying for the cost of treatment and compensation for the injured. Andrawos Oweida from the political office of the Maspero Youth Movement objected vehemently, saying that the movement will protest and is completely autonomous from the Church.[1] The same scenario was repeated a few days later, when the pope announced that those who participate in acts of civil disobedience are contravening religion, which demands that they obey the ruler. The Maspero Youth announced and participated in the civil disobedience campaign initiated on 10 February 2012 by the youth coalitions. Equally important, where the Church leadership response was to maintain silence in reaction to sectarian assaults, the Maspero Youth Movement took to the streets to protest, made public statements of condemnation, and was generally able to make the political stance that no one expected the Church to assume any more.

The outcome of the movement's activism was twofold. First, it challenged the Coptic Orthodox Church's position as the only political spokesperson for the Copts without actually delegitimizing it. In other words, it did not displace the Church, but rather filled in the political vacuum created by the absence of independent civil Coptic voices advocating on behalf of the cause. Second, the Maspero Youth Movement's open protests had a ripple effect by emboldening other Copts to take to the street at that particular political moment in Egypt's transition (a time of sustained and continued protest).

The *Zabbalin*: A Case of Acute Dispossession and Spontaneous Protests

While the *zabbalin* (garbage collectors) comprise a very particular group due to their profession, their participation in spontaneous protests nevertheless offers us insight into the cumulative impact of persecution that subsequently manifests itself in acts of protest in solidarity with Coptic grievances.

On 8 March 2011, at around noon, a group of 150 to 300 *zabbalin* living in the *zabbalin* settlement of Manshiyat Nasir on the Muqattam Hills went to the Autostrade, the highway linking north and south Cairo, to hold a vigil against the burning of the church in Sol and in solidarity with the other protesters who had congregated in Maspero. Some placards said, "No to destroying churches," while others read, "Muslim, Christian, one hand." As they assembled for a silent vigil on the road, traffic became heavy, commuters began to complain that the protesters were blocking the road, and a fight soon broke out. Rumors quickly spread in the surrounding neighborhoods of Sayyida 'Aisha and Khalifa that the Christian *zabbalin* were on their way to burn the Sayyida 'Aisha mosque. Thugs armed with guns and knives, joined by many residents of the surrounding areas, set upon the *zabbalin* with Molotov cocktails and knives, setting fire to and burning the *zabbalin*'s garbage collection trucks. In response, the *zabbalin* youth threw bricks, stones, and glass to defend those approaching their settlement. One young man, enraged by the burning of the trucks, stole a microbus, emptied it of its passengers, and drove up the hill. Rumors spread that the garbage collectors had taken people hostage in a microbus and had driven up on the hill where they were stripping women of their veils and raping them. Meanwhile, many witnesses said that the local sheikh in the Sayyida Zeinab mosque was inciting people to go "save your fellow Muslims from the Christians . . . the Christians are killing the Muslims" and "go to jihad."

At about 4:45 p.m., according to witnesses, the army arrived with two tanks. "They started firing in the air to dissipate the crowd . . . nobody was budging. The two tanks then headed toward the entrance of Muqattam," said one witness, adding that he was surprised that the tanks moved in the direction of Muqattam, since he would have thought that the army would assign a tank at Sayyida 'Aisha and another at Muqattam in order to separate the crowds.

Several witnesses whom the researcher spoke to were injured in the twelve hours that followed, not only by residents of Sayyida 'Aisha but also by the army. "One army officer told us to flee to the hills because the army is going to shoot on us," said one witness. According to several witnesses, the army began to shoot live bullets randomly at the *zabbalin*. Among those I interviewed in April 2011, some were shot in their thighs, backs, and stomachs while trying to save the injured.

The fighting continued until approximately 3:00 a.m., with witnesses saying that the people from Sayyida 'Aisha and surrounding areas were attacking from behind the army tanks. During this period, some of the residents had reached Manshiyat Nasir, property was looted and burned, some women were assaulted, and houses were destroyed. Some of the Muslim residents of Manshiyat Nasir came to the defense of their Christian neighbors and one Muslim man died while trying to defend his Christian neighbor against the violence. In the midst of this, some witnesses noted that property was not burned randomly, but that Christian property was specifically targeted (Christian households in Muqattam are identifiable by the religious pictures that usually adorn their façades).

The crowds, according to witnesses, blocked a fire truck from entering the area and would not let an ambulance through. Residents, both Muslim and Christian, came to the rescue of the injured by driving them in private vehicles either to nearby hospitals or to the medical clinic up in Manshiyat Nasir.

By dawn, ten *zabbalin* were dead (nine Christian and one Muslim) and around 150 were injured, some with lifelong disabilities. Guirgis, who was transferred to al-Dimirdash Hospital, where he was treated for a bullet in his arm, recalled that he found himself with many of the young revolutionary groups who were being treated for injuries, some received at the hands of thugs. Ironically, when some of the patients began to shout anti-Christian messages, the young revolutionary groups lashed at them, insisting that Christians have always lived with Muslims: "They came to me and said, 'Never mind, Guirgis, don't listen to them, they are ignorant, they have a sick mind.'"

Another member of the *zabbalin* community, who had received a bullet from the army in his stomach and was transferred to al-Zahraa Hospital, said that when he woke up from anesthesia, the doctor told him, "I saved your life and did not discriminate between Muslim and Christian despite the fact that you were attacking us."

Having learned from experience that victims are often framed as villains, some of the members of the *zabbalin* community, such as lawyer Maged Adel, set about documenting the events visually and through interviews with the injured and through the collection of evidence (such as cartouches, bullets, and so on). Regrettably, the mainstream official narrative represented the *zabbalin* as the instigators of the violence. In an article in *al-Ahram*, for example, Muhammad Abd al-Latif reported that the Muslims of Sayyida Zeinab decided to take action "after they heard of the detention of three Muslim women at the top of the Muqattam hills and that the Christians were coming to burn the mosque of Sayyida 'Aisha, after which the Muslims and Christians clashed."[2] The reporter in no way suggested that these were rumors rather than facts. Moreover, his report suggests that the *zabbalin* blocked the Autostrade, that they were throwing stones from the top of the Muqattam Hills, and that they were attacking the residents of the neighborhoods nearby.[3]

A formal complaint was filed with the Prosecutor General's Office against the assault on the *zabbalin* by the army and the residents of the surrounding areas. Until 1 February 2012, no action was taken by the general prosecutor. Compensation was sought for the injured and the families of the deceased. Forty injured individuals who had applied for compensation managed, after a long struggle, to obtain payment.

The situation was far more complex as regards the deceased. In order for their families to be given state compensation, the victims would have to be recognized as martyrs of the revolution. According to Maged Adel, the criteria for recognition as a martyr is that the person must have died while protesting in a city square or in front of a police station in the period between January and March 2011. The government refused to recognize the *zabbalin* who had been protesting at the Autostrade as martyrs as they did not fulfill these criteria. On the other hand, the Coptic protesters who had died at Maspero, together with those who had died in the clashes downtown (in Muhammad Mahmud Street, the area near the People's Assembly, and Qasr al-'Aini Street) were recognized as martyrs (see chapter 9) by special decree of the prime minister. Why the government would choose to recognize the protesters who died at Maspero and not those who died at the Autostrade has much to do with issues of advocacy, voice, and power. Human rights organizations, many political activists, and the youth revolutionary groups spoke out vociferously against the massacre at Maspero. The matter was given much media attention and became the subject of sustained public debate. By contrast, there was hardly any advocacy or lobbying on behalf of the *zabbalin*, nor did the matter receive much media attention or public visibility. The Coptic Orthodox Church leadership did not make any public claims on their behalf. Maged Adel sought a special decree from the prime minister to have the *zabbalin* acquire the status of martyrs, but until 1 February 2012, such efforts had not had any effect. It occurred to Adel and others to take the ten families of the deceased to protest in front of the Cabinet building. "But people are now scared and we knew that because they were *zabbalin*, we would not gain people's sympathy and no one would join is. Besides, if they detained anyone, what would we do then?" said Adel. For these ten families, the struggle to have their deceased loved ones recognized as martyrs is not primarily driven by a desire for financial compensation, even though many of them are in dire economic straits, but by the quest for public recognition that their relatives were killed because the state failed to protect them while they were exercising their most basic of rights, namely that of public protest.

An examination of the *zabbalin*'s history, in particular their predicament during the last decade of Mubarak's rule, would suggest that their initiative in holding vigils or spontaneously protesting is driven not only by their sense of solidarity with Christians who have been assaulted but also by the cumulative impact of their own persecution. They had gone out spontaneously to protest after the bombing of the church in Alexandria, they had gone out to protest when their pigs were culled, and they had gone out to protest when private companies encroached on their livelihood with no compensation being offered. In effect the *zabbalin*'s trajectory is one of dispossession and exposure to multiple forms of discrimination on the basis of profession, social class, religion, and geographical location.

Background: Cumulative Injustice
The *zabbalin* have a long tradition of using pigs to consume organic waste, which allows them to extract valuable recyclable material from garbage that can in turn be sold. This system allowed them to deal with a large amount of waste in a cost-effective way. According to Marie Assaad, the *zabbalin* recycled more than 90 percent of all garbage, thus doing the environment a favor by minimizing the waste that needed to be dumped, buried, or burned.

The largest *zabbalin* community in Manshiyat Nasir is situated in the Muqattam hills, once an area on the outskirts of the city, but now very much a part of it. Manshiyat Nasir is part of the governorate of Cairo. The community is estimated to be made up of around thirty thousand people. The second main community of *zabbalin* is based in Ard al-Liwa, a haphazard squatter settlement sandwiched between Dokki and Mohandiseen, upper-class and upper-middle-class suburbs of Cairo respectively, and Bulaq al-Daqrur, another squatter settlement. The *zabbalin* population of Ard al-Liwa is estimated to be around seven thousand people. This community falls partly within the Giza governorate and partly within the governorate of Sixth of October. The third *zabbalin* community is in 'Izbit al-Nakhl, a highly populated urban squatter and slum settlement north of Cairo. The community is part of the Qalyubiya governorate. One of the common features of the *zabbalin* in all three settlements is that the majority belongs to Egypt's 10 percent Christian minority. While the communities are part of Greater Cairo, their affiliation to different governorates is significant in that they are subject to different governors' policies, which may vary greatly. Interviews were deliberately conducted with *zabbalin* who had recently lost their livelihoods to the pig cull in all three settlements in order to capture any difference between them. To protect them against possible political reprisals, the *zabbalin*'s names have been omitted.

The *zabbalin* communities are most heavily concentrated in Cairo (where there is the most garbage) and are almost all Christians who migrated from Upper Egypt in the twentieth century. The neglect of Upper Egypt under the centralized government of Nasser in the 1950s, which pursued an intensive industrialization policy, led to a growing population and an increase in the number of poor landless peasants who migrated to Cairo in search of work. The narratives of the first *zabbalin* to settle in Cairo from other areas, whether from 'Izbit al-Nakhl, Manshiyat Nasir, Muqattam (south of Cairo), or Ard al-Liwa (central Cairo), are almost the same. Lacking jobs, they came to Cairo in search of work. They met with people from *al-wahat* ('the oases', people who had originated from Egypt's oases and settled in Cairo), who were engaged in garbage-related work and who introduced them to the garbage collection profession. Subsequently, they were introduced to the idea of breeding pigs in order to expand their work from garbage collection to garbage sorting. Once they were settled, other members of their families migrated to Cairo. Extended families belonging to the same tribe settled in close proximity to each other. Intermarriage was the custom, and the social norms and traditions of the original rural community were maintained. Their experience was one of dispossession. They settled in obscure areas out sight of the government or on the fringes of the city (in areas such as Muqattam and 'Izbit al-Nakhl). As Cairo's population increased, these settlements on the city fringes became attractive to new governors, and the residents would be evicted, moving to a new settlement until the same thing happened again. In most instances, the difficulty in obtaining formal ownership of the land obstructed their access to adequate infrastructure. Many *zabbalin* recount at least four different relocations before settling in their present community. For example, a migrant who would eventually work in the garbage profession might arrive at Imbaba, then relocate to 'Arab al-Tawayla, before moving to 'Arab al-Hisn, before finally settling in 'Izbit al-Nakhl. Many of the *zabbalin* at Ard al-Liwa also tell a similar story: "The government evicted us from one place to another. They say we are polluters of the environment. We arrived at Imbaba, then moved to 'Ayn al-Sira, then to Hudn al-Gabal (also known as Batn al-Baqqara), and then Mazalakn Ard al-Liwa, where again, the government came to level us with the bulldozers, so we went to Shaf'i and then were evicted to Ard al-Liwa." With each move, the families would take their pigs and belongings and establish a new pigsty with an adjoining area for the storage of garbage and as a living area (sometimes using the same area for both).

There are hierarchies within the profession. At the bottom of the ladder are the garbage scavengers who wander the streets of Cairo with their donkey carts in search of any recyclable materials thrown in garbage bins or on the sides of roads. Slightly better off are the *zabbalin* who collect the garbage from residential homes. The fees paid to them are a pittance, often amounting to less than LE5 (US$1) a month per residential home. The prospects of earning a livelihood from garbage collection lie in the district covered—the wealthier the area, the more likely is its garbage to be rich in recyclable material, which is where the real opportunity for income generation lies. *Zabbalin* collecting garbage from urban centers of Upper Egyptian towns or from the villages tend to be the poorest because the recyclable material is very limited, while *zabbalin* based in Muqattam and 'Izbit al-Nakhl are usually better off because they collect garbage from upper-class districts of Cairo. *Zabbalin* who rely exclusively on the collection of garbage without owning pigsties have fewer income-generating prospects. The collected garbage used to be transferred to the *zabbalin* who ran pigsties. While the men were responsible for gathering the waste from locations around the city, the women were tasked with taking care of the pigs. After the pigs had removed the organic waste from the garbage, it was left to the women to complete the most tedious, and hazardous, job of all: sorting the remaining garbage in their homes.

The wealthiest members of the garbage collectors community were those who had well-established recycling industries, which were both capital- and machine-intensive, with several paid laborers working for them, and which sold raw recycled carton, metals, plastic, and other elements to exporters to China and elsewhere. They were the least likely to be affected by the culling of the pigs.

Social and political exclusion have meant that health and educational opportunities have often been compromised. Those better off in 'Izbit al-Nakhl, Ard al-Liwa, and virtually all the inhabitants of Muqattam have a work area separate from the living area. The poorer *zabbalin* often use the space for garbage sorting as well as for their living space. Women in Ard al-Liwa talk of giving birth in the pigsties amid the pigs and garbage. Yet the narrative of the *zabbalin* who owned pigsties is about neither the hardship of their lives nor the daily exposure to hazards. It is not their livelihood that is a source of agony; it is the government's persecution of them.

In 2002 the Egyptian authorities contracted private international companies to assist in the disposal of garbage in the main governorates of Cairo and Alexandria, although their efficiency and scale of operation were questioned a year later. In the same year, the Giza governorate signed an agreement with two private companies (one Spanish and the other Italian) to collect the three thousand tons of garbage produced daily by the governorate and dispose of it.[4] That year, the *zabbalin* protested that their role was being totally neglected in the contractual agreements and that they were against being governed by the Italian company. A company spokesman is reported to have said: "I don't know what all the fuss is about; we are ready to accept the experienced labor in our business, but we are against the old fashioned non-environmental technique of garbage collection."[5]

In early May 2009, the Egyptian government announced that it planned to cull all of the nation's estimated 300,000 pigs. This action was necessary, the government stated, in order to control the spread of so-called swine flu,[6] which was declared a "public health emergency of international concern" by the World Health Organization. The decision to cull the pigs, approved by parliament, was taken to protect the country from the pandemic even though there was not at that point in time a single confirmed case of H1N1 influenza in the country.

The intensity of sectarian sentiment in the Egyptian street was far greater than that in parliament or the media. Marie Assaad recounts that in the period preceding the decision to cull the pigs, "Egypt was sitting on a sectarian volcano about to erupt in the most violent way. People were saying 'the Christians are going to kill us. This is part of the west's plan to eradicate Muslims. We have to kill the pigs before they kill us.'" Assaad said that the garbage collectors had legitimate reason to fear a mob taking matters into their hands and attacking them.

However, counter-arguments suggest that while the narrative may have been sectarian, the government's adoption of a pig-culling policy was in fact more a result of poor governance than religious discrimination. The government's record in handling natural or man-made disasters, particularly health issues such as avian influenza, certainly indicates poorly established and implemented policy responses that are severely lacking in transparency and accountability. The institutional processes for engaging with crises are characterized by a top-down, inconsistent, and sporadic implementation of policy, with no regard for the socio-cultural context in which a policy is applied. Nonetheless, the actual implementation of the culling suggests a sectarian coloring in three ways: the inhumane manner of killing the pigs (by throwing acid on them and burying them alive); the unjust compensation received by the *zabbalin*; and the persecution to which they were subjected as potential carriers of disease (H1N1).

Both society and state are implicated in these acts of persecution. Society has stigmatized the *zabbalin* because of their profession and lowly socio-economic status, while the fact that most are Christian subjects them to additional persecution. Human rights and advocacy groups have failed to acknowledge and defend them. The highest echelons of the Coptic Orthodox Church leadership ignored them and in the instance of the H1N1 crisis served as a complicit party in their repression. The Coptic Orthodox Church leadership, represented by Pope Shenouda III, was also able to score political points: by supporting the cull it could appear to take a 'patriotic' stance in relation to the crisis, and given the marginalization of the *zabbalin* within the Christian minority, the Church could do so at no major internal political cost. As for the state, not only has it failed to provide the *zabbalin* with the modicum of rights accorded to other citizens, it has actively persecuted them, under Mubarak's and post-Mubarak regimes alike. The *zabbalin* were among the first targets of SCAF's use of live bullets against civilians. Yet the *zabbalin* have exercised their agency in various forms of resistance and subversion of the status quo. They have protested, performed sit-ins, and gone on strike.

Their narrative of dispossession and persecution, and the kind of assaults they have been exposed to, whether in 2011 or 2009, is only likely to further radicalize a group within the *zabbalin*. This is critical to explaining why Copts who are not part of movements, such as the *zabbalin*, and who have been politically inactive would spontaneously participate in a vigil or a protest. Their involvement in one-off protests is the outcome of a cumulative buildup of a sense of marginalization that is catalyzed by the right political circumstances and political moment.

Such forms of civil and political activism in Egypt have in effect challenged the mediation of citizenry via the Coptic Orthodox Church, opening possibilities for more diverse, vocal, and, at times, successful contestations of state-sponsored sectarianism.

In the next chapter, I examine one incident each of Coptic protest and Copts in protest that became symbolic of a dual struggle—to liberate Egypt of the military regime and to protest the escalation of violence against Copts. This dual resistance became epitomized in another new movement, the Mina Daniel movement, named after a young man who was celebrated both as a revolutionary and a 'martyr.'

9 | Egypt's Bloody Sunday and Its Ripple Effects

The Maspero Massacre, which resulted in the death of between twenty-seven and forty civilians and the injury of over three hundred others, represents a critical moment in the history of Egypt's political transition from authoritarian rule. It reflected the single worst assault by an Egyptian ruling authority against a non-Muslim minority in modern Egyptian history. It also led to heightened tensions between the Coptic civil movement and the Church leadership over the management of sectarian assault. Moreover, instead of having the impact of thwarting all Coptic resistance movements, it spawned the creation of new ones. Finally, it marked the beginning of a new phase of heightened animosity between the army and the revolutionary movements.

While the army had attacked unarmed civilians since the ousting of Mubarak, the scale and intensity of the assault at Maspero led many to the realization that perhaps the army and the people were not one hand after all, despite the fact that the army had emerged triumphant as the protector of the people in the 25 January Revolution. The fateful prediction by Copts, "It is us today, you tomorrow," became true less than a month after Maspero. Maspero became part of a broader narrative about military repression, with people referring to Maspero, Muhammad Mahmud, and the Cabinet in a single breath as milestones in the ongoing conflict between SCAF and the revolutionary movements.

The official reaction to the Maspero Massacre epitomizes the denial, demonization, and distribution of blame that had become characteristic of political life during the Mubarak era, but it had some critical ripple effects within the wider Egyptian political scene, on the Coptic resistance movement, and on Church–society relations.

Churches into Rest Stops

As usual with violence against Coptic Christians in contemporary Egypt, disputes emerge at the local level and then smolder until a national crisis erupts. The church burning in al-Marinab on 30 September 2011 is a case in point, both in terms of how it happened and why.

Probably the most accurate account of the events that led to the blaze in al-Marinab, near the town of Edfu in Aswan, Egypt's southernmost Nile province, is found in the report submitted to Prime Minister Essam Sharaf on 4 October 2011, five days before the Maspero Massacre. The "national justice committee" of the government cabinet had charged a fact-finding commission with investigating the arson. The commission reported that the church's license as a house of worship was valid and that the state had issued a permit to rebuild the church from the ground up because it was too dilapidated for simple renovations. Hostile residents of al-Marinab organized a protest against the church reconstruction, however, claiming that the structure was a private residence that has been used as a 'rest stop' *(istiraha)*. Further, they complained that the new steeple was three meters higher than the height allowed by the license. Concurrently, the church leaders sent a copy of the license to SCAF, asking it to intervene.[1] The generals did nothing. Rather than interpreting and enforcing the law, provincial authorities convened a "reconciliation meeting" for the village elders, who agreed that the church would shorten its steeple and that it would not install a cross, bell, or microphone at the top. Construction was brought to a halt and a contractor was hired to knock a few meters off the steeple. But it was not long before a mob intervened to torch the church and several other properties belonging to local Christians.

The fact-finding commission submitted its report to Prime Minister Sharaf along with a series of recommendations: the governor of Aswan should resign; the arsonists should be tried; and the state should assume the expense of rebuilding the church. The prime minister took no action. The commission's findings and recommendations were later published in the newspaper *al-Yawm al-sabi'*.[2]

The report did not include another set of facts, which have been documented elsewhere.[3] A local sheikh, who remains unnamed and unaccountable, stirred up worshipers against the church during his Friday sermon on 30 September, likely goading them into launching the attack. The actual arsonists were held for a very short time and then released with fines of LE500 (around US$83).

This account of the Marinab incident is not what Egyptians were reading in the lead-up to the Maspero demonstration, however. It is striking, indeed, that both state-affiliated and independent newspapers consistently misreported the circumstances of the church burning and its immediate aftermath, raising serious questions about the ethics (or perhaps the skills) of journalists in the post-Mubarak era and suggesting, again, that SCAF's penchant for censorship and press intimidation was on a par with that of the deposed regime. In the 1 October 2011 editions of the independent *Al-Masry Al-Youm* and *Nahdat Misr*, as well as the official *al-Ahram* and the former opposition *al-Wafd*, front-page or page 3 stories showed considerable empathy with Muslim villagers' anger at the church's purported "illegality." The *al-Ahram* headline echoed the canard that the church was a "rest stop."

As for the state, its sympathies were as plain as day. Mustafa al-Sayyid, the governor of Aswan, appeared on state television to deny that a church had been burned down. He repeated the line that the torched building was a "guest house." Al-Sayyid said that he had issued a permit for a structure 10 meters high, not the 13-meter edifice that was erected, and blamed the church leaders' delay in addressing this alleged violation for causing the sectarian strife.[4] This statement threw fuel on the fire, prompting Copts in Aswan to demand al-Sayyid's resignation in protests before the governorate's main offices. The Gama'a al-Islamiya, one of Egypt's most prominent Islamist groups, stepped into the fray, pledging to intervene further if SCAF bowed to Coptic pressure on the matter of the church. In his Friday sermon on 7 October, Sheikh Khalid Ibrahim al-Kusi, the amir (spiritual and political leader) of the Gama'a al-Islamiya, insisted that the Coptic Church apologize for a priest who had threatened SCAF head Field Marshal Muhammad Hussein Tantawi with action should the church not be rebuilt, labeling the priest's interjection as humiliation of a Muslim ruler by a non-Muslim subject.[5] The priest had said, "Tantawi knows well what we can do. We will show them a march that the country has never seen, ending inside Maspero."

On 4 October, around ten thousand Copts across the country began open-ended protests organized by the Maspero Youth Movement and the Free Copts, two lay groups independent of the Coptic Orthodox hierarchy. In the capital, the protesters assembled at Maspero. An army unit deployed to the broadcasting headquarters assaulted eight protesters, sending two to the hospital in serious condition, including one young man beaten severely on the ground by a gang of soldiers. This youth's ordeal was taped and widely disseminated on YouTube.[6] The protesters made specific demands on the government: immediate restoration of the church in al-Marinab; the Aswan governor's resignation; justice for those assaulted; compensation for Aswan Christians whose property was damaged; and a quota for Copts in the parliamentary elections coming up in late November.

On the same day, Judge Noha al-Zeini said that the National Justice Committee of which she was a member had presented its findings to the prime minister. Al-Zeini said that the committee made two recommendations, which they relayed to the minister of local development and which were made available to the prime minister that very night (4 October). According to al-Zeini, members of the committee present had unanimously reached two decisions, the first being that the governor of Aswan must resign immediately and the second that all places that are used by Christians for worship must be officially registered. Yet in the end the prime minister did nothing. In reaction to the prime minister's inaction, al-Zeini in protest froze her membership of the committee. She argued that the government had ignored the committee's recommendations and was trying to find excuses and justifications in order not to implement the necessary measures, much in the way of the old regime. She argued that the governor of Aswan was responsible for the escalation of events, his management of the crisis had failed, and he publicly announced to the media that the church had violated the law and "'our Muslim youth' had dealt with this violation" (that is, had brought the church down).[7] Al-Zeini concluded that had the prime minister announced the resignation of the governor of Aswan on 5 October, matters would not have escalated to the degree that they did.

From Shubra to Maspero

The Maspero Youth Movement, which organized the protest on 9 October, had notified the authorities in question, as required in Egypt, of its intention to walk from Shubra to the Maspero television broadcasting station. The protest started at about 4:00 p.m. at the Shubra roundabout, at the heart of one of Cairo's most densely populated middle-class suburbs, historically known for its high Christian population. The march involved the participation of many different political movements and coalitions, including the April 6 Movement. At the head of the protest were Fathers

Matthias and Philopateer, who were joined by a large number of boy and girl scouts, all dressed in white. As the march proceeded from Shubra to Maspero, more people joined in and the marchers were met on the way by thugs who threw stones at them and sought to beat up some of the protesters. There was no security intervention to protect the protesters, but the protest remained peaceful. There were Christians but also Muslims in the ranks, men and women, including women wearing the veil.

As in many previous protests, there were people who came holding large pictures of saints and those who held large wooden crosses. There were also large banners carrying biblical verses about faith and perseverance in the face of hardship and persecution. Others held up slogans and banners that were clearly revolutionary, such as those calling for the fall of Field Marshal Tantawi and proclaiming that although Mubarak was out, his regime was still in control. Many youth used the same chants and slogans they had used during the first days of the 25 January uprisings against Mubarak to stir people to join in. These included *"Ya ahalina indammu lina"* ("Our people, join in with us"), *"Inzilu min biyutkum, rayhin nigib hukukum* ("Come out of your homes, we are off to get your rights"), and *"Kum ya Mina, kum ya Bilal, asl al-thawra salib we hilal"* ("Rise Mina, rise Bilal, for this revolution is that of the Cross and the Crescent"). These revolutionary slogans resonated with many of those citizens who had participated in the 25 January uprisings, and they joined the march because of their firm belief in the importance of solidarity with their co-citizens.

Other protesters were more focused on the discriminatory practices of the state, using slogans such as *"Ya Tantawi sakit liih, di kinisa mish kabarih"* ("O Tantawi, why are you silent, this is a church, not a cabaret").

The participation of the people grew as the march moved forward, while some joined in front of the Maspero building. At Maspero, the country witnessed one of the worst assaults in contemporary Egyptian history launched against unarmed civilians—and the perpetrators were its own army.

The Bloody Hours of Sunday
What happened on Sunday, 9 October 2011, in the hours that followed the march to the Maspero building looked at first like a repeat of the worst instances of state brutality witnessed during the 25 January uprising. Security forces deployed tear gas, live bullets, and armored vehicles in an effort to disperse peaceful protesters. What happened next, however, was

worse than any single incident of state violence in January and February 2011. Captured live by the cameras of the Al Arabiyya satellite channel, armored personnel carriers bearing army markings sped toward the protesters, at one point crossing a sidewalk, and crushed several to death underneath their massive treads. By night's end, seventeen demonstrators were dead and three hundred more injured, some in critical condition. There is no definitive death toll because it is believed that some bodies were dumped in the Nile, but the estimate is between twenty-seven and forty dead.[8] The army's claim to fame during the January–February popular uprising—that it would not, under any circumstances, shoot at Egyptians—was exposed as the definitive lie.

How it all started is hotly debated. At a press conference on 12 October, a representative of SCAF insisted that the army did not attack and that a "third party" was involved. Some put forward the notion that the army was provoked under assault from the protesters. Others argue that "thugs" of unknown provenance infiltrated the demonstration to foment chaos and prompt the army's retaliation. Yet the overwhelming thrust of eyewitness accounts, both Muslim and Christian, is that the army initiated the violence, first throwing stones, then wielding batons, and then firing live ammunition, before taking the grim final step of grinding protesters into the sidewalk. Certainly, several protesters threw stones as well, but eyewitnesses insist that they did so in response to the bullets being shot at them.

Appearing on Al Jazeera on that bloody Sunday, General Mahmud Zahir of the Interior Ministry placed the blame squarely on the protesters' shoulders. "Some incident worth less than three milliemes [nearly worthless in today's economy, one thousand of which equal an Egyptian pound] in Upper Egypt and people congregate at Maspero," he said, dismissive in his anger. Yet the tensions leading to the supposed three-millieme incident had been escalating for more than a month, with no government or SCAF remedy applied.

The Politics of Deceit (or Denial)

The official reaction to the bloody Sunday of 9 October was consistent with state responses to attacks on non-Muslim citizens in the Mubarak era. It can be summed up in three D-words: denial, demonization of protesters, and (specious) distribution of blame equally among all the parties involved. Much of the Egyptian media and many important public figures also reacted in one or more of these ways.

On the evening of 9 October, Information Minister Usama Haykal went on air to deny that the army had been involved in any act of aggression against protesters, even as Al Arabiyya broadcast pictures of the camouflage-painted army vehicles running down Maspero demonstrators at high speed. SCAF released a statement expressing its condolences to the victims, but claimed no responsibility for the army's acts, instead warning of plots that aimed to create friction between the army and the people, in line with the conspiracy theories of the Mubarak years. Prime Minister Sharaf delivered a televised speech in which he also pointed to "hidden hands, domestic and foreign," as drivers of the violence. (The Muslim Brotherhood later employed the same phrase in its first commentary on Maspero.) At a press conference held on 12 October, SCAF maintained its stance that army officers and soldiers did not fire on the Coptic protesters. They did not have live ammunition. A third party may be implicated. "We are not circulating conspiracy theories, but there is no doubt that there are enemies of the revolution," said General Mahmud Higazi.

As for the seemingly obvious visual evidence of army involvement rocketing around the world on television and the Internet, SCAF spokesmen offered a baroque non-explanation. It is against army doctrine, they said, for armored vehicles to run over human beings, even enemy soldiers in battle. The instances of crushing captured on camera were not "systematic" and were possibly the panicked acts of soldiers desperate to escape the roiling crowds. "None of you has experienced what it is like to face death," General 'Adil 'Imara told the journalists. An investigation, the army promised, would show who was responsible for inciting the violence and firing the live rounds.

Initially, Usama Haykal and state television announcers claimed that army officers were also killed at Maspero. The 10 October headline of *al-Ahram* read in part: "24 Soldiers and Demonstrators Dead." One version of the reports that day claimed that three soldiers were among the dead. SCAF denied that story, but remained silent about the number of army casualties or the victims' identities. Many analysts therefore doubt that the army suffered any losses at all. At the press conference, the generals displayed fuzzy footage of a military policeman being stabbed.

Independent documentation of the violence and grass-roots fury among Copts have been sufficient to push the Coptic hierarchy, usually loath to contradict the official narrative of sectarian incidents, to speak out. On 12 October, the day of the SCAF press conference, Pope Shenouda broke his long silence about Maspero, pronouncing in his regular Wednesday meeting that the protesters had been peaceful and unarmed. For the first time in the Church's contemporary history, he continued, a single day's events had produced twenty-four martyrs. The pope pointed out that forensic reports indicate that two-thirds of the dead were killed by live ammunition, with the remaining third crushed to death.[9]

State-Sponsored Civil Strife

Before the denials, however, there were two immediate actions by the authorities as events unfolded that fateful Sunday night. The first was that the army stormed the offices of the two television stations whose personnel had managed to tape soldiers firing on the protesters—the Egyptian January 25 channel, set up by revolutionary activists, and the U.S.-sponsored Arabic-language satellite network al-Hurra. The goal was to intimidate the stations into going off the air. At al-Hurra, soldiers carrying automatic weapons entered the studio while Cairo anchor 'Amr Khalil was conducting an interview about Maspero. "I'm Egyptian, you guys! I'm Egyptian!" Khalil exclaimed, as the noises of forcible entry were heard off-camera. The anchorman went on to explain to viewers that "angry" soldiers were searching the premises for "persons" who had done something wrong. "Maybe they'll find someone on the couch," he quipped before proceeding with his interview.[10] Soldiers also assaulted a news correspondent at the site of the protest.

The second action was to announce on state-run television that "Copts" had put the army itself in peril. Subtitles at the bottom of the screen read: "Urgent: The Army Is Under Attack by Copts." The presenter called upon all "honorable citizens" to go to Maspero to help defend the soldiers. Around this time, a report was also circulated that two officers had been martyred at Coptic hands. Viewers at home were not unmoved. Indeed, that evening, many residents of Bulaq and other nearby working-class districts armed themselves with clubs and other weapons before heading off to Maspero to assist the army in beating up and even killing protesters. One corpse had its head split in two, clearly by a sword or other sharp instrument, not an army-issue weapon. Renowned political activist Nawara Nigm, daughter of poet Ahmad Nigm, who was witness to the carnage wrote in her testimony:

We were surprised to find the honorable citizens [Nigm was using the term sarcastically to refer to the television broadcasting station] arriving from Sixth of October Bridge near Ramsis Hilton [hotel] and they were shouting "Islamic, Islamic" and "Raise your head high, you are a Muslim" and behind them were the Central Security Forces followed by the army. Some of the youth approached them and one of the central security forces officers held one of the youth and saw his hand and found a cross [tattooed] and threw him toward the honorable citizens, telling them "Christian" so they dragged him [on the pavement] up to the beginning of Sahil al-Filal street and did not stop hitting him.[11]

Later, on her way to the Coptic Hospital where many of the injured and deceased in the Maspero Massacre had been transferred, Nigm said she saw the following: "On my way to the Coptic Hospital I found a bearded man wearing a short *jilbab* (white, loose-fitting coat-like attire) telling people to change direction. I asked him for the reason and he said the Nazarenes are firing on the Muslims . . . when I arrived at the hospital I did not find any 'Nazarenes' firing any bullets but I found them trying to find shelter in the hospital while the honorable citizens threw stones at them." Nigm said she could identify some of these "honorable citizens" as affiliated to the Ministry of Interior—they were familiar faces from previous protests. Nonetheless, many citizens had genuinely believed that the Egyptian army was under attack by the Christians and some were shocked to hear the truth.

At its 12 October press conference, SCAF stuck to its story that the protesters had placed the soldiers, and by extension the institutions of the state, in danger. The army spokesmen showed footage of the priest who had threatened the march on Maspero, predicting as well that the Aswan governor would be killed if he were not dismissed. The carnage at Maspero could have been much worse, the generals claimed, were it not for the soldiers' "self-restraint" despite their terror. "Thank God the soldiers didn't have live ammunition or else it would have been a real catastrophe," said 'Imara.

The demonization of the Maspero protesters is partly in keeping with standard operating procedure for the Egyptian state in dealing with political dissidents, whether they are Copts, workers, or activists. The state always presents itself as protecting a silent majority from an unruly few. When the dissidents are Christian, however, the demonization is served up with a twist: Copts are implicitly or explicitly depicted as lacking patriotism, even as traitors. This portrayal extends beyond the state into the wider public realm. When such groups as the Maspero Youth began to be active, prominent commentators did not celebrate Coptic agency independent of the Church but suggested that young Copts had become too big for their boots. Worker protest is demeaned as "special-interest" pleading, but Coptic protest is denounced in stronger terms as divisive. This state of affairs persists despite the fact that Copts are not calling for additional rights but simply due respect for their citizenship and proper application of Egyptian law amid a backlash targeting existing churches and other property, as well as people. Hasan Abu Talib, editor-in-chief of the prestigious annual *al-Ahram Strategic Report*, told Al Arabiyya that the Maspero demonstrators had provoked the public sentiment against them by asking for international protection, although this request had been nowhere on the protest's agenda. The army and the 25 January Revolution are "one hand," and the army is the protector of Islam, Abu Talib continued, so Egyptians are bound to react negatively to such veiled criticism of the institution. The fact that the protesters made very specific demands for civil rights makes no difference to the upholders of such a discourse, because protest under the banner of Coptic identity is seen as illegitimate.

On 9 October, however, SCAF and the state media went well beyond the usual insinuations that protesting Copts are overly demanding, ungrateful, or unduly provocative. The messages crawling along the bottom of the television screen were an open incitement to civil war.

In the aftermath of the Maspero events, the same thinly disguised gripes about Copts reappeared in the public arena. The Muslim Brothers, for example, issued a statement on 10 October beginning, "Does what happened last night at Maspero make sense? To those who took turns praying each Friday in Tahrir Square, with Christians pouring water for Muslims to perform ablutions with, those who belong to two religions calling for love, peace, kindness, and fairness? And all, supposedly, because of a small incident in the far south of the country?" The Brothers went on, "All the Egyptian people have grievances and legitimate demands, not only our Christian brothers. Certainly, this is not the right time to claim them."

What is most disconcerting is that the bloodiest clashes since the downfall of Mubarak did not at that point in time serve as a wake-up call for the country as a whole. By and large, Egyptian public opinion was sympathetic (if quietly) to the army's version of events and susceptible to believing that the army may have been, in some sense, the victim. Columnist Wa'il al-Sammari wrote that after the crowds had dispersed on that Sunday night, he strolled the streets of downtown Cairo and asked what had happened. "Someone told me that twenty officers from the armed forces had been killed at the hands of Copts, and that they are determined to kill our officers so that we remain without protection," he recorded. "When I told him that the army protects us all, Muslims and Christians, he said, 'Are you asleep or what? The army is ours alone. As for the Copts, they are protected by America. And we will see: Us or America!'"[12] Al-Sammari found it particularly depressing that many of the youths who responded in this way were apolitical and did not seem to be especially religious. Many, indeed, had come downtown to defend the army and told the columnist that, if need be, they would fight Copts to defend Islam. The comments posted after Arabic-language Internet news stories very much suggest that the army's narrative was widely trusted. Several commenters expressed their outrage at Coptic belligerence and disrespect for the armed forces and Muslim society. On talk shows, callers took umbrage at the fact that Coptic protesters held up wooden crosses. Almost all of them seemed to be sure that the Copts had attacked the army, a belief that the Internet images of flattened bodies did not seem to have shaken.

Most political forces in today's Egypt are wary of seeming to side with Copts or acknowledging their grievances, in all likelihood for fear of losing popularity. Deputy Prime Minister Hazim al-Biblawi tendered his resignation on 10 October, telling a television interviewer, "The government failed in its main responsibility, which is to provide security, and it should at least acknowledge its failure to give this issue the effort it needed and apologize." The government promptly rejected his resignation. Informants within the Egyptian Social Democratic Party, to which al-Biblawi belongs, assert that he could not back down for the party was exerting tremendous pressure not to back down from his resignation.

Hence, like the weak transitional government, various parties jockeying for position in advance of the parliamentary elections held in November 2011–January 2012 issued anodyne calls upon all parties to show self-restraint lest an outbreak of sectarianism undermine the progress of post-revolutionary Egypt. Such equalization of responsibility obstructed movement toward a policy of zero tolerance for religious discrimination. When there is no perpetrator and no victim but only two competing sides, the question of justice is sidelined. Some liberal thinkers and activists have pressed for measures of justice: accountability for the army officers who issued the order to fire; Information Minister Haykal's resignation; and the sacking of the news team responsible for inciting sectarian violence on live television. These liberals, however, do not comprise an aggregate voice of adequate political weight. As for politicians, they may feel uncompelled to pursue the votes of Copts, who are, after all, a geographically diffuse 10-percent minority in an overwhelmingly Muslim country.

The equalization of blame also obscured the truth, meaning that the identity of instigators of sectarianism could remain concealed. The priority was to restore calm. The sheikh who preached arson in al-Marinab, the governor of Aswan who falsified information, the people from Bulaq and elsewhere who set upon protesters, and, most important, the army officers who crushed citizens under their tanks, all fade into the background, as do calls to bring them to justice. Yet while political calculations may explain the muted reaction of most political forces to Maspero, what is less easily understood is the scale and ferociousness of the army's attack and the accompanying sectarian propaganda.

There are several possible explanations, all of them wanting. Perhaps the most convincing is the application of Mubarak's standard recipe of divide and rule. If the polity is divided and there appears to be chaos on the ground, then this would justify its hanging on to power and its public image as the arbitrator of conflict, without whose presence Egypt would collapse.

A second possible explanation is the flexing of the army's muscles to send a signal that protests and uprisings would no longer be tolerated, under the rubric that Egypt is being externally targeted and law and order must be regained. It chose to strike against Copts because they are the weaker party in society. It may have sought to bank on strong anti-Coptic sentiment in society, confident in its ability to mobilize prejudice to its advantage. This would have sent a stern warning to the revolutionaries that violence will be used when the army is faced with continued dissidence.

A third possible explanation is that SCAF panicked and struck at the protesters haphazardly and aimlessly without a strategic plan. This seems the least likely explanation given that eyewitnesses said that the tanks were running over protesters in a systematic and organized way and that their actions did not seem to be responding to any real threat on the ground.

Maspero's Ripple Effects

Whatever the motives for the military's actions, Maspero backfired badly on SCAF. While on the day there was a genuine risk of the country falling into a state of civil war, a number of misguided policies on the part of SCAF served to radicalize the wider polity against them.

A number of politically significant ripple effects emanated from the Maspero Massacre. First, it sounded alarm bells loud and clear to the revolutionary forces that SCAF and the people are not one hand and that the former will use military might against peaceful civilians. Second, it spawned a new movement, the Mina Daniel movement, which has kept the memory of the massacre alive and made an Egyptian Copt an iconic figure of a young revolutionary, perhaps one of its most renowned martyrs. While the numbers of the movement are not large, the Mina Daniel movement has come to symbolize the revolutionary youth who died for a patriotic cause and who did not have to abandon or subsume their Coptic identity in order to be Egyptian. Among the young revolutionary groups, Mina Daniel was highly esteemed for his sustained struggle against Mubarak's regime and its remnants. For Coptic Egyptians, he became one of the most famous, most revered martyrs. Third, it unleashed a more intense backlash against the activists involved, bringing about an international outcry. Fourth, the Coptic Orthodox Church's handling of the Maspero Massacre made it lose face even more, and, by default, increased the political popularity of nascent Coptic movements.

In effect, Maspero became the precursor to bloodier uprisings against SCAF and the government and the intensification of the battle to remove it from power. The first of such misguided policies was to announce that civilians would not be referred to military courts *except* those implicated in the Maspero events because of their direct assault on members of the army.[13] The arrest of Alaa Abd El-Fattah, a blogger and human rights activist, on charges of inciting the protesters against the army at Maspero generated an international outcry against SCAF. Abd El-Fattah refused to collaborate with a military court and requested he be transferred to a civil one. The military refused and he was detained for a period of over two months. The victims of Maspero became the accused. In addition to Alaa

Abd El-Fattah, two priests from the Maspero Youth Movement, Father Matthias and Father Philopateer, were accused of inciting the masses against the army, as were dozens of others. It was a major embarrassment for SCAF when human rights organizations announced (and the military denied) that on the list of those accused of mobilizing the masses and who were called for questioning was Mina Daniel. Mina Daniel was one of the revolutionary youth of Tahrir Square who was killed in Maspero.

The campaign against the referral of civilians to military courts was stepped up. It ignited the youth revolutionary movements and coalitions to mobilize against the authoritarian rule of the military regime. The quest for SCAF to cede power intensified, and in retaliation in December 2011 young revolutionaries protesting in Muhammad Mahmud Street and in Qasr al-Aini Street were met with internationally prohibited tear gas, live bullets, and brutal assaults. Over thirty people died. This not only intensified the revolutionary fervor among the youth, but ironically unified Coptic youth movements and al-Azhar. Sheikh Emad, an al-Azhar scholar who had gone to Qasr al-Aini in an attempt to broker a peace deal between the army and the youth, was shot dead. The Coptic-led Maspero Movement joined in the mourning of Sheikh Emad, who together with Mina Daniel became a symbol of the killing of Egyptians by a tyrannical military regime.

Moreover, the second misguided policy on the part of SCAF that antagonized political forces even further was its failure to allow an independent judicial committee to investigate the perpetrators of the Maspero Massacre. A report was issued by the National Council for Human Rights that was criticized by many human rights activists as evading the difficult questions and deliberately subverting the question of injustice. The investigations undertaken by the Military General Prosecution (al-Niyaba al-'Askariya) were considered to be a farce given the fact that those implicated in the very acts of assault were those investigating the incident. Not surprisingly, the Egyptian government refused to conduct an investigation. It became very clear that in the absence of truly autonomous and free local institutions, it was not possible to undertake a transparent investigation or hold SCAF accountable. SCAF promised that an independent inquiry would be undertaken by the Cabinet and its results publicly released. Such a report never materialized. Similar promises were made to release the findings on the assaults on the youth in Muhammad Mahmud and Qasr al-Aini Streets, which were also never met.

Maspero had another important ripple effect on the question of voice and legitimacy. SCAF was seeking to exert its power over the Coptic Church leadership to quickly close old files (such as Maspero) and contain angry Coptic sentiment. However, in post-Mubarak Egypt, a vibrant political society meant that the pope and his entourage of bishops found it increasingly difficult to exert political authority over the lay population. A number of crises related to Maspero brought this to the forefront. The most notable incidence of this perhaps, recounted via informants within the Coptic Orthodox Church, was that Sharaf's government called one of the high-ranking bishops close to the pope[14] to stop Copts who were demanding that the victims of Maspero be recognized as martyrs. The pope was presiding over the funeral prayers for the victims and this particular bishop sought to convince the families not to go ahead with the demands for martyrdom recognition, arguing that it is preferable for the victims to be put to rest and not be referred to forensic doctors (a necessary step to document the cause of death). Independent Coptic voices told the families that it is their right to have their sons and daughters recognized as martyrs, and the families were convinced. Against the will of the Coptic Church hierarchy, most families filed their cases. Under tremendous pressure and a series of sustained protests to demand justice for the victims of Maspero, Sharaf conceded and through a prime ministerial decree announced that those killed in Maspero were martyrs.

The aftermath of the Maspero Massacre highlighted the extent of marginalization of the Coptic Orthodox Church's leadership and the growing internal critiques against its application of old strategies of engagement in a new political age. On 24 October 2011, Pope Shenouda met with Field Marshal Tantawi. The press reported that the two men agreed that the interest of the nation/homeland should supersede all. On the surface, it seemed that the meeting was intended to be a conciliatory one with respect to the Church, as the press reported that Tantawi offered to deal with all pending issues associated with Christian places of worship. In effect, what was offered illustrated that Pope Shenouda had very little political weight in relation to SCAF. For example, it was decided that the church at al-Marinab would be recognized as a community services center with the possibility of holding masses in it. The meeting and its conclusions stirred the wrath of the Coptic intelligentsia, who were quick to criticize it openly on the Internet. Many wrote that it was about time the Church leadership realized that the kind of ententes it established with the authorities were detrimental to securing the rights of Copts and that the Church leadership should seek to regain its independence from the ruling powers. The SCAF regime followed the same strategy of punishing the victim as did Mubarak's. In March 2012, the priest in al-Marinab was tried for increasing the height of the Marinab church steeple and received a three-year prison sentence. It is ironic that none of the members of the armed forces who had crushed demonstrators or shot live ammunition received sentences, nor did those who instigated the attacks on the church in the first place, and yet the priest in al-Marinab was incriminated. This was a clear case of blaming the weaker party with the purpose of intimidation and containment as part of a strategy to force the Coptic Orthodox Church to approach the authorities in a bid to arrive at an agreement so as not to subject its clergy to incarceration. The strategy worked and the Court of Cassation of Edfu announced on 12 May 2012 that the case has been dropped after the parties arrived at reconciliation informally.[15]

This policy of incarcerating the weaker party in order to force it to seek informal agreement in return for its release has been a key element of the authoritarian functioning of the state. It is applied to all dissenters, and has been consistently applied to Copts in incidents involving violence against them. The Church leadership, in particular Pope Shenouda, suffered a serious blow on 6 January 2012, on Coptic Christmas Eve. The Maspero Youth Movement and other Coptic movements held protests to express their objection to the idea that the very army generals responsible for the Maspero Massacre would be welcomed to the Christmas Eve mass, to be greeted by the pope. During the mass, as the pope took an interval to greet his visitors—the army generals—and to thank them and pay them compliments, the youth at the back of the church shouted at the top of their lungs, "Down, down with military rule!"

The Coptic intelligentsia and the revolutionary movements were highly sympathetic to the Maspero Youth's stance, wondering why SCAF would include the chief of military police, Hamdin Badin, in its delegation to wish the pope and Christians a merry Christmas. General Badin was in command at the time of the Maspero Massacre. They wondered whether it was a deliberate move designed to offend or a matter that was overlooked by SCAF. In both instances, it spoke of a clear disregard for Coptic sentiments and an over-assurance of the extent to which they would not be subjected to scrutiny.

Against this backdrop, the civil Coptic youth movements were growing stronger and gaining the respect and sympathy of many Copts. Father Matthias pointed out in an interview with me that, a few days earlier, the pope's secretary had summoned him and asked him to deflect the protests being planned against SCAF's visit on Christmas Eve. Father Matthias recounted that he had informed the secretary that this was out of his hands, for although he was a member of the Maspero Youth Movement, decisions were made by the movement as a whole and he could not impose his will upon it. When Pope Shenouda made statements on 22 October 2011 against the internationalization of the Maspero case, Ramy Kamal of the Maspero Youth Movement announced that "the Church can talk as it wishes on spiritual matters but it is the families of the victims and the Coptic activists who determine whether to internationalize the matter or not. It is a legal right according to the international conventions to which Egypt is a signatory."[16]

The Maspero Youth Movement was gaining ground among Copts, who continued to join organized protests in large numbers and increasingly contested openly and publicly the Church's stance on politics. It became very clear that rather than intimidating Copts into retreating behind church walls, the Maspero events propelled them onto the streets with even greater vigor.

10 | The Copts' Islamist Experience

There is a growing body of literature on the position of Islamists toward the Coptic question (Tadros 2012a; Scott 2010; Fawzi 2009; Morcos 2006a; Ali 2005). Much of this scholarship focuses on Islamists' perspectives on the position of non-Muslim minorities in Egypt, and their rights and duties in an Islamic state as conceived by Islamists. Some of this literature was written against the backdrop of the Muslim Brotherhood's growing participation in formal political life in the 2005 parliamentary elections and the underlying question of the positioning of Copts should they come to power. The literature often focused on Islamists' ideas and views as conveyed in parliament or in party platforms. The reverse—Copts' perceptions of Islamists; their sense of positioning within the Islamist framework; and their conception of the relationship among Islamist groups, the Coptic citizenry, and the state is far less documented. Such a gap in the literature is due to the fact that, unlike the Muslim Brotherhood, Copts do not constitute a political entity per se, while the historical weakening of Coptic civil society since 1952 has meant that voices from within the Coptic community that have actively articulated their own perspectives on such matters are few and far between. Finally, it cannot be emphasized enough that Copts, like any other group, are not homogenous.

While it is beyond the scope of this chapter to document the full spectrum of Copts' perspectives on Islamists' visions of state governance, the first part of the chapter takes a brief look at some of the predominant positions taken with regard to Islamists by some Coptic lay members and Church leaders since the inception of the Muslim Brotherhood and up to the ousting of Mubarak. The second part of the chapter analyzes why the demise of the Mubarak regime did not lead to Copts turning a new leaf in relation to Islamists. The chapter then discusses the establishment of Islamist parties and the extent to which their emergence violated the constitutional principles prohibiting the formation of religious parties. It exposes the way in which the most prominent Islamist parties deceived the public regarding the real numbers of non-Muslims who joined them while evading any accountability. By examining the profile and prerogative of some of the Coptic members who joined some of these parties, and inquiring as to their expectations and assumptions about them, it dispels some of the assumptions about what motivated these citizens to join.

Copts, the Church, and Islamists Historicized

When Hassan al-Banna established the Society of the Muslim Brothers (often referred to as the Muslim Brotherhood) in 1928, he was keen to convey an image of the organization as having no hostility toward non-Muslims. Certainly, al-Banna's project was the revival of the Islamic caliphate, which he sought neither to deny nor hide. However, his position was that it is not possible for non-Muslims to live in a Muslim-majority context, unless they willingly wish to be ruled by an Islamic state. Al-Banna argued that Copts, like their Muslim counterparts, have an allegiance to Islamic civilization that is greater than their affinity with western civilization, which was imposed upon Egyptians by colonial powers. Al-Banna's other major argument was that Copts had nothing to fear from living in an Islamic state since shari'a guarantees all of their rights. Responding once to the accusation that the Muslim Brotherhood's impact on the nation is divisive, Hassan al-Banna responded by insisting that there is no fanaticism in Islam, and that the Prophet supported the idea of unity among the different sects of the *umma*, or Islamic nation, on the basis of national interest.

At the personal level, al-Banna's ability to build a vast source of social capital also incorporated non-Muslims. Some of the stories cited about al-Banna's positive relationship with Copts are included in his own biography *(Mudhakkirat al-da'wa wa-l-da'iya)*. For example, while he was living in Ismailiya and teaching at a school, a Christian of anonymous identity submitted a complaint to the administration that al-Banna was a fanatic teacher leading a fanatic association (the Muslim Brotherhood). Once this complaint reached the headmaster, it was completely rejected by the Christian community in Ismailiya, which sent a delegation to the school to refute such claims (al-Banna 1986: 102).

It was also widely publicized that the only Egyptian to have broken the government cordon and attended al-Banna's funeral was the renowned Coptic politician, Makram Ebeid. The Muslim Brotherhood also pointed to the Christians that served as councilors to the Brotherhood's Guidance Bureau as evidence of the absence of fanaticism within the group. Tawfiq Doss was the legal councilor to the Guidance Bureau and, together with Akhnukh Labib Akhnukh and Karim Thabit, represented on the Higher Council of the Muslim Brotherhood. Despite the prominence of these names, the Higher Council had no authority or influence on the society's internal decision-making apparatus, being a consultative, non-binding committee.

On the other hand, one of the fiercest sustained sources of opposition to the Muslim Brotherhood came from Father Sargious, a Coptic leader renowned for his patriotic stance against British colonialism and his solidarity with al-Azhar in demanding Egyptian independence. He launched several attacks on al-Banna personally and continuously lobbied the Egyptian government to liquidate al-Banna's organization through his publication *al-Manara al-misriya*. For example, in October 1948, Sargious drew up a petition calling for the dissolution of all organizations that mixed religion and politics and were thus detrimental to equality (Carter 1986: 276). Banna in return accused Sargious of treachery and attacked him for being sectarian (Carter 1986).

In terms of the movement's wider engagement with the Coptic citizenry, relations were not always characterized by the collegiality found between al-Banna and some Coptic figures. The Brothers were implicated in the burning of a church in 1949 and "they were also involved in a number of minor incidents like removing crosses from the tops of churches" (Carter 1986: 277). Copts who lived in Shubra shared anecdotes about members of the Brotherhood painting crosses on their houses to "single them out" from among the Muslim population. Incidents of strain in Muslim–Christian relations as a consequence of Brotherhood instigation were also reported in several villages.[1] Throughout the history of the Brotherhood, there have been instances at a local level where strong friendships emerged between members of the movement and Coptic figures, whether lay or clergy. However, on a political level, the relationship between Coptic citizens and the Brotherhood has tended to be very strained on ideological grounds.

The following vignette may shed light on this. In 1992, under the leadership of Ma'mun al-Hodeibi, the Brothers attempted a rapprochement with Copts, and sought to do so strategically by approaching lay Copts as opposed to the Church leadership. In December 1991, a group of Coptic intellectuals and some leading members of the Muslim Brotherhood began to meet at the Muslim Brotherhood headquarters in al-Tawfiqiya on a regular basis. The Copts included former member of parliament and one-time minister of housing Milad Hanna; Sueliman Qilada, renowned writer; Maged Attia, member of the Wafd Party; and businessman Amin Fakhri 'Abd al-Nur. Representing the Muslim Brotherhood were al-Hodeibi, Salah 'Abd al-Mu'ati, Muhammad Emara, Sayyid Disuki, and Salah 'Abd al-Maqsud. It is claimed that Ahmad Seif al-Banna, the son of Hassan al-Banna, and former Supreme Guide Muhammad Mahdi Akef also attended. There were several purposes to the meetings reported in the press. One explanation was that the dialogue sought to find common ground for addressing heightened sectarian tensions in Egypt. Others suggested that the purpose was to see whether there were possibilities for attracting Copts to become founding members of a proposed new political party, which would minimize the prospects of accusing it of establishing a religious party.[2]

The dialogue faltered. According to Milad Hanna, "After five sessions they presented us with the Islamic cultural project to rule Egypt in the face of the western civilization project . . . we were expected to give it our stamp of approval but we refused and I told them, let us examine the Egyptian cultural project which recognizes religious pluralism and the right to citizenship, Copts and Muslims, on the basis of equality."[3]

Shortly following the Muslim Brotherhood's victory in parliament, Akram al-Sha'ir, a Muslim Brotherhood MP from Alexandria, invited distinguished Coptic members—all lay members—for a dialogue. Yusuf Sidhom, the editor-in-chief of *Watani*, regarded as a Coptic mouthpiece, hosted a dialogue with members of the Brotherhood at the newspaper's premises. He confessed that Copts were deeply critical of those who participated in the dialogue, but conceded that there must be room for common ground. He argued that the reaction of Copts stemmed from their deep suspicions of the Brothers as a result of the disconnect between the latter's stances on equal citizenship and their more liberal discourse. He also attributed the mistrust to the politicization of religion by the Brothers, which had a detrimental impact on fostering citizenship.[4] While Sidhom was openly very critical of the Brothers' agenda, claiming that it was premised on the establishment of an Islamic state that is at odds with a civil state, he insisted that dialogue with the Brothers was necessary because it was preferable to boycotting them. His openness to dialogue with the Brothers was exceptional for Coptic leaders at the time.

The Brotherhood–Coptic lay leaders' dialogue occurred against the backdrop of various Coptic figures' open expression of heightened opposition to the Brothers' ascendancy to power. Milad Hanna became renowned in 2005 for saying, in the wake of the 2005 elections, that if the Brotherhood came to power, he would pack his bags and leave Egypt.[5]

At the same time other prominent Coptic figures expressed their fears regarding the Muslim Brotherhood's governance of Egypt. Prominent historian and scholar at the Al-Ahram Center for Political and Strategic Studies, Yunan Labib Rizk, said that his fears focused on the erosion of the concept of citizenship for all, in view of the Brotherhood's primary allegiance to a universal conception of the Islamic *umma*, the boundaries of which are not territorially limited to those of Egypt but extend to the wider Islamic world. He argued that historically no religious movement upon accession to power has respected the idea of full citizenship for those who do not share its religion because it always views them with superiority.[6]

Former MP Mona Makram Ebeid, the daughter of Makram Ebeid, argued that the Muslim Brotherhood's political slogan "Islam is the solution" undermined the validity of its framework of "a civil state with an Islamic reference," since it is premised on the Islamization of all aspects of life. She argued that one of the impacts of their political role has been the creation of rifts between people based on religion.[7] Other Coptic writers, such as Sameh Fawzi and Samir Morcos, have also criticized the Muslim Brotherhood's ability to engage with the Coptic question through the prism of equal citizenship (Fawzi 2009; Morcos 2006a; Morcos 2006b). I examined the writings of the Coptic intelligentsia in the past fifty years. Despite the diversity in background, political orientation, and self-identification, it became apparent that all spoke of the Brotherhood's vision, history, and agenda as an anathema to full citizenship for all, including Copts. Their stance was based on their reading of how the Brotherhood engage in the public arena as a political movement (in particular vis-à-vis the instrumentalization of religion), and their stances on matters such as equality in places of worship. The one exception has been Rafik Habib, who has consistently said that Copts have nothing to fear from the Muslim Brotherhood, as its Islamic framework is the most ideal for securing their rights. Well before he was appointed deputy head of the Freedom and Justice Party (FJP) in 2011, Habib's stance was that the Muslim Brotherhood's position toward Copts is that they are equal partners in the nation and that many of the fears that the Copts have are illusionary. Further, he held that a secular system of governance was not in the best interests of Copts since it would, for example, deny them their own personal status law. He also argued that it would not be in Copts' favor to adopt a position that ran counter to that of the majority, and that if the Islamic *marja'iya* was held by the greater part of the population, then there would be no reason to oppose it.[8]

Relations between the Coptic Orthodox Church and the Muslim Brotherhood had been at times lukewarm, at other times suffering from heightened tensions, but rarely friendly (see Tadros 2012a). There were particular moments of tension between the pope and the supreme guide. In the 1990s, a comment made by then Supreme Guide Mustafa Mashhur to the effect that Copts should not be conscripted into the army and that they should pay the *jizya* stirred the wrath of Copts. A high official delegation from members of the Muslim Brotherhood and the Islamist Labor Party visited the pope as a gesture of reconciliation and to encourage the Brotherhood's friendly relations with the Church. Relations also experienced a phase of strain when Mahdi Akef became supreme guide in the 2000s. Relations between him and the late Pope Shenouda occasionally verged on open conflict. Akef argued that the Church supported the Mubarak regime, which it should not do, while various Church leaders accused the Brotherhood of using religion for its own political ends. There were persistent reconciliatory gestures on the part of the current supreme guide, Muhammad Badi', to build a bridge with the late Pope Shenouda and the Coptic Orthodox Church leadership. The nature of the relationship that will evolve between the new patriarch, Bishop Tawadros, who was officially made pope on 18 November 2012, and the Muslim Brotherhood will be partly determined by the relationship between Bishop Tawadros and Muhammad Morsi, the new Egyptian president.

Some predicted that the demise of Mubarak would present an opportunity to turn over a new leaf, in particular since a prevailing discourse then was that it was the former regime that was inciting sectarian hatred, not any of the non-state actors (see chapter 5). However, relations between the Muslim Brotherhood and the Coptic Church entered a state of confrontation over the struggle for political power among different political groups. Informally, the Muslim Brotherhood accused the Coptic Orthodox Church of assuming a political role by encouraging its followers not to vote in favor of the constitutional referendums of March 2011, and not to vote for Islamists in the parliamentary elections. By the same token, the Coptic Orthodox Church leadership informally accused the Muslim Brotherhood of instrumentalizing religion to win votes and using religion in the most divisive manner.[9]

The political battles that were played out in 2011 are briefly narrated below.

The Constitutional Referendum Litmus Test: Paving the Way for the Parliamentary Elections

On 19 March 2011, SCAF held a constitutional referendum on a number of revisions to the Egyptian constitution of 1971. The proposed constitutional referendum immediately polarized SCAF and the Islamists on the one hand, who favored the revisions, and the youth revolutionary groups and all liberal forces on the other, who rejected them. The official position of the Coptic Orthodox Church was that each Copt should vote on the referendum as he or she saw fit. However, at the parish level, Coptic parishioners who had been exposed to liberal voices were clearly in favor of a no vote in the constitutional referendum. The Muslim Brotherhood and Salafis used their access and full control over an overwhelming number of mosques to push for a yes vote. Religion was instrumentalized to the maximum to show that good Muslims should vote yes, and that only infidels and unbelievers would vote no. This in effect brought Islamists and Copts to a clear battle of the wills, and into the realm of open war.

According to Ahram Online's accounts of the day's voting, in Marsa Matruh, Salafis and Muslim Brotherhood members tore down posters put up by the leftist Tagammu' Party calling for a no vote, replacing them with yes posters. In electoral voting offices, particularly those in more rural and remote areas of the country, members of the Muslim Brotherhood prodded citizens to mark the green spot, which in Egypt symbolizes the color of Islam. The Brothers told people that to mark the green color was to be in favor of Islam and to mark the black color was to take the un-Islamic path. Informants, however, said that in many circles what was specifically said was that black marked the color of the priest's headwear (*'imma*) and therefore whoever marks black is in favor of the Christian unbelievers.

The constitutional referendum produced a result of 77 percent in favor of the constitutional amendments. The level of fraud was minimal and there was a 41 percent turnout, far greater than any turnout in Egypt's limited electoral history. The people, Islamists declared, had freely made their choice for the first time in over sixty years. There were no doubts that what the constitutional referendum had shown was the strength of the Islamists' ability to mobilize the people.

Clearly, the post-Mubarak era paved the way not for a more conciliatory relationship but a more conflictual one between Coptic citizens and Islamists, who were edging ever closer to power. However, there are particular nuances that are important to note. First, there was an attempted media differentiation between Salafis and the Muslim Brotherhood regarding their position on the Copts. Salafis' statements openly declared Copts to be unbelievers. The Muslim Brotherhood's statements were more reserved on the matter, which gave the sense that they were more 'moderate' or 'enlightened' and therefore a better choice for Copts. On the other hand, there was a general attempt by all Islamist movements to assure Copts that their rights would be secured should Islamists come to power. This was true of both Salafi and Muslim Brotherhood forces, who stepped up their assurances during the parliamentary elections and even after they had secured the majority of seats in parliament. For example, during the Christmas of January 2012, many Copts noted that for the first time ever many Islamist-oriented colleagues and acquaintances made a point of calling them up to wish them a happy Christmas and to insist on the fraternity between Muslims and Christians. This seems to be an almost universal observation on the part of many middle-class Copts, to the point of suggesting a policy systematically pursued and applied as opposed to random, individual gestures. Moreover, for Christmas Eve mass, the Muslim Brotherhood sent high-ranking members from the movement and the FJP to the Patriarchate to wish the Coptic Orthodox Church leadership a happy Christmas.

The Muslim Brotherhood made a number of attempts to engage Coptic youth groups, but the latter shunned such advances on the grounds that they did not want to be approached in their capacity as Christians as opposed to Egyptian citizens with different political orientations. Kamal Zakhir, the coordinator of the Coptic lay movement, found the Muslim Brotherhood's attempts to allay fears among Copts regarding the Brotherhood's rise to political power via the Church problematic because they assumed that the Church spoke politically on behalf of Copts. "They are trying to gain legitimacy in the eyes of the Coptic youth through the Church, which in my opinion is the real reason behind this initiative," said Zakhir.[10] He argued that by singling out Coptic youth for dialogue, they are "treating them as a separate entity to the rest of the Egyptians. If they had ideas they wanted to represent to the country's youth, what is the point of sending this invitation only to the Copts?"

A number of attempts to forge a bridge between the Muslim Brotherhood and the Coptic Orthodox Church were made. This cultiminated in a meeting between Muslim Brotherhood leader Muhammad Badi' and Pope Shenouda III in the Patriarchate on 7 March 2012, ten days before the pope died. While Badi' hailed the meeting as one characterized by mutual esteem, we do not have any church accounts of the content of the conversation. Presumably, since these were the pope's last days, his health had deteriorated rapidly, and the encounter was very brief, it may be that this was no more than a courtesy call as opposed to a substantive meeting.

Coptic Members of Islamist Parties

SCAF issued Law No. 12 of 2011 to reform some of the stipulations of Law No. 40 of 1977 specific to the political parties system. Article 4 of Law No. 12 cited among the conditions of the formation of political parties that for a party to acquire a permit, there is to be no discrimination in its principles or programs, its implementation of activities, or its choice of leaders or members based on religious or class difference, interest group, or geographic location, or grounds of sex, language, or creed.

Article 4 of Law No. 12 was repeatedly rejected by the Muslim Brotherhood during Mubarak's era on the basis that Article 2 of the constitution stipulates that shari'a is the principal source of legislation and thus Islamist parties are compatible with the constitution.

Following the fall of Mubarak, public opinion was overwhelmingly in favor of emphasizing the necessity of integrating the Muslim Brotherhood into Egypt's political life. The concerns expressed during Mubarak's era by political forces across the spectrum that the Muslim Brotherhood could not become a political party as long as its political premise remained a specifically religious one ceased to be raised after February 2011. The focus on integrating Islamists into political life was driven by a number of intertwining factors: recognition that Islamists had been harshly treated by the Mubarak regime and had suffered much repression; keenness to build a new Egypt where all political factions are included and none marginalized; the participation of Islamists (even if not at the beginning) in the uprising against Mubarak; and, of course, the presence of an alliance between SCAF and the Islamists that blessed the latter's accession to power.

Even so, the revised political parties law that was issued by military decree maintained the prohibition on the formation of political parties based on religion. Concurrently, it was no secret that SCAF was collaborating closely with the Muslim Brotherhood, a factor that would no doubt influence how the political parties law would be interpreted.

On 19 February 2011, the Parties' Affairs Committees of Egypt's State Council approved the establishment of the centrist Wasat Party, led by Abu al-'Ila Madi. Madi, the party's founder, had resigned from the Muslim Brotherhood in the mid-1990s to form his own party. The party, which has prided itself on being more liberal than the Muslim Brotherhood (for example allowing women and Copts to assume the position of the country's president) is still considered an Islamist party, on the premise that it advocates a civil state with "an Islamic reference." It is unclear on what premise the Parties' Affairs Committees decided that Wasat, though firmly grounded in an Islamic reference, is not a religious party. Certainly, its acceptance also paved the way for the establishment of the Freedom and Justice Party (FJP) by the Muslim Brotherhood, which also identifies itself as one that believes in a civil state with an Islamic reference.

All three Islamist parties, Wasat, the FJP, and the Salafist Nour Party founded shortly after the 25 January Revolution, were keen widely to publicize the fact that they had women and Copts on their lists of founders as evidence that they are not religious parties and are open to all Egyptians. The Wasat Party, which was widely publicized as having Christians among its founding members, in fact had just one, Azmi Abadir (interviewed; see page 217). However, in the absence of mechanisms of transparency or accountability, both the FJP and the Nour Party misled the Egyptian public with regard to the real number of Copts joining them. The FJP widely publicized the fact that it had ninety-three Copts among its founders. The real number is twenty-three—three in Cairo, one in Giza, one in Gharbiya, one in Sharqiya, one in Minufiya, two in Qalyubiya, three in Minya, two in Damietta, two in Beheira, two in Beni Suef, one in Fayoum, two in Asyut, one in Sohag, and one in Aswan.

The Nour Party leadership announced that there were fifty Copts among the party's founders but refused to announce their names. The official list obtained through the Parties' Affairs Committee reveals that there are only five Copts among the founders—three in Alexandria, one in Minufiya, and one in Gharbiya. None of them occupies any organizational position within the party.

One of the ways in which these statements can be verified is to scrutinize the names of founders, which by political party law must be published in the national newspapers. Yet tracing the Coptic members of these political parties proved to be a very difficult task. Journalists who approached Islamist parties for a list of their Coptic founders were met with hostility. There seemed to be a deliberate intention to enforce a media blackout on the matter. Similarly, the Cabinet's political committee refused to share information regarding non-Muslim founders of Islamist parties, again showing a deliberate attempt to conceal such information for reasons unknown. To question the openness, inclusiveness, and representation of the Islamist parties would be in effect to question the very grounds upon which they were established (that is, contravention or otherwise of Law No. 12 of 2011). It seemed as though there was a consensus not to raise a question that could be explosive— three leading independent newspapers refused to publish a number of interviews conducted with Copts who had joined Islamist parties as founder-members (see below). The single exception, of course, has tended to be Rafik Habib, deputy head of the FJP, who was a long-time consultant to the Muslim Brotherhood's Guidance Bureau, well before the FJP was established.

Here, I include three of the unpublished interviews mentioned above and additional ones specifically conducted for this research. It is important to note again that these Copts' views do not represent those of the Coptic community. The interviewees consistently reported that when they informed their families and acquaintances of their decision to join the Islamist parties, they were met with opposition. In view of the difficulty in collecting information on Copts in Islamist parties in a systematic way (December 2011 to January 2012), the interviews provided here are the ones that were accessible. Hence the intention here is to present some insight into certain case studies in terms of profile, motives for joining, how these founder-members came to be part of the party in question, what their expectations were, their relationship to the Church and the Christian community, and how they conceive of the agenda and practices of the Islamist parties they joined.

Profile

The profiles of the Copts interviewed were all, with one exception, founder-members of the FJP. The single exception was a founder-member of Wasat. We could not identify any founders in the Salafist Nour Party. These interviews are instructive in challenging some of the possible hypotheses that may have been put forward regarding the 'type' of Copt who may agree to be a founder of an Islamist political party. For one thing, in the sample of nine interviewees, not one member was poor or socially deprived. In other words, the motive for joining was not one of extreme poverty (and the possible promise of economic betterment or at least some form of handout). To the contrary, these men tended to be mostly middle class, either owning their own businesses or having a middle-rank position in a government ministry or post.

Second, all the interviewees in the sample were educated. Magdi Mikhail Sami, forty-seven, is an architect and the owner of a jewelry store. Muhib Makram Isra'il Yusuf, thirty-nine, is a secondary school teacher with an undergraduate degree in philosophy and an advanced studies degree in the history of art. Nassef Henry, fifty, is a veterinarian by training but occupies a senior managerial position in an Emirates-owned pharmaceutical company with a branch in Egypt. Emad Fakhry is the bursar for the government telecommunications office in Ismailiya. Shuhdi Sidki Rashid is an engineer, Nabil Ramzi Shakir occupies a senior managerial position in the Ministry of Education, Saad Morcos Saad is a computer expert who runs his own business, Azmi Abadir is a university professor of mathematics, and Salah Makram Elia is a deputy head teacher for al-Tiba preparatory school.

As this shows, all the interviewees in this sample were educated, some of them graduate-degree holders. So again, the notion that the Muslim Brotherhood tapped into a segment of Coptic society that was susceptible to a particular message due to lack of exposure does not hold up.

Third, all of the interviewees identified themselves and their families as being affiliated to the Coptic Orthodox Church. In other words, these were not men who were kicked out of the Church or who had taken a position against the Church and were therefore seeking an alternative accommodating space.

How they came to join

An informant within the FJP told me that the party had exerted tremendous effort to try to invite Copts to join and that in many cases it encountered much resistance. Hence, the question of how these particular Copts came to join Islamist parties was critically important. In most cases, the Copts who served as founding members were approached by members of the Muslim Brotherhood who were personally known to them. These Copts were not approached because of their political activism. In fact, they all pointed out that they had never been politically active before and that this was the first party they had ever joined. In most instances, they were approached by friends and neighbors who asked them to become founding members. In some instances, they were approached by colleagues or through work.

The fact that the Muslim Brotherhood relied on personal ties for its recruitment drive is significant because it meant that Coptic founder-members were not sought publicly and systematically through propagation of the Islamist platform to the wider Coptic citizenry. This may also explain why none of the nine interviewees had any prior history or experience of political engagement/activism.

Nabil Ramzi from Maghagha in Minya said he was approached by a colleague who was an FJP member, who explained the program to him and asked him if he would like to join. Shuhdi Sidki was also approached by a member of the Muslim Brotherhood who said the movement would like him to be a founding member. Azmi Abadir joined through Abu al-'Ila Madi, a friend and former student of his.

Why join?

This was one of the most difficult questions to answer because the reasons the interviewees cited for joining were often vague and indirect. It was therefore necessary to read the answers in the context of wider narratives.

Muhib Makram said he joined because the FJP was a strong party capable of leading Egypt through its transition, and besides "many of the people in the party are my friends and I know them well." Throughout the interview, Makram repeatedly emphasized that they were his friends, known to him, suggesting that this was key not only to how he joined but also to what motivated him to agree to do so.

Nabil Ramzi said that he read the FJP's party program and noticed that it mentioned that in matters of personal status, the party took the view that to each according to his own shari'a. Ramzi said that it was this reference to one's freedom of creed that led him to support the FJP's party political platform, since it implied that Muslims would be subject to their religious laws and members of other religions to theirs.

Shuhdi Sidki said that he chose the FJP because they believe in the duality of systems, one for Christians according to their own faith and one for Muslims according to their own faith. Hence, he felt that the FJP was the only party that explicitly acknowledged Copts' right to live according to their own religious jurisprudence.

It is noteworthy that most of the interviewees were keen to distinguish between the Muslim Brotherhood as a religious movement and the FJP as a political party. Nabil Ramzi said that if religion or political party were mixed or if anything conflicted with his own religious values, he would resign from the party. In response to the question of whether they felt there was a conflict between their identities as Copts and the Brotherhood's program, all the interviewes said no because they drew the distinction between the Muslim Brotherhood as a movement and the FJP as a political party. Muhib Makram Isra'il argued that there was a difference between the Muslim Brotherhood and the FJP in terms of objectives and ideologies. According to Makram, from a logistical point of view a distinction is made by the organizers between the Muslim Brotherhood and the party, and this distinction manifests itself in their approach and terms of engagement. For example, his religious affiliation is of no concern to the party, "and some of the objectives of the party are in conflict with the objectives of the Muslim Brotherhood and this conflict is understandable since the Brotherhood is a proselytizing movement but the party is about politics." The same distinction has repeatedly been made by others who argue that they joined the party because they thought it would be completely separate from the movement, ideologically and organizationally.

When asked how they feel about Islamist parties using a sectarian approach to mobilize the Egyptian street in their election campaigns, many of the respondents suggested that the Egyptian people are by nature religious. Magdi Mikhail Sami went further, arguing that sectarianism is so diffuse as to make this argument meaningless, since all are responsible for it.

The notion of loyalty, so central to the followers of the Muslim Brotherhood, did not seem to be so evident in the case of the members interviewed here. For example, they argued that in the instance that the values of the Muslim Brotherhood conflicted with theirs, they would immediately express opposition, with some saying that they would resign.

Some of the interviewees claimed that they would be able to serve Copts by joining the FJP. Shudhi Sidki argued this on the basis that the FJP would one day form a government and appoint governors and local councils. He would therefore be in a position to serve Copts if they needed anything, in line with what is practicable and right.

Another argument put forth was that to participate in the FJP is the reverse of being passive. It is to play a proactive role in political life, with the understanding that Copts' voices must be represented in all political parties and political trends.

These Copts, for the most part, have not denied their Coptic identity, nor have they denied the centrality of issues such as religious equality in their narratives. However, in some members' discourse, there is an attempt to distinguish themselves from other Copts who harbor fears of the Muslim Brothers. These they represent as 'conservative' or cocooned or politically marginalized. Hence, there is a sense in which engagement with the Muslim Brotherhood is pitted against political passivity. In his conversation about his role as a founding member of the FJP, Muhib Makram presents himself as a positive role model to other Christians, as a Copt who is a founding member and not maligned by the Brothers: "I try to tell them that the Brothers do not bite. These are people who do politics. We have to put our hands together in the next period and I say to them, I am an example before you."

Interestingly, as founding members, some of the interviewees have admitted that they have to pay a financial contribution, but when asked they would not disclose how much. For example, Muhib Makram replied to the effect that "these are the party's political matters which I cannot disclose."

Some had high expectations that they would be made to occupy a distinctive position in the party. Others had joined but seemed to have no politically active role. In all cases, it was unclear whether any had substantive powers or whether they were simply being positioned in the party for window-dressing purposes.

Some interviewees mentioned that since some Copts have a "phobia" of Islamists, this makes it difficult for them to join their parties. They urged that Copts not act in a way to exclude themselves from wider society. They all mentioned that the Church had never interfered in their personal choices.

The interviews suggest that in cases where these Copts were approached by FJP advocates through professional relationships, their joining may have been motivated by a concern for their image within the work community (for example, not wanting to appear prejudiced or fanatical) or by fear of loss of business (for example, if clients or partners are affiliated to the Muslim Brotherhood). One such case is Magdi Mikhail Sami, a jewelry store-owner. Since the 1970s, Christian jewelry store-owners have been the target of attacks by militant Islamist groups, and it is possible that the rise of Islamist groups to power may have given Sami a sense of insecurity regarding the future of his business. He may have thought that to be more closely aligned with the party that is affiliated to the Muslim Brotherhood might provide him with some protection. He bluntly said in the interview, "I am anxious about my money and my property."

How are they positioned within the Freedom and Justice Party?

None of the Copts who joined as founders in the FJP occupy any positions of influence, although they claim that they are active participants in the party and hope that more Christians will join. Only one or two claimed that they believe that their presence in the party will have a positive impact on encouraging other Copts to join.

When Magdi Sami was asked whether he was appointed to or offered any influential positions within the FJP, he said that realistically he did not expect to be placed on any of the party's nomination lists because it would strategically undermine the party's chances of winning: "Just as the Nour Party use religious slogans, they, too, use religious slogans. The Nour Party today say that the FJP are a Copts' party."

Makram Elia was also of the belief that by joining the FJP as a founder, his voice would carry weight and he would therefore be able to influence positively the Copts' predicament: "Perhaps this [my joining] will stimulate dialogue and make the other [the Muslim other] consider my needs and specificities [as a Copt] in his decisions and we become the reason for the Copts to enjoy more peace and security." Elia said that what particularly encouraged him was the fact that Rafik Habib was the deputy head of the party.

Between the lines

Unlike in closed organizations such as the Muslim Brotherhood, in political parties there is a certain degree of easy entry and exit, and the FJP is no exception. The Coptic members' entry seems to have been easy. The exit option did not seem out of the question. For example, Nabil Ramzi, when asked how he accounts for the fact that Christians, although constituting 35 percent of the population of Minya governorate, make up just 1 percent of the FJP, said that Copts harbor distant fears of the party, but "what is the problem? If I enter the party and if there is something [I don't like] I present my resignation, and I give it a try and won't lose anything." The fact that the exit option is one that he puts forward as a course of action to be considered if necessary suggests that his level of loyalty to the party itself is not very high.

Azmi Abadir, one of the few Copts to have joined the Wasat Party, also expressed his intention to resign from the party. He felt that he had been placed in the party merely as a token and was completely marginalized, despite the fact, in his own words, that the leaders of the party, Abu al-'Ila Madi and Essam Sultan, repeatedly showcased his membership to demonstrate that the party is open to Christians. He expressed his intention to leave Wasat and join one of the liberal political parties. He would not write the reasons for his resignation from the party in his letter "because they are all my friends." In effect, he concluded, he joined Wasat out of *mugamla*—as an act of friendly courtesy toward his friends. Interestingly, the same word appeared in the narrative of Salah Makram Elia, who spoke of his enduring relationship with neighbors and friends to whom he had been bound since 1986 with "strong friendship characterized by *mawadda* [conviviality], *irtibat* [connectedness], and *mugamalat* [reciprocation of favors to strengthen ties]."

It can be gathered from these interviews that these individuals, unlike Rafik Habib, are not ideologically committed to the Islamist school of thinking, and that their strategy of joining is driven by pragmatic considerations. In the next chapter, the instrumental role of religion in the parliamentary and presidential elections is discussed with a focus on its impact on social cohesion and sectarian relations.

11 Winning for God: Sectarianism in the Parliamentary and Presidential Elections

The parliamentary and presidential elections that followed the 25 January Revolution were supposed to be milestones on Egypt's path to democratization. While many of the ills of the elections witnessed during Mubarak's regime were also witnessed in the transitional phase, such as vote buying, rotating votes, and the violation of publicity rules as well as ceilings on campaign funding, one of the most striking characteristics of these two elections was that they were among the most intensely sectarian witnessed in Egypt's history. This chapter examines ways in which religion was instrumentalized in these elections, their implications for different actors, and their possible long-term impact on social cohesion and participatory politics.

It will be argued that the elections both represented a manifestation of the extent of communalization and were a contributing factor to its exacerbation and intensification by framing messages around religion rather than party agendas; by circulating rumors about candidates' religious affiliations and whether they were in God's camp or not; and by using religious symbols, spaces, and discourses to mobilize support.

The 2011–2012 Sectarian Elections

The first parliamentary elections in post-Mubarak Egypt occurred in a context of extreme political uncertainty, as the youth revolutionary groups were protesting against SCAF in Tahrir Square and there were question marks as to whether the elections would go ahead at all. The elections did go ahead, over three stages from November 2011 to January 2012. Egypt's electoral system was a mixed one, combining party proportional lists and single member districts (SMD). According to the constitution, 50 percent of the seats were supposed to be allocated to party proportional lists and 50 percent to single member districts. However, the electoral law—in violation of the constitution—allowed parties to compete for over two-thirds of the seats. In reality parties ignored the law altogether and in many cases put forward their own candidates even for the single member district seats (Rabi' 2012: 50).

Not surprisingly, the legitimacy of the parliamentary composition was from the very start called into question. In the end, in a historical ruling in June 2012, the Supreme Constitutional Court deemed the 2011–2012 parliament null and void due to the violation of the proportional list–single member ratio.

The elections witnessed an unprecedented level of political engagement in Egyptian politics: 10,251 candidates competed for 498 seats, almost double the number of candidates who competed in the 2010 elections and 2005 elections (5,411 and 5,177 respectively) (Rabi' 2012: 358). There were 49 political parties competing, compared to 22 political parties in the 2005 and 2010 elections respectively (Rabi' 2012: 360). While the general level of political activism was high, the nomination of Copts as candidates was extremely poor. It is estimated that nationwide only 120 Christians put themselves forward—all on party proportional lists (Rabi' 2012: 362).

Two principal coalitions fielded candidates during the parliamentary elections. Al-Tahaluf al-Dimuqrati (Democratic Coalition) was composed of twelve political parties including the FJP, Karama (Nasserite), Ghad al-Thawra (liberal), and a number of smaller political parties. The Kotla coalition comprised three parties: the Free Egyptians, the Egyptian Social Democratic Party, and the leftist Tagammu' Party. The Salafist Nour Party had pulled out of the Democratic Coalition out of disapproval for the list of nominees and formed its own coalition of Salafist parties. Moreover, socialist parties came together to form a coalition called al-Thawra Mustamirra (The Revolution Continues). From the very outset, there was a clear polarization between the Islamist (Democratic Coalition) and so-called liberal (Kotla) camps, although when the FJP and Nour were vying for seats, competition between them was vicious. While violations during these elections were not on a par with those that had marred the 2010 parliamentary elections under Mubarak, they were in some electoral districts serious enough to be referred to court. If there is one word that best describes these elections, it is sectarian.

While the use of religion in campaigning is as old as time in Egypt, every phase of the 2011–2012 elections was deeply sectarian. The most common way religion was used was to prop up a candidate's campaign or to slam the opponent's character. Certainly the Muslim Brotherhood and Salafis were better positioned than all of the other political forces to win the elections as a result of their decades-long citizen engagement through mosques, one of the few spaces in Egypt through which people freely and collectively congregated. Their welfare services extended through NGOs established in the 1970s, and their significant funding base, allowed them a vast reach. However, the newly formed political parties were founded by renowned national leaders. For example, the Free Egyptians was founded by Coptic business tycoon Naguib Sawiris and the Social Democratic Party founded by Muhammad Abul Ghar.

Islamists launched a systematic campaign against the Kotla as being driven by crusaders, apostates, unbelievers, and those with intentions to undermine Islam. Their campaign alluded to Sawiris's party as evidence that the Kotla was being led by a Coptic unbeliever. Further, the fact that the Social Democratic Party had a higher representation of Copts fielded on its lists than any other party exposed it to accusations of being the party of the Copts. Finally, it became an open secret that the Coptic Orthodox Church leadership had instructed all its parishioners to vote for the party lists of the Kotla and those running for individual seats selected by the Kotla. Islamists and the Wafd Party in particular launched a systematic campaign against the Church for supporting the Kotla, accusing it of deepening sectarianism.

While the Coptic Orthodox Church did in effect encourage its citizens to vote for the Kotla, this cannot be considered sectarian because, in practice, it meant supporting political forces not on the basis of the religion of the candidates but their political affiliation. The fact that the Church is situated in the civil society arena means that, like other civil society organizations, it is entitled to lobby and advocate for its interests, which it clearly determined to be associated with the endorsement of the liberal forces against the Islamist wave. Since the FJP has long rested its case for the right to engage in politics on the basis that it is a political and not a religious party, the Church's stance should not have been interpreted as religious but political.

The case against the Church also rested on the fact that its premises throughout the country were supposed to be sites for religious worship and not political mobilization. This is true, but then mosques in Egypt were used for political mobilization without reservation and in a way that challenged the religious-political divide in more dangerous ways. The FJP leadership claimed that it is completely separate and independent of the Muslim Brotherhood, yet in practice the Muslim Brotherhood's mosque base was used as one of the main instruments of citizen mobilization. In view of the fact that the FJP had declared that neither its program nor its practices were religious, this constituted a flagrant violation of the political parties law. Opponents were regularly referred to as Christians (even when they had overtly Muslim names) in order to discredit them. In the Egyptian context, where in most cases citizens are able to distinguish a person's religion by his or her name, even candidates whose names were clearly Muslim (such as Amr al-Shubki, running in the middle-class Cairo district of Dokki) were called Christian in an effort by Islamists to discredit their candidature among the voters. This tactic was used systematically across the whole country. In fact, when competition grew intense between a Salafi and a Muslim Brotherhood candidate, the Salafis would seek to smear the FJP as not being truly loyal to Islam because they allowed Copts into the party. The whole approach was astutely summarized by one political commentator as "catch a Christian" (that is, catch a thief). The instrumentalization knew no limits. In Upper Egypt, it is a social taboo to ever mention a person's mother in a derogatory way in public, yet in Asyut, where one candidate, Ziad Ahmad Bahaeddin, was running under the party list of the Kotla, Islamists sought to undermine him by going to the villages telling people, "Don't vote for the son of the Christian woman!"

In some places, when the candidates went out to meet with the people, the latter would say in surprise, "So you are Muslim like us, why did they spread rumors that you are from the unbelievers?" Since the believer/unbeliever divide ran very deep, all candidates could do was to reassure their constituencies that they were indeed good Muslims. As a counter-strategy, in some instances the Kotla responded by also raising the banner of Islam, declaring that they are in favor of shari'a and hence are on Islam's side.

The cumulative impact of so much instrumentalization can only be a deepening religious intolerance toward the unbelieving other and the creation of an environment for mistrust and antagonism. Sectarian attitudes were expressed not only by the parties but also by judges and those presiding over voting stations. In some voting stations, certain judges who had strong sympathies with Islamist movements violated electoral law by not requiring women in *niqab* to show their face, which meant that women who were able to collect other people's I.D. cards were able to vote over and over again. In the voting station at al-Salih in Old Cairo, the judge adamantly refused to allow Christian women to vote on account of the fact that they were not veiled.[1] Similar violations were documented in other electorate areas.

Election Outcomes

The elections saw a relatively high percentage of voter participation, averaging 60 percent across the three rounds of voting.

Table 5: Number of seats won by different coalitions

Party	Party proportional lists (PPL)	Single member districts (SMD)	Total seats	Percentage of parliament
Freedom and Justice coalition*	127	100	227	45.58
Nour coalition**	96	21	127	25.50
Wafd	36	2	38	7.63
Kotla***	33	1	34	6.83
Wasat	10	0	10	2.01
al-Islah wa-l-Tanmiya	8	1	9	1.81
al-Thawra Mustamirra	7	0	7	1.41
Independent candidates		27	27	5.42
Other			19	3.82
Total parliamentary seats			498	100

Source: Rabi' (2012: 378–79).
* These included ten non-Muslim Brotherhood members; the majority are Islamist sympathizers.
** These included fourteen members of the Gama'a al-Islamiya
*** These included thirteen seats for the Free Egyptians party, eighteen seats for the Egyptian Social Democratic Party, two for Tagammu', and one seat for the coalition overall.

The Islamist parties represented a clear majority in parliament, comprising 69.7 percent of the total seats. The Islamist parties comprised the FJP, Nour, Hizb al-Bina' wa-l-Tanmiya (Building and Development, the political party formed by the Gama'a al-Islamiya after the 25 January Revolution), Wasat, and al-Assla (Abu Zeida 2012: 407). The Muslim Brotherhood's FJP won 42.7 percent of the votes, Nour won 22.1 percent, al-Wafd 7.5 percent, the Egyptian Social Democratic Party 3.4 percent, the Free Egyptians 2.8 percent, the Building and Development Party 2.4 percent, Wasat Party 2 percent, the Reform and Development Party 1.8 percent, and the Socialist Populist coalition 1.4 percent. The remaining percentages were negligible and also include those who ran as independents (Abu Zeida 2012: 405).

The 2011/2012 parliament was one characterized by the political marginalization of women, youth, and Copts. The first post-Mubarak parliament represented almost a replica of the old parliament in its political marginalization of groups that have been historically sidelined. Women acquired only 9 seats of 498 in parliament, five of which belonged to the FJP, representing 2 percent of parliament. This represented a significant drop from the previous (2010) parliamentary elections, which saw women's attainment of 64 seats. Youth representation was equally negligible (Rabi' 2012: 390–92).

Of the 498 *elected* MPs, six were Copts, representing 1.2 percent of parliament. Five were men, and one was a woman. Of the six, three belonged to Kotla, one belonge to Wafd, one belonged to Karama, and one belonged to Hurriya. Three came from Cairo, two from Upper Egypt (one Minya, one Asyut), and one from the Red Sea governorate. What is striking is that all of the elected Coptic MPs won on the party proportional lists. Not a single Coptic candidate won on the single member district. The fact that they all won on party proportional lists is commensurate with the body of literature mentioned in the introduction that minorities have consistently fared better in party proportional lists, where they were embedded in and backed by a party. The fact that not a single Copt was able to win in a single member district may be due to a number of factors, such as the lack of individual appeal of the candidate or the strength of the competing candidate. However, it may also be as a consequence of the deepened religious lines in Egypt, which would inhibit the Muslim majority from voting for a candidate seen to belong to the "opposite" faith.

In addition to these six elected Coptic members of parliament, an additional five Coptic members were appointed by SCAF. The head of state has the right to appoint ten of the 498 members of parliament and these appointees were usually Copts and women to mitigate the gap in representation. In the absence of a president, it was SCAF that made the selection. Conventionally, the head of state selected the Coptic appointees in consultation with the Church leadership. Since such a process tends to take place behind the scenes, it is difficult to tell whether the choices were the result of a combined SCAF–Church will or whether SCAF simply rubberstamped the Church's choice of appointees.

Thus, the total number of Copts in parliament (whether elected or appointed) came to eleven, representing 2.2 percent of parliamentary seats. This is more or less commensurate with previous election results (in 2010 there were ten members comprising 2 percent; in 2005, there were six members representing 1.4 percent; and in 2000 there were seven members comprising 1.5 percent) (Rabi' 2012: 416).

In addition to the Copts' poor representation in parliament, Abu Zeida notes the complete absence of Copts in the parliament's sub-committees. There are nineteen subcommittees in the Majlis al-Sha'b, or People's Assembly, including sub-committees for foreign affairs, defense and national security, human rights, health and environment, youth, and so on, and they have substantial powers. The FJP led twelve out of the nineteen, while three were led by Nour and four by the other political forces (three of which are known for their Islamist sympathies). There was not a single Copt in either the leadership or membership of these committees, despite the fact that they were present in such committees in previous parliaments (Abu Zeida 2012: 416).

The Short-lived Parliament:
The Islamic National Democratic Party?

The Muslim Brotherhood assumed leadership of parliament by virtue of the clear majority of seats won by the FJP in the parliamentary elections and the election of FJP's Muhammad Saad al-Katatni as the speaker of parliament. Moreover, as mentioned above, the Muslim Brotherhood assumed leadership of the majority of parliamentary sub-committees. Where the Brotherhood did not hold leadership, the usual runners-up were Salafis. The FJP had promised that parliament would be run democratically, decisions arrived at through consensus politics, and active measures taken to involve and engage with MPs from across the political spectrum. Instead, the FJP ran parliament on the principle of majoritarian politics, relying on the implicit coalition between Muslim Brotherhood and Salafi MPs to further particular political initiatives. In the process, certain voices, such as those of the non-Islamist revolutionary youth and politically liberal MPs, were sidelined. Some began to compare the FJP in their governing of parliament to their predecessor in the time of Mubarak, the National Democratic Party. Despite the FJP's rhetoric of recognizing and promoting the citizenship of all Egyptians, it failed the first real test it encountered when the sectarian strife at al-Amiriya was referred to parliament.

Emad Gad, an MP belonging to the Egyptian Social Democratic Party, requested from FJP Speaker of Parliament Muhammad al-Katatni that the matter be discussed in parliament. Al-Katatni refused on the basis that it may stir people's feelings if it were openly discussed in a session that is likely to be broadcast on television. Gad threatened that unless the matter was taken seriously by parliament, he would resign. After much press coverage condemning these reconciliation meetings, the human rights committee affiliated to the parliament sent a fact-finding mission to the village and announced its rejection of the reconciliation committee decision to expel the families and its insistence on matters being relegated to the court system. However, the fact-finding mission from the People's Assembly did not condemn the reconciliation committee meetings and only mentioned the return of five out of the eight families. Moreover, the topic of compensation for the families whose property had been attacked was not broached.

Perhaps the most disconcerting aspect of the fact-finding mission was its reluctance to criticize the management of sectarianism through the reconciliation committees. The question of who is charged with the responsibility to mediate in these reconciliation committees is one of legitimacy—the populist legitimacy of Islamist leaders or the legitimacy of the rule of law. In view of the weakness (deliberate or incidental) of the police in enforcing the rule of law, there would be no guarantee that further attacks on vulnerable members of the community would be stopped unless the relevant local powers complied with it. In such a context, even if non-Salafi members were to mediate in the reconciliation committees, would they have the authority to exercise morally binding decisions that would protect non-Muslim members of the community from further assault?

The fact-finding mission also attacked the media and human rights organizations for inflaming sectarian sentiment by giving the matter more attention than it was due. This rhetoric was very much reminiscent of Mubarak's policy of sectarian denial and reflected how the new status quo also sought to vilify anyone who challenged injustice based on religious grounds by saying this increased sectarianism rather than dampening it.

The Presidential Elections

The presidential elections took on an intense sectarian coloring on par with that of the parliamentary elections. The first round of presidential elections was held on 23 and 24 May 2012 and the second round was held on 16 and 17 June 2012. The leading candidates during the first round were Abdel Moneim Abul Fotouh, a former Muslim Brotherhood member; Amr Moussa, former secretary general of the Arab League and one-time foreign minister under Mubarak; Ahmad Shafiq, briefly prime minister under Mubarak during the 25 January Revolution and retired air marshal; Muhammad Morsi, a leading figure in the Muslim Brotherhood and chairman of the FJP in the wake of the 25 January Revolution; Hamdeen Sabahi, leader of the Nasserist Karama Party and long-standing opposition figure under presidents Mubarak and Sadat; and Khaled Ali, a young Egyptian lawyer and labor activist.

The first round of elections gave Ahmad Shafiq and Muhammad Morsi the lead, while in the second round Morsi won the vote by almost 3 percent. The fact that both men took the lead in the elections was not surprising to anyone in touch with the Egyptian street, although for the revolutionaries, the fact that Egyptians voted in such large numbers for Shafiq was considered an insult to the revolution, and conspiracy theories of outside intervention were rampant. However, not all Shafiq supporters were *filul* (or 'remnants' of the old regime), and many had originally been very sympathetic to the 25 January Revolution and participated in the mass demonstrations that led to Mubarak's downfall. Their vote for Shafiq was not an indication of their yearning for the Mubarak regime, but for something else. There were two pressing issues that made people tilt toward Ahmad Shafiq: security and economic well-being. From the 25 January uprisings, the police had staged a vendetta against the Egyptian people. Consequently, many Egyptians talked of *inflat amni*, or 'lax security,' describing a situation in which gangs and thugs ruled supreme, police stations turned a blind eye to crime, and there were daily rumors of kidnappings of men, women, and children. This sense of fear for one's safety and that of one's family was shared across all classes in the country.

In socially deprived areas, men no longer felt that it was safe for women to walk in the streets alone after dusk. Women who were accustomed to visiting family and doing errands found themselves asking for their husbands' accompaniment. Children who used to go to school on their own or in groups were being taken and picked up by their parents. Crime rose tremendously. The keys to dealing with this widespread lack of security were in the hands of the ruling military—after all, during the parliamentary and presidential elections when SCAF willed that there be no threats to human security, none had occurred. People in voting lines during the first round of the presidential elections talked of the need for a strong leader who could fix the security situation and resume law and order.

The second factor that drove many citizens to vote for Shafiq was desperation for their economic well-being. The economic situation prior to the 25 January uprising had admittedly been dire, but things became considerably worse after the revolution. Many Egyptians lost their jobs, experienced a drop in wages, or found themselves working hugely increased hours just to be able to put enough food on the table. Factories closed down, tourism came to a virtual halt, and prices skyrocketed. In Shafiq, voters hoped to find a resumption of "the wheel of production."

Yet the announcement of the verdict on 2 June 2012 of the trials of Mubarak, his sons, and members of the security apparatus and Mubarak's business cronies worked in favor of the Muslim Brotherhood. After the results of the first round of presidential elections, they realized that they had lost a substantial constituency among those who had voted for them in the parliamentary elections. The FJP's performance in parliament had cost them a considerable amount of support. Hence in response to the results of the first round of presidential elections, the Muslim Brotherhood changed their strategy from asking people to vote for the FJP to pressing them not to vote for the so-called *filul*, represented by Ahmad Shafiq. The acquittal of six of the former regime's key actors and the right awarded to Hosni Mubarak and Habib al-Adli, the notorious ex-minister of interior, to appeal against their life-imprisonment verdict generated a strong sense of indignation among a significant proportion of the population, prompting the return of *milyuniya*s (though with smaller turnouts). The Brotherhood seized the opportunity to champion these protests and announced that in the event that it came to power, it would avenge the blood of the martyrs of the 25 January Revolution.

During the presidential elections, the Coptic electoral vote featured prominently. The Copts' vote in the first round was split among Shafiq, Sabahi, and Moussa. Sabahi was a favorite among Coptic youth, while Shafiq and Moussa fared better among the older generation.[2] Assurances from Islamists both in Morsi's and Abul Fotouh's presidential campaigns that Copts would enjoy full rights of citizenship under their rule, and that they would be governed by their own religious code, were for the most part met with suspicion.

Opposition among Coptic voters to any Islamist candidate was intense. This was partly ideological, Islamist identity being seen as anathema to Egyptian identity, and partly as a consequence of the backlash against equal citizenship for Copts experienced during the recent rise of Islamists. In focus groups undertaken with Coptic women in May 2012, many said they would vote for Shafiq because in addition to economic instability and lax security, their experiences of religious discrimination had intensified in the past year. They spoke about more subtle changes happening as a consequence of the growing powers of Islamists in society and politics. For example, in some of the schools in the poor informal settlement of Mu'assasat al-Zakat, Christian and Muslim children were separated into two classes, and incidents of heightened discrimination against non-Muslim pupils were reported. According to the Coptic women living in Mu'assasat al-Zakat, the rhetoric of *kuffar* (infidels) was becoming increasingly common in daily interactions, and those deploying it were the Muslim Brotherhood and Salafis. For many Copts who had supported the revolution, what they desperately yearned for was a leader who could rein in the Islamists, which they believed would necessarily reduce the level of animosity toward them in society.

Irrespective of whether the Copts voted for Shafiq, Sabahi, or Moussa in the first round of the presidential elections, a minute percentage would in all likelihood have voted for Abdel Moneim Abul Fotouh and an even smaller percentage would have voted for Morsi. The Coptic voting pattern infuriated Islamists, who launched an intense campaign to vilify Copts for their "sectarian voting." The Gama'a al-Islamiya issued a statement declaring that among the most important reasons for Shafiq's success was "the sectarian vote endorsing Shafiq since the Copts gave their votes to Shafiq in accordance with the directions given by the Church and this is something to be sorry for."[3] Prominent judge Noha al-Zeini remarked that while the Coptic Orthodox Church leadership did not officially endorse any one candidate, priests were of course supporting non-Islamist candidates via the churches. This, she explained, was a natural reaction to the mobilization of voters in mosques prompting them not to vote for a liberal candidate, a *kafir* (infidel), and through the media in which Copts were repeatedly referred to by the Islamists as *ahl al-dhimma* (historically, the non-Muslim citizens of an Islamic state or polity). She argued that Copts were not to blame if their reaction was to vote against the Islamist candidates, and that it is the majority that should be blamed for starting this sectarian voting in the first place.[4] Nabil 'Abd al-Fattah, political analyst at the Al-Ahram Center for Political and Strategic Studies, was also of the opinion that of the five million who voted for Shafiq, the great majority were Copts and that greater effort was needed to reassure them so that they did not feel driven to voting against Islamists.[5]

However, the contention that Shafiq's large number of votes was due to the Coptic vote is ill-grounded given that the bulk of the votes in his favor came from the Delta governorates (Sharqiya, Minufiya, Gharbiya), where Copts comprise a minute percentage of the population. This would suggest that the highest number of votes for Shafiq came from Muslims. In fact, the governorates conventionally associated with the highest proportion of Copts (Minya, Asyut, Cairo, Giza, and Alexandria) provided Shafiq with only a marginal proportion of his overall votes (see below).

Table 6: Number of votes for Ahmad Shafiq, according to governorates with highest votes, first round

Governorate	Number of votes	Percentage of candidate's overall votes
Cairo	934,198	16.95
Sharqiya	627,808	11.39
Minufiya	586,345	10.64
Gharbiya	459,637	8.34
Daqahliya	418,855	7.60
Giza	411,286	7.46
Qalyubiya	395,553	7.18
Minya	265,402	4.8
Alexandria	212,219	3.85
Asyut	193,503	3.51

Even if all the Copts in Minya, Asyut, Cairo, and Alexandria had voted for Shafiq, this would still not have been enough to put him in the lead in these governorates because the percentage of citizens voting in the two governorates was high.

Table 7: Number of votes for Muhammad Morsi, according to governorates with highest votes, first round

Governorate	Number of votes	Percentage of candidate's overall votes
Cairo	589,710	10.41
Giza	556,630	9.83
Sharqiya	536,634	9.48
Minya	407,201	7.19
Beheira	392,487	6.93
Daqahliya	381,639	6.74
Qalyubiya	302,352	5.34
Fayoum	289,485	5.11
Alexandria	269,455	4.76
Beni Suef	260,041	4.59

Nevertheless, the first round of elections showed that there was a very close contest between Morsi (24.8 percent of votes) and Shafiq (23.7 percent of votes). In terms of numbers, a few thousand votes would have made a difference. In other words, even if Copts were a minority, they had the political weight in this case to make a difference. Coptic electoral patterns during the May–June 2012 presidential elections therefore had two key implications, the first of which was that although Coptic citizens were often treated as passive political actors, inconsequential to the political scene, they were an important political constituency in their own right, one that could not be sidelined. In short, as political commentator and television show host Bassem Youssef pointed out, they cannot simply be dealt with as a powerless minority.[6] This necessarily raised questions regarding the percentage of Copts in the population at large. The second implication of the public attention to Copts' voting patterns was an intimidation campaign in the second round of elections to dissuade them from going to vote. Coptic citizens were in some areas exposed to direct verbal assaults and threatened with grave consequences should they vote for Shafiq in the second round of the presidential elections. While a segregation of votes on religious grounds is not possible, it is likely that a drop in votes for Shafiq in the Upper Egyptian governorates of Minya and Asyut is partly attributable to a drop in Copts' participation in the elections. In the second round, Morsi won the presidency by a small margin of votes (51.73 percent) compared to Shafiq (48.27 percent). In Minya and Asyut, and particularly in areas with a high concentration of Copts (such as Dayrut and Abu Qurqas), citizens were told that if they went to the polling stations, their homes and property would be burned down, and that even if they did not vote and Shafiq won, their houses would be burned down anyway.[7]

The use of intimidation against Copts went largely unreported in the media as the focus was on what was happening inside the polling stations. However, the National Council for Human Rights (NCHR) highlighted in its report on the second round of elections that Copts were prevented from going to the voting stations and that assaults were instigated against them. Of the complaints the NCHR received, the highest number (thirty-two) was related to incidents of campaigning for a particular candidate within the voting station, which is prohibited by law, followed by attempts to influence voters (twenty-nine), incidents of preventing Copts from going to polling stations (twelve), and assaults on Copts (nine) (NCHR, Unit for Support of Elections memo, June 2012, Indicators of the second round). Nonetheless, the report concluded that these violations were not sufficient to obstruct citizens' free exercise of their agency. This is a somewhat perplexing conclusion to draw, if one portion of the Egyptian population (Copts) were terrorized out of going to polling stations. How can this not be sufficiently inhibitive as to undermine the election results, at least in the electoral districts where such violations occurred?

Farouk Sultan, announcing the results of the presidential election on behalf of the Supreme Presidential Electoral Commission (SPEC) on 24 June 2012, did not deny that such violations vis-à-vis Coptic voters had occurred.[8] He said the electoral commission was not able to discover the identity of the perpetrators and whether their intention was achieved or not. He added that in the village of Abu Henes in Minya, the turnout was 2,437 in the first round and 2,464 in the second, and hence the SPEC had decided to dismiss the claim of intimidation. The justifications given for dismissing the claims are interesting. Since the prevention of Coptic Christians from voting occurred in more than one village and more than one governorate, it is difficult to arrive at the conclusion that neither the prosecutor general nor the police were able to identify the intimidators and the impact of their behavior in any of the villages. Moreover, the fact that there was an increase in turnout in the village of Abu Henes does not preclude the possibility that the threats did have an impact on voters who had not voted in the first round but who wished to vote in the second. SPEC's decision to dismiss such complaints sent a clear signal to all political actors that the Coptic Christian minority's exclusion from the political process would be tolerated. It remains to be seen if this precedent (of dismissing the terrorization of Copts in order to prevent them from exercising their right to vote) will influence the political strategies deployed by contenders in future elections, whether on a local, parliamentary, or presidential level. SPEC's verdict on these violations has also sent a clear signal to Christians to consider political isolation as they need not participate.

When the results of the first round of elections were announced, the FJP's first strategy was to encourage people not to vote for the *ancien régime*. The focus of their strategy was to remind people of the horrors of Mubarak's regime and how, by voting for Shafiq, they were reinstating that very system. They were backed in their plea by some of the revolutionary forces, such as the April 6 Movement, which also believed that any option would be tolerated except that of having Shafiq in power. When that strategy did not seem to work, the FJP changed its approach and focused on why voting for Shafiq would be voting against Islam and voting for Morsi would be voting for Islam. This instrumentalization of religion was also catalyzed by the fact that there was no distinction between the Muslim Brotherhood as a movement that engages in *da'wa* on the ground and the FJP, which is prohibited from using religion for political ends.

When Morsi won the presidential elections, he vowed repeatedly to be the president of all Egyptians and in his early speeches sought to assure Copts that their citizenship rights would be secured. In view of the fact that the elections exposed the extent of sectarian sentiment in Egypt and also contributed to its intensification, it remains to be seen whether or not Morsi has the political will to adopt an integrationist stance toward Copts or whether there will be a division of roles in policy whereby an official discourse claims one thing and unofficial practice pertains to another. It also remains to be seen how responsive different nodes of power within the Coptic population (Church, youth movements, lay members) will be to the new president.

Conclusion: Walking next to the Wall, inside the Wall, and away from the Wall

"We are now going through a phase where we are not required to walk next to the wall, but walk in the wall."
    – Prominent lay leader within the Coptic Orthodox Church
        on the state of sectarian relations in Egypt in 2011

In *Hassan and Morcos*, a highly acclaimed film about Muslim–Christian relations in Egypt, featuring prominent actors Omar Sharif (playing the Muslim Hassan) and Adel Imam (playing the Christian Morcos), there are two scenes in particular that are laden with humor and very telling about the state of Christian–Muslim affairs. Since the film script has been published (Mo'aty 2008:17), it is worthwhile quoting the relevant parts:[1]

Scene 5
Strict security procedures surrounding a large building; we see police cars and central security forces surrounding the building. The camera angle rises to show us a sign—"the 51st conference on national unity." We see sheikhs and priests entering the electronic gates.

The [news] correspondent:
The 51st conference on national unity advocates national unity, bringing together Muslims and Christians on the land of the Crescent and the Cross.

Then we see to the side two priests walking together, one whispering in the other's ear:

Priest one: What conferences, Luka! Even if we live for a hundred years in this country, we won't get anything. We can't build a church and we can't fix a toilet in a church without getting a permit that takes a year to obtain!

Priest two: And it is not just that! Not one of our own [people] gets appointed in a position in the state. Tell me how many Christian ministers do you have in the government!

Priest one: It is all kisses and hugs and conference announcements, but what is in the heart is in the heart!

Two sheikhs crossing the road to the entrance of the conference are whispering:

Sheikh one: Oh, Sheikh Gad, what persecution are they talking about? We are the ones persecuted! Every time we build a mosque they build a church next to it. Three quarters of the country's wealth is in their hands. They have left nothing [no trade] that they don't work in!

Sheikh two: And bank managers and all the CEOs of the large investment companies are Christians!

Sheikh one: They kept on saying "our feast is not a [public] holiday" until all their feasts have become holidays and together with ours, nobody works in this country any more, we are spending our days on holiday!

Scene 6
Inside the conference hall, one of the sheikhs is speaking at the podium:

Sheikh: Our religion has called upon us to treat our Christian brothers well and I feel that the sentiments of love and fraternity that bind us have reached their height . . . as for the fanatics and terrorists that bear upon the Islamic *umma* and bring us ill repute, they have nothing to do with Islam, and Islam is innocent of them, the innocence of the wolf from the blood of Jacob.

Intense applause and people nodding with their heads and we see all four men, the two priests and two sheikhs calling out, hugging, and shaking hands:

All: Long live the Crescent with the Cross, long live the Crescent with the Cross!

And the scene continues.

These two scenes encapsulate well the disconnect between the publicized discourse in the formal arena and the hidden narratives of informal spaces. It seems that there are spaces in which there is an expectation of a particular discourse, a modus operandi of how to engage with sectarian matters. There is then another space, away from the official glaze, where the insecurities, the deep sense of grievance, and the rumors circulate. The situation is almost schizophrenic, with the official discourse manufacturing a mantra of unity that at times seems artificial and contrived. This situation typifies what James Scott terms the official versus the hidden transcript, which reflects the dynamics of a particular power hierarchy. The side conversation between the two priests, which is very different from the publicized stance, reflects what Scott (1990: xii) observes, namely that "every subordinate group out of its ordeal creates a hidden script that represents its critique of power spoken behind the back of the dominant." The narrative of exposure to persistent religious discrimination (in relation to places of worship and equal representation) based on an inherent fanaticism that runs deep shows an acute awareness on the part of many Copts of their predicament as second-class citizens, and this hidden transcript represents a resistance to it as it shows a subversion of the politically correct account of perfect fraternity and harmony based on equality and mutual acknowledgment.

Yet those in a dominant position also share a hidden transcript, which is critically important in highlighting how power hierarchies are justified. As Scott reminds us, "The powerful for their part also develop a hidden transcript representing the practices and claims of their rule that cannot be openly avowed" (1990: xii). This manifests itself in the hidden transcript of the two sheikhs. Beyond the gaze of the media, the sheikhs are aware that Copts talk about persecution, and they find no grounds for this in reality— they reiterate the rumor that Copts have asserted a powerful presence in the realm of the market and trade. They negate Copts' sense of a lack of recognition by the majority by making reference to the fact that some years ago, the government made 7 January (Coptic Christmas) a public holiday for all, Muslims and Christians. They wonder if granting citizens this additional day off has undermined the work ethic just in order to please the religious minority. In other words, they feel that the minority is being appeased at the expense of the country's national interests.

This duality of discourse, an official one and a hidden one, reflects the state of sectarian denial Egypt is in, which is in turn indicative of a power hierarchy that wishes to maintain the status quo. Occasionally this official discourse is punctured by brave attempts by those who wield power to articulate inequalities and propose active measures to redress them. The Oteify Report, published at a time of intense discrimination, is one of them. Regrettably, these official stances are few and far between and are never followed through at an implementation level because resistance to challenging the status quo runs very deep.

The challenges of fostering unity while recognizing pluralism are not particular to Egypt. The structural causes of the rise of sectarianism and the proposed policies, approaches, and frameworks needed to manage and mitigate religious tensions have been time and time again developed, deliberated, and disseminated. Yet the political will to pursue a policy of unity through pluralism is weak, and no amount of flagrant exposure of the persistent social and political cost of ignoring sectarianism seems to alter policies.

This concluding chapter summarizes ways in which the findings presented in this book challenge some of the normative values and arguments related to sectarian conflict in Egypt and discusses some of the possible scenarios for the future.

The Three-D Policy:
Denial, Demonization, Distribution of Blame

One of the striking patterns of engagement with sectarian assaults on Copts in Egypt is a policy pursued by parts (but not all) of the media and by officials that involves denying that the assaults are sectarian. This entails denying that reactions are driven by hostility toward the religious other and lead to demonization of the victims—the implication being that they have done something to incur the wrath of the reasonable majority—and the distribution of blame, which occurs literally by arresting victims and perpetrators and morally by denying that there are injustices perpetrated through power inequalities. Such a pattern can be seen in many of the sectarian acts of violence that took place in Mubarak's era, as well as post-Mubarak, as is evident in the case of the treatment of the *zabbalin* (garbage collectors) or the Maspero Massacre.

This three-D policy may take various forms. Sometimes the sectarian nature of an incident is not denied but represented in a way that downplays its severity or its scale, or conceals the real perpetrators behind it. It obstructs the possibilities for addressing the structural causes of ruptures in social cohesion and by default increases the mistrust on both sides. There is a need for the emergence of local, collective, non-state actors that can expose violations, press for their recognition, advocate for policy action, and carry the political weight to hold accountable those who are in power. At the moment there are efforts of this kind on the ground but because they lack a strong collective will behind them and the kind of political weight that derives from a clearly defined constituency, they remain quite weak.

Social Cohesion is under Threat
from *within* Communities Themselves

As highlighted in the quantitative analysis, one of the key triggers of communal tensions is when, on a local level, an ordinary, day-to-day dispute that has nothing to do with religious differences assumes a sectarian character. This raises alarm bells regarding the extent to which the social fabric in society has come under strain. It is telling that in one focus group in May 2012 in a poor squatter settlement of Cairo (Mu'assasat al-Zakat) one Coptic woman confided that what worried her the most now was the speed with which things that have nothing to do with religion whatsoever rapidly develop into sources of sectarian conflict. She said that she had stopped allowing her son to play football with his friends in the neighborhood alleys in case they had a routine disagreement (as children do when playing) and the matter assumed a sectarian dimension, with Muslims taking the side of the Muslim boy and Christians having to remove the Coptic boy from the scene before rumors spread and violence ensured. This is in no way to suggest that this kind of strain on social cohesion represents the situation across the entire country. It is to say, however, that against the backdrop of the salience of religious difference in everyday life for a considerable part of the population that has been denied opportunities for awareness raising, education, and social and economic well-being, the conditions are often ripe for severe ruptures in communal relations arising out of the most insignificant, marginal everyday life occurrences.

Two particular triggers are significant in virtually all the cases of the instigation of sectarian violence explored: the power of rumor and speedy mass mobilization. As the documentation of incidents shows, rumors of conspiracies to assault Muslims or denigrate Islam and its symbols become central to the mobilization of bias. These do not happen in a vacuum and often there are actors who assume the role of mobilizing the crowds to act. What is alarming is the speed with which people mobilize and engage in torching, looting, and plundering targeted homes and property. At its height, it has put Egypt in danger of civil war, as when SCAF called upon "honorable citizens" to defend the Egyptian army it said was under attack by Christians. The discourse then did not become one of defending the Egyptian army only, but of defending Islam itself. Similarly, when, following the clashes in front of the presidential palace (al-Ittihadiya) in December 2012, Muhammad al-Beltagi, the head of the FJP, claimed that 60 percent of the protesters who were demonstrating against President Morsi were Christian, this was in the context of a deeply polarized political scene a highly inflammatory statement inciting anti-Christian sentiment among the pro-Morsi camp.

Sectarian assaults on non-Muslims increased during Egypt's first year of transition both in frequency and in severity. This challenges the notion that communal tensions can be solely attributed to the Mubarak regime and will die down as political spaces open up. This is commensurate with democratization literature, in particular that which draws on the experiences of Eastern European countries, where transitions from authoritarian rule unleashed social and political forces that heightened the potential for ethnic conflict. However, as with several Eastern European examples, ethnic difference did not mean that ethnic conflict was inevitable. By giving due recognition to minorities and taking active steps to create an inclusive political order, these countries ensured that the conditions for pluralistic societies were laid. In Egypt, the ousting of Mubarak offered a golden opportunity to put in place the foundations of an inclusive political order. The repertoire of good will built at Tahrir Square, the images, stories, and songs about Muslims and Copts as Egyptians joined in a common struggle for a better future for themselves and for their children could have been reproduced and reinforced for the purposes of a genuine discussion about a new era of national unity. Operationally, it would have required two policies: a zero-tolerance policy toward sectarian assault on non-Muslim minorities and active measures to include them in all policy-making positions. Neither policy was adopted. What emerged was a political order that seemed to put in place the procedural elements of a democracy (such as elections) but suffered from the tyranny of a majoritarian political order that was by no means inclusive: excluded were the youth who led the revolution, the women who had stood side by side with men in every single public square, and the Copts, who had participated in the revolution at every level and every point in time.

While it is important to emphasize that SCAF dealt with all revolutionary liberal forces with ruthlessness and repression, it is also important to recognize its role in fostering a status quo of religious persecution. SCAF became the perpetrator of sectarian assault, as was witnessed in the firing of live ammunition on demonstrators in Muqattam and in its responsibility for the Maspero Massacre. SCAF became complicit in administering injustice, giving its blessing to the Islamist-led informal reconciliation committees. One can only speculate as to why SCAF assumed such a discriminatory policy. I would argue that it stemmed from two realities: its informal pact with Islamists and the fact that SCAF itself is not a separate island, for religious bias permeates its ranks in the way it does the rest of the Egyptian population.

In the previous chapters, it has been argued that the SSI assumed a key role in 'managing' the 'sectarian file' in Egypt. In so doing, it was on occasion responsible for instigating sectarianism by turning a blind eye to reports of rumors spreading, flyers being distributed, and so on. It has also played a central role in mismanaging sectarian conflict to the point of complicity. The reconciliation committees were run by the SSI, and it is owing to its mediation that injustice was delivered. In other instances, it played a key role in positively deflating tensions and using hard power to prevent sectarian assaults from being launched. Much depended on who presided over the SSI in a particular geographical location as well as the nature of the instructions they were receiving from headquarters. In post-Mubarak Egypt, there are signs that the SSI is still involved in managing sectarian matters under the new umbrella of "the National Security apparatus," although it has assumed a more covert role.

At the same time, it would be inaccurate to suggest that without the SSI, there would be no sectarian conflict. The SSI was only able to play such a role because there were so many enabling environmental factors arising from the growing religiosity of the wider Muslim population that made it possible for them to divide and rule so effectively in this way.

The policies and practices of Islamist actors who assumed political power in government and on the streets between February 2011 and February 2012 have directly undermined social cohesion and contributed to an escalation of sectarian tensions. While 2011 was far bloodier than 2012 in terms of lives lost in sectarian attacks, the number of sectarian assaults increased from 70 in 2011 to 112 in 2012. Despite the pronouncement of several reassuring statements that Copts have nothing to fear from Islamists being in power, the role of Islamists in contributing to a divisive social and political reality manifests itself on several fronts:

- The return of the discourse of *dhimmi*s and Nazarenes and the issuance of public statements and fatwas that encourage religious hatred.
- The mobilization of the masses in public displays of rejection of the non-Muslim other.
- The organization of public dissent against the appointment of a governor who is a Coptic Christian on the basis that Christians should not rule over Muslims is a case in point.
- The calls for jihad to free allegedly Muslim women from the shackles of imprisonment by the Church manifested itself in sustained campaigns involving the mobilization of hundreds. It ended, in one case, with the burning of two churches, in Imbaba.
- The enforcement of unjust agreements following sectarian assaults through the infamous reconciliation committees. The replacement of these reconciliation committees by Salafi and Muslim Brotherhood leaders after the 25 January Revolution only served to enforce the notion that there is no rule of law and that there is only the rule of the majority. In effect, it represents one of the most conspicuous cases of the erosion of the fundamental precepts of citizenship, since it sent clear signals that the only way to avoid becoming vulnerable to assault is to seek the patronage and protection of the Islamists who rule the street.
- The instrumentalization of religion in the constitutional referendum of March 2011, the parliamentary elections of November 2011–January 2012, and the presidential elections of May–June 2012 in a way that deepened the religious divide. Clearly there was a disconnect between the discourse that assured Copts that their full citizenship rights were recognized and the reality on the ground.
- More generally, the rise of the Islamists to political power emboldened Islamist groups and movements on the streets to tell non-Muslim women, who happen to be predominantly Christian, to cover up. It

also allowed them to adopt other measures to enforce public compliance with their moral code. It has emboldened those in any position
of power, even if they are not part of the Islamist movement, to act
openly on their fanatic religious beliefs in ways that would have been
more covert during Mubarak's era. The case of a local council civil
servant denying a citizen permission to upgrade his house because he
might convert it into a church is a case in point.

Nonetheless the deep politicization of Egyptian society that has
occurred as a consequence of the 25 January uprising has also meant
increased resistance on the part of newly emerging Coptic actors. In this
book it has been argued that there has been a reconfiguration of power
dynamics vis-à-vis Coptic agency that started well before the 25 January
uprisings but that has been further consolidated in its aftermath. Such
a reconfiguration has had a positive impact by encouraging Copts to
become much more assertive in their demand for equal citizenship rights.
The emergence of civil Coptic movements with a known constituency
has proven to be a powerful source of resistance to the escalation of violence and to the growing powers of Islamist movements. While resistance
does not always produce the impact that is desired, as the Maspero Massacre has shown, it has nevertheless been successful in effecting change
in small ways, such as forcing the army to rebuild a church, forcing the
Ministry of Education to change examination dates so that Christian students can enjoy Christmas, and forcing the government to invite them to
engage in dialogue.

While Coptic resistance movements are likely to thrive in a hostile
political environment as Islamists grow increasingly intolerant of their
activism, their powers will rest on a number of strategic balances:
• Maintaining their autonomy from the Coptic Church hierarchy without exiting the Coptic Church itself;
• Building a strong constituency from within the ranks of Coptic
  Church followers while building strong alliances and coalitional links
  with opposition movements;
• Maintaining their raison d'être, which is to play an advocacy role
  in religion-based injustice while withstanding accusations of being
  sectarian;
• Allowing for diversity within while maintaining a strong, united front;
  and

- Preventing the radicalization of members if sectarian assaults increase, while preventing the co-option and infiltration of the movement by various state actors.

Future Pathways and Directions: Some Possible Scenarios

On the Coptic Orthodox Church front, the new pope may choose to rebuild a pact with the new government based on the same conditions that governed relations between Pope Shenouda and President Hosni Mubarak: securing his standing and positioning within the Coptic community and the outside world in return for public support for the government's policies. However, this is likely to backfire in the long run as it will generate the same compromises that were witnessed during the last years of Mubarak-Shenouda rule, namely that sectarian assault will be met with complacency, that the pope will rely on a number of key actors within the government, but that others within the government will circumvent those relationships and attempt to subvert them, and the highly politicized role of the Church will generate opposition from within its own ranks. On the other hand, the next pope may choose to keep a safe distance from the state, which would ultimately place him in a more marginal position politically with fewer political concessions at his disposal. However, such a position will ultimately maintain the Church's autonomy. In such a scenario the Church may choose to distinguish itself from the emerging Coptic civil society, recognizing its role in advocating Coptic rights without either appearing openly to support or oppose them. This would certainly be an ideal situation; however, it is partly dependent on the political will of the new pope, Tawadros II, and of Muhammad Morsi and other central players. For example, will the SSI return to openly playing a central role in governance, and the leading role in mediating Christian–Muslim relations? It will also ultimately depend on the Muslim Brotherhood's strategy of engagement. Will the Muslim Brotherhood in power wish to govern relations with the Coptic minority through the old millet system? The Brotherhood has been keen to focus on its belief that Copts should be governed according to their own religious laws. The Brothers were keen to show displays of respect for and solidarity with the Copts when Pope Shenouda III died in March 2012. If citizenship is going to be mediated through religious identity, then this would ultimately increase the power of the Coptic Orthodox Church in representing the Copts. The Muslim Brotherhood may wish to adopt such a stance in order to undermine the civil Coptic movements whose advocacy on Coptic grievances will undoubtedly represent a thorn in its side.

There are three possible scenarios for how the the Muslim Brotherhood-led government will engage with the Coptic question:

First scenario: revenge and containment

In view of the open and hostile opposition of Coptic citizens to the ascendency of the Muslim Brotherhood, the Brotherhood leadership might be tempted to seek to contain forms of Coptic resistance (such as the independent civil movements), put pressure on the new pope, and basically "put Copts in their place," all falling under the rubric of protecting the unity of the nation in a time of transition. Its ability to adopt a policy of containment in relation to Coptic dissidence will partly depend on the signals it is receiving from the west, in particular the United States, regarding the extent to which it will turn a blind eye to this. It is also partly dependent on the strength and unity of the internal political opposition to the Muslim Brotherhood and other Islamist groups.

Second scenario: winning over the Copts

Once the Muslim Brotherhood have consolidated their hold on power, they may feel less under threat, and may choose to adopt a conciliatory stance toward Copts as part of a wider strategy of engaging in consensus politics. Such a policy may include appointing token Copts to positions of authority and making public appearances with the new pope, granting him particular concessions regarding the building of a few more churches. The benefits to the Brotherhood of such a policy would be to demonstrate to the international community that Islam and democracy are compatible and to coopt what they would regard as radical Coptic voices within. In view of the deep mistrust felt by a large proportion of Copts toward the Muslim Brotherhood, it will take a series of concerted and consistent measures to win over a sizeable Coptic constituency. However, it is also possible that the Brotherhood may choose not to adopt such a conciliatory stance for fear of losing support from within its own rank and file and in particular of incurring the hostility of Salafis, who were important allies to the Muslim Brothers during the presidential race.

Third scenario: division of roles among the different Islamist players

I would argue that this is the most likely scenario, given that it would be in tune with the policy the Muslim Brotherhood adopted when its affiliate party, the FJP, assumed majority power in parliament. Such a policy would involve the president and the highest echelons of government deploying a discourse of equal citizenship, respect for the rights of all, and so on, while in practice giving Islamists and the general public the liberty to inhibit, suppress, and subjugate Coptic citizens. This is not to suggest that members of the public will necessarily always participate, but it is to say that the mobilization of people on religious grounds is a possibility. The benefits of such a tactic for the Brotherhood is that it would seem detached from any discriminatory policies and impress the international community with its moderate discourse while, in reality, one of its most belligerent enemies is being contained with minimal populist resistance from the majority.

Possible Future Scenarios

However, these scenarios would not occur in a vacuum, and their implementation and outcome are just as likely to depend on how social and political forces, including Copts, interact.

For the future, there seem to be three possible courses of action:

Integration

One possible scenario is the integration of Copts into the life of the nation as citizens. It has been argued in this book that the only kind of political order that would allow for this is a secular, inclusive democratic system. By secular I do not mean the negation of the role or meaning of religion in people's lives, but the acceptance of the notion of pluralist frameworks and reference points under the rubric of an Egyptian polity rather than an Islamist one. As I have argued, there is a very real tension between the Islamist political vision and that of Copts. Attempts at forcing Copts to accept Islamic civilization as the basis for a common identity are likely to backfire, as they have historically.

As for inclusive democratic policies, they can take many different forms. While this is highly controversial, I would argue that affirmative action is needed for both women and Copts in Egypt, since the level of social hostility toward their acceptance in positions of power runs very deep. Without affirmative action, both groups are likely to be excluded from the centers of power. However, quotas are a prerequisite but insufficient measure to create an inclusive democratic order. Such measures will have to be implemented in conjunction with other interventions in relation to security and the executive, judicial, and legislative branches of the state, in addition to social, cultural, and economic development. The introduction of quotas in a highly exclusionary political order will only lead to the appointment of token Copts who have no genuine links to a wider Coptic constituency. Further, the adoption of decentralization measures, which are a popular element of inclusive democratic policy programs, without fundamental changes in governance will also have a minimal impact on addressing structural causes of inequality. For example, the decentralization of decision-making to a local council level with respect to the construction and renovation of churches will be met with the same hostility and foot-dragging as when it was managed at a governorate level. Unless laws are reformed and rigorous implementation followed, decentralization will be pointless.

Another important dimension of inclusive democratic policies is the promotion of rule of law. In the case of Egypt, for example, it would mean replacing the informal reconciliation committees with proper recourse to the law and the mediation of these matters through court. However, unless the judiciary is reformed it will also rule through highly discriminatory verdicts. In short, inclusive democracy based on a common Egyptian identity (without negating religious plurality and allegiance) is necessary for the integration of the Coptic citizenry into Egyptian public and political life. However, policies will have to go beyond the procedural dimensions of liberal democracy to deal with some of the substantive socio-cultural aspects of change.

Assimilation

Assimilation differs from integration in that it necessarily requires the subjugation of one element of one's identity in order to fit in within a wider polity. During Nasser's era, for example, all identities, whether Egyptian or religious or particularistic, had to be subsumed under the pan-Arab identity. Since the Muslim Brotherhood assumed political power first in parliament (although that parliament was later declared null and void by the Egyptian Supreme Constitutional Court) and then through the presidential election, there has also been the expectation and concern that the primary allegiance of Egyptians is to the notion of the Islamic *marja'iya*. As mentioned by Rafik Habib, and before him by Yusuf al-Qaradawi, the influential Islamic theologian, Islam is an aspect of Muslim identity by virtue of Muslims' faith and civilization and for Christians by virtue of their belonging to Islamic civilization. This kind of assimilationist approach, which looks to finding common ground in the Islamic identity for Christians and Muslims, is becoming quite diffuse in many circles. In an obituary for prominent Egyptian thinker Anwar 'Abd al-Malik, Diaa Rashwan described him as faithful to his Coptic Orthodox Church but also bearing strong allegiances to the Islamic civilization to which he belonged. Rashwan described him as a person whose identity was difficult to fathom: sometimes he appeared Christian, at other times Muslim, and unless one posed a direct question regarding his religious affiliation, it would not be possible to pinpoint it.[2] This praise for Abd al-Malik, for this sense of his belonging to an Islamic civilization while being a Copt, is meant to send a message on the salient normative values around identity.

However, Copts' assimilation to an Arab identity is probably far less problematic than their assimilation to an Islamic identity, since the former does not clash with their identity whereas the latter does. Certainly there will be more Copts who will espouse the banner of Islamic civilization as the unifying base for all Egyptians. However, for the majority, they will simply retreat from public life to the greatest extent possible. If assimilation is pursued, it is likely to lead to a high level of political, social, and economic marginalization of all but the smallest number of Copts.

The expression that Copts "walk inside the wall" is intended to reflect this sense of going beyond the assumption of a marginal position to one of invisibility. It would in effect involve adopting a process of cocooning, or finding refuge in the Church to an extent far greater than that witnessed during the decades of marginalization under presidents Nasser, Sadat, and Mubarak.

Open conflict

Another possible scenario is for the Muslim Brotherhood or any other political actor in authority to increase the level of persecution and for this to be met with open resistance by Copts. In other words, if Copts collectively rise in protest as they did on previous occasions at Maspero, 'Umraniya, and in the aftermath of the Two Saints Church bombing, this will not be met with much tolerance on the part of the wider community. Already the 'hidden transcript' shared by many Egyptian Muslims is that Copts have become too big for their boots and are provoking the wrath of the majority through their protests and antagonistic marches. It is impossible to predict how Copts—or citizens in any country for that matter—will react to persecution or growing perceptions of persecution. They may retreat into a cocoon or they may choose to revolt. There are many reasons why they may not necessarily choose to adopt an accommodationist, compliant stance. First, revolt may be catalyzed by a cumulative sense of oppression based on religious identity (the case of the *zabbalin* being the most extreme example of this, although others, in particular the inhabitants of poor rural and urban areas who have experienced exclusion in a systematic way, also fit this category). Second, for many, there is a strong sense on the part of many Coptic activists of no going back; that they cannot relinquish the idea of equal citizenship even if it is not practiced. Just as the uprisings of 25 January were as much about dignity as about bread and social justice, so too the Coptic revolts were about restoring dignity and social status as much as about materialist demands.

Moreover, if Coptic movements are met with extreme repression, this may drive some underground and generate radicalized offshoots that would then play a catalytic role in mobilizing Copts. If such conflict occurs, it will pose a serious threat to all Egyptians, as it will destabilize relations in both society and politics. Finally, there is the option of emigration for the very few who qualify and who can afford it. Yet for the majority of Copts, the response to rising sectarianism will vary according to both contextual and personal factors. For many, survival strategies will include at times accommodation to their realities ("walk inside the wall") and at other moments subversion (in ever more covert ways), while in particular instances people will resort to open resistance. The question is: What will the long-term implications be for Egypt, politically, economically, and socially?

Notes

Notes to the Introduction

1 Minority Rights International, http://www.minorityrights.org/11338/press-releases/

2 Gamal Nkrumah, "Hail the Holy Synod," *Al-Ahram Weekly*, 22–28 March 2012.

3 For literature on Copts in the diaspora from a Coptic perspective, see Khalil 1999. For a study on Copts in the diaspora reflecting mainstream critiques of the diaspora in lobbying for Coptic rights back home, see al-Banna 2001.

4 Romania has a population of about 22 million, of which 89.5 percent are Romanians, 6.6 percent Hungarians, 2.5 percent Roma, 0.3 percent Ukrainians, 0.3 percent Germans, 0.2 percent Russians, 0.2 percent Turkish, and 0.4 percent others. According to these estimations, more than 10 percent of people living in Romania belong to national ethnic minorities (Filipescu 2009).

5 *Al-Masry Al-Youm*, 5 March 2011.

6 Britain's Department for International Development (DFID) definition of a political settlement.

7 This period was chosen on the basis of the availability of the day-by-day screening of more than fifteen key newspapers by the Coptic Culture Center and their dissemination in a daily report. Hani Morsi, a brilliant doctoral student at the Institute of Development Studies, then undertook data analysis and compiled the results in a classification system, presented in this book.

8 The data relied on a daily scanning of over fifteen newspapers undertaken by the Coptic Cultural Center in Cairo over the aforementioned period. Daily and weekly newspapers were thoroughly reviewed by trained researchers for news items featuring, directly or indirectly, matters pertaining to Copts, and all articles were scanned and uploaded into a daily report.

Notes to Chapter 1

1 See him, for example, appearing on al-Azhar's satellite television, Azhari TV, http://www.youtube.com/watch?v=5C7mGS5oghEat
2 For the history of Egypt during this period, see Asaf 1995.
3 "The Number of Copts in Egypt," *Akhir Sa'a*, 18 June 2012.
4 Pew Research Center, "Ask the Expert," 11 May 2011, http://pewresearch. org/pubs/1770/ask-the-expert-pew-research-center#christians-egypt
5 M. Basha, "al-'Awa bi-l-Mansura: al-fitna sababha al-'atifa," *al-Ahram*, 17 May 2011.
6 See Abou al-Ella Mady's article in *al-Karama*, 11 June 2007.
7 *al-Kiraza*, the official Church monthly magazine, issue no. 6, 1977, p. 2.
8 *Nahdat Misr*, 12–13 July 2007.
9 Gabir al-Qarmuti, "Dr. Tharwat Bassili yufajjir mufaja'a: 'adad al-Aqbat fi Misr 18.5 nasma," *Bawwabat al-Ahram al-'Arabi*, 7 January 2012, http:// arabi.ahram.org.eg/NewsQ/947.aspx
10 Heikal was a close confidant of Gamal 'Abd al-Nasser and was highly skeptical of Anwar al-Sadat's policies. He was imprisoned by Sadat in the wave of the mass arrests that took place on 3 September 1981.
11 Mustafa Kamil (1847–1908) was a prominent Egyptian nationalist political leader and writer who opposed the British occupation of Egypt. He founded the National Party in 1907 and sought to revive the concept of the Gama'a al-Islamiya.

Notes to Chapter 2

1 By 'sectarian incident' I refer to cases in which (a) there was a direct incitement to violence against an individual/group on the basis of their religion; for example, sermons, the distribution of flyers, and the dissemination of rumors, particularly if such incitement led to violence; (b) citizens were mobilized to act against others because of their religion; (c) there were one-on-one acts of assault; (d) there were instances of communal violence arising from perceived religious antagonisms.
    Instances where the parties to a conflict had different religious affiliations but where the incident in question was not about religion were discarded from the data set.
2 M. 'Abd al-Khaliq, "Majma' al-buhuth al-islamiya yarfud qanun dawr al-'ibada al-muwahhad wa yutalib bi-akhar li-bina' al-kana'is." *al-Ahram*, 18 October 2011, http://gate.ahram.org.eg/News/128006.aspx
3 M. Abul Nil, "al-Azhar wa-l-kana'is yarfudun qanun dawr al-'ibada." *Al-Ahram*, 17 October 2011, http://www.ahram.org.eg/The-First/News/107230.aspx.
4 Noha al-Zeiny in an interview with Wael el Ibrashy, Dream TV, http:// www.youtube.com/watch?v=vF_B1gwjS6o
5 A. 'Abd al-Aal, "Behind Every [sectarian] Strife in Egypt Is a Woman," *al-Ahram al-raqmi*, 18 March 2011.

6   I. Eissa, "Jokes that Lighten the Tragedy," *Al Dostour Online*, 15 February 2012.
7   K. Gabr, "The Emotional Buildup and the Sectarian Explosion." *Rose al-Yusuf*, 20 November 2010.
8   K. al-Araby, "Abeer and Camilla Have Appeared, Will Sectarian Strife Disappear?" *Ikhwan Online*, 2011 (in Arabic).
9   *al-Musawwir*, 31 December 2004.
10 *Watani*, 29 October 2006.
11 *Watani*, 29 October 2006.
12 Islamway (portal), unauthored, 5 March 2009: "The conversion of Copts and the stance of al-Azhar."

Notes to Chapter 3

1   Perhaps the most thorough historical account to date on the relationship between the state and the Church in the nineteenth century and up to the 1950s is Tarek al-Bishri's *al-Muslimun wa-l-Aqbat fi itar al-jama'a al-misriya* (Muslims and Copts in the Framework of the Egyptian National People, 1981). Also excellent articles containing relevant information include McCallum 2007 and Sedra 1999.
2   For example, the Church can be particularly beneficial in instilling positive attitudes among Copts with regard to good citizenship, for example, calling upon Copts to participate in union and syndicate elections.
3   Guirgis Gouda, at the time of writing of his book *al-Sadat wa-l-Aqbat* (Sadat and the Copts), was the president of the American Coptic Association of Southern California and a strong lobbyist on behalf of the rights of Copts. He was also a strong supporter of Pope Shenouda and was fiercely opposed to the papal committee that was established to take over the responsibilities of the pope when he was placed under house arrest by Sadat. He was one of the activists who lobbied the Copts living in the American diaspora not to cooperate with the papal committee.
4   He was also the editor-in-chief of the government mouthpiece, *al-Gumhuriya*. Sabry, who was a Copt Orthodox, had very strained relations with the Church.
5   See earlier references on the Sadat–Shenouda crisis.
6   The Oteify Report was based on a fact-finding mission on the burning of a church in al-Zawya al-Hamra, the findings of which were shared with parliament.
7   The construction, repair, and maintenance of churches was historically regulated by an Ottoman decree dating to 1854, commonly known as *al-Khatt al-Hamayuni*, and ten conditions laid out by the government in 1934 that are considered highly restrictive and discriminatory (see Bebawi 2001).
8   According to the Church mouthpiece, *al-Kiraza*, the Holy Synod unanimously agreed to the cancellation of all celebrations of Easter for that year

and the retreat of all metropolitans and bishops to the monasteries. The pope retreated to the monastery, and the cathedral where he resided was closed (*al-Kiraza*, 4 April 1980).

9   *Mayu*, 7 September 1981.

10   http://www.sis.gov.eg/VR/conts/en/2.htm

11   As a form of resistance to the proposed legislative changes, there was a call for fasting for three days from 31 January to 2 February 1977 to call upon God to bestow "his people with unity of heart and peace to the nation and wisdom and success to its leaders." The call was made by members of the clergy and the Majlis al-Millis and representatives of the people of Alexandria in a conference held at the Patriarchate premises in Abbasiya, Cairo, on 17 January 1977. This fast, while a religious act, was also a symbolic form of open and covert political resistance. The executive recommendations and conference documents are available in 'Abd al-Fattah 1984.

12   Consider, for example, Bishop Athanasious' relations with the authorities in Beni Suef, which were considered highly amicable.

13   Pope Shenouda's change of policy and tactic are discussed in the next part of the chapter. However, it is noteworthy that immediately upon the termination of his house arrest, Shenouda espoused a highly conciliatory tone, as is evident from the letter he sent Mubarak thanking him for his message of good wishes for Christmas and emphasizing that "Christians and Muslims in Egypt look forward to a bright future under the great leadership of President Mubarak" (*al-Dustur*, 1 April 2007).

14   For example, when Pope Shenouda cancelled the Easter mass in 1980, a church delegation approached Vice President Mubarak hoping that the latter would act as mediator between Sadat and the pope, possibly arranging a meeting between the two that would help to restore dialog between them and ease tensions. Accounts indicate that Mubarak rejected the idea and expressed his extreme anger at the actions of the pope, which he insisted were orchestrated to undermine Sadat's planned visit to the United States. An account of this meeting was published in *al-Dustur*, 1 April 2007.

15   See, for example, Hassan 2003.

16   This report, authored by Nabil 'Abd al-Fattah and the first of its kind, provided a rigorous analysis of the various religious movements, organizations, and institutions in Egypt and their relationships with each other and with the government in historical and contemporary contexts. It was published by one of Egypt's leading think tanks, the Al-Ahram Center for Political and Strategic Studies. Two reports on the subject were published by the Center, after which publication stopped ('Abd al-Fattah 1995).

17   This does not however, suggest that they will necessarily follow suit blindly, although given the influence of the clergy on Copts, its impact cannot be underestimated.

18 Such as, for example, when a bishop visits one of the churches in his arch-diocese or on the occasion of a funeral.

19 Although it is significant that Pope Kyrollos also gave instructions to all the churches to ring their bells to celebrate Nasser's retraction from his decision to resign as president (*Rose al-Yusuf*, 10 April 2007).

20 A liberal party that is an offshoot of the famous Wafd Party.

21 Father Philopateer, who later became famous for his leadership role in the Maspero Youth Movement, was also vocal in his criticism of the manner in which the government handled the sectarian incidents that erupted in December 2005 in Alexandria. It is significant that Father Philopa-teer's sentence would have been for three years but the pope granted him clemency in June 2007. This decision on the part of the pope may be inter-preted as a political message to the government that the Church leadership was no longer pursuing the policy of supporting the NDP at all costs. The toleration for anti-government elements within its ranks is an overt policy indicative of heightened tensions (*al-Dustur*, 16, June 2006; *Al-Masry Al-Youm*, 16 June 2007).

22 *al-Arabi*, 1 April 2007.

23 *al-Ahram*, 27 May 2007.

24 *al-Fagr*, 20 August 2005.

25 *Al-Masry Al-Youm*, 23 May 2007.

26 *Rose al-Yusuf*, 14 April 2007

27 *Al-Masry Al-Youm*, 19 January 2007.

28 It is ironic that a few days prior to Pope Shenouda's announcement of his position in support of the current wording of Article 2, which holds shari'a to be *the* principal source of legislation, his official spokesman, Bishop Morcos, requested the revision of the article so that shari'a is said to be *a* but not *the* principal source of legislation. He also emphasized that Copts in Egypt did not want to see this article revised so that shari'a does not take precedence over other sources of legislation. Later, shortly after Pope Shenouda's pro-Article 2 position was announced, Bishop Morcos somewhat retracted his earlier statement, claiming in another press interview that in light of the current leadership/regime, Copts did not have reservations about the current wording of article 2 (*Rose al-Yusuf*, 15 February 2007).

29 The movement known as al-Haraka al-'Imaniya (the Lay Movement) held two conferences. The first, held in November 2006, discussed lay visions of priorities for Church reform. The second conference, held in April 2007, discussed Church trials as well as Copts' engagement in civil society.

30 American–Coptic statement issued on 20 March 2007, http://www.christi-annewswire.com/news/367392535.html

31 *Nahdat Misr*, 13 July 2007.

32 *al-Ahali*, 8 December 2004; *al-Ahram*, 10 December 2004.

33 Later that evening, after the pope had already left the cathedral, it was announced that the religious guidance meeting (which should have been held some time ago) was going to take place at one of the residential homes belonging to the Coptic Orthodox Church (as opposed to the premises of the state security apparatus). A fortnight later, the pope returned from the monastery, and in a press conference on the occasion, Bishop Bassanti declared that the crisis had yet to end, making reference to the twenty-one youth in detention and to other conversion cases that had not yet been resolved (*Al-Masry al-Youm*, 23 December 2004).

34 *Al-Masry Al-Youm*, 23 December 2004.

35 The same is emphasized in the coverage of the press conference given by the bishops, in which there was an open and scathing critique of the state security apparatus' handling of the affair (*al-Arabi*, 12 December 2004; *Asharq Alawsat*, 12 December 2004). Bishop Bachomious said that although there were objections from the governor of Beheira and from the secretary of the NDP to the delay in granting him access to Constantine, it was the security apparatus that insisted on pursuing matters this way (*al-Arabi*, 12 December 2004). Also, one of the monks at the monastery to which the pope had withdrawn told the press: "The problem is not in the disappearance of a priest's wife; every person has the right to choose his faith but [the problem] is in the way that the crisis was managed. The Church did not escalate the crisis but we wanted to know the priest's wife's position and in effect, the pope promised the protesters that the lady would return but the security broke its promise and the pope had [no choice but] to leave" (*al-Hayat*, 10 December 2004). According to Bishop Bishoy's statement, the pope was "extremely upset" about the way he was treated despite "all that he gave for Egypt in terms of the patriotic stands that has made him one of the Christian personalities that have most defended the Arab causes" (*Al-Masry Al-Youm*, 12 December 2004).

36 *al-Ahram al-masa'i*, 30 December 2004.

37 *al-Ahram al-masa'i*, 30 December 2004.

38 *al-Usbu'*, 20 December 2004.

39 *al-Usbu'*, 20 December 2004.

40 *al-Usbu'*, 20 December 2004.

41 See, for example, Muhammad Emara in *al-Ahram*, 21 December 2004; Habib 2005; and al-Bishri 2005.

42 *al-Ahram*, 21 December 2004.

43 For coverage of the events from a Coptic perspective, see *Watani* newspaper, 12 December 2004, which includes a detailed account of how the state security apparatus failed to keep its part of the deal in resolving the crisis.

Notes to Chapter 4

1 E. Fawaz, "El Adly Warns against the Copts' Heightened Protests and Demands the Intervention of the Pope," *al-Karama*, 2 August 2010 (in Arabic).

2 Maximos had begun a lawsuit against the Ministry of Interior for not recognizing its official seal/stamp. The court ruling denied Maximos' appeal and justified its decision on the premise that there is only one patriarch for the Coptic Orthodox Church in Egypt, Pope Shenouda, and that Maximos' church had not fulfilled the legal requirements for establishing a new denomination according to Egyptian law. The details of the ruling are presented in *Sawt al-umma*, 31 December 2008.

3 A rank in the ecclesiastical order of the Coptic Orthodox Church lower than priest.

4 As recounted by Max Michel himself in an interview published in *Nahdat Misr*, 13 July 2006.

5 *al-Mujaz*, 24 July 2007.

6 These rumors featured widely in the Egyptian press; see, for example, *al-Wafd*, 8 July 2006.

7 *al-Fajr*, 17 July 2006.

8 *Al-Masry Al-Youm*, 8 July 2006.

9 *al-Ahram*, 7 July 2006.

10 *Al-Masry al-Youm*, 11 July 2006.

11 *al-Ahram*, 12 July 2006.

12 *al-Midan*, 13 July 2006.

13 *al-Midan*, 13 July 2006.

14 *al-Dustur*, 8 January 2010.

15 *al-Shuruq*, 1 January 2011.

16 Interview with Bishop Moussa, April 2011.

Notes to Chapter 5

1 Gamal Essam al-Din, "Questions about Human Rights," *al-Ahram Weekly*, 18–24 February 2010.

2 *al-Dustur*, 4 February 2010.

3 *Al-Masry Al-Youm*, 12 January 2010.

4 *al-Dustur*, 7 January 2010.

5 A. Hussein, "Hundreds of Copts Continue Protesting for the Second Day over the Disappearance of the Der Mowas Clergyman's Wife," *al-Dustur*, 24 July 2010.

6 A. Shaaban, "Camillia Returns," *al-Wafd*, 25 July 2010.

7 S. Salah, "Protests Call for the Release of Der Mowas' Clergyman's Wife," *al-Wafd*, 4 September 2010.

8 *Al-Masry Al-Youm*, 22 September 2010.

9 H. al-Wakil, "Protest in Alexandria Condemns Disappearance of Camillia and Calls on Mubarak to Interfere," *al-Dustur*, 25 September 2010;

"Protests in Cairo and Alexandria Calling for Prosecuting Bishoi and Releasing Camillia," *Al-Masry Al-Youm*, 23 October 2010.

10   W. Wahid, "Protest in 'Amr ibn al-'As Mosque in Support of Camillia," *al-Wafd*, 11 September 2010.

11   H. Abu Shakra, "Large Protest at Qaed Ibrahim Mosque in Alexandria Demanding Release of Camillia Shehata," *al-Dustur*, 6 November 2010.

12   "Sheikh al-Mahallawi Leads Salafi Protest Calling for Camillia Shehata's Release," *al-Dustur*, 9 October 2010.

13   I. Eissa, "al-Aqbat al-Muslimun wa-l-lahma," *al-Dustur*, 27 September 2010.

14   Interview with informants in S. 'Abd al-Rahman, "Violent Clashes Between Security Forces and Coptic Protesters over Stopped Church Construction in Giza," *Al-Masry Al-Youm*, 25 November 2010.

15   E. Khalil, "Copts Protest Cessation of Umraniya Church Construction, and Giza Governor Interferes," *Al-Masry Al-Youm*, 23 November 2010.

16   The case studies presented in this section are retrieved from Nader Shoukry's excellent book, *Lijan al-sulh wa-l-Aqbat* (The Reconciliation Committees and Copts, 2010).

17   A. Seif al-Nasr, "Muslims and Christians Clash in Fayoum Village after Alleged Kidnapping of Christian Wife Who Converted to Islam," *al-Badil*, 22 June 2008 (in Arabic).

18   A. Seif al-Nasr, "Police Aborts New Sectarian Clashes Due to Elopement of Muslim Wife with Christian Man," *al-Dustur*, 30 June 2008 (in Arabic).

19   A. Shantir, "Clashes Continue in Nag Hammadi, Bahgoura Village and Ezbet Turki," *al-Wafd*, 10 January 2010.

20   O. El-Sheikh, "Six Injured in Clashes Between Muslims and Christians in Beni Suef," *Al-Masry Al-Youm*, 4 July 2009 (in Arabic).

21   O. El-Sheikh, "Sectarian Clashes in Beni Suef Village," *Al-Masry Al-Youm*, 18 July 2009 (in Arabic).

Notes to Chapter 6

1   K. Kamal, "Egypt's Policy of Denial," *Al-Masry Al-Youm*, 6 January 2011 (in Arabic).

2   S. Muntasir, "Egypt is Ancient," *al-Ahram*, 3 January 2011 (in Arabic).

3   A.Y. Ahmad, "Necessary Reflections on the Saints' Church Massacre," *al-Shuruq*, 6 January 2011 (in Arabic).

4   Hasan Nafa', "Coptic Extremism," *Al-Masry al-Youm*, 6 January 2011 (in Arabic).

5   *Al-Masry Al-Youm*, 5 January 2011.

6   Excellent examples would be, from the state-run press, 'A. Mikha'il, "Priests and Intellectuals: Coptic Protests Promote the Terrorists' Agendas," *Rose al-Yusuf*, 4 January 2011, and from the opposition press, 'A. Sha'ban, "Ministers Went to the Cathedral to Extend Condolences and Angry Copts Met Them with Stones and Slander," *al-Wafd*, 4 January 2011.

7   See W. 'Abd al-Magid, "Youth Anger in Egypt and Tunisia: What Is the Difference?" *Al-Masry Al-Youm*, 7 January 2011 (in Arabic), and 'A. al-Shubaki, "How Was Sectarianism Deepened?" *Al-Masry Al-Youm*, 6 January 2011 (in Arabic).

8   The immediate lead-up is referred to here as opposed to the accumulation of the more long-term structural causes of instability in Egypt, such as extreme corruption, police abuse, and so on.

9   "The Three Churches Denounce the 25 January Protests and Call Upon the Copts Not to Participate" (E. Khalil, *Al-Masry Al-Youm*, 24 January 2011).

10   M. Adel, "The Pope Warns Copts against Participation in the Protests," *Rose al-Yusuf*, 25 January 2011 (in Arabic).

11   H. Sholkamy, "From Tahrir Square to My Kitchen," *50.50 Inclusive Democracy*, 14 March 2011, http://www.opendemocracy.net/5050/hania-sholkamy/from-tahrir-square-to-my-kitchen

Notes to Chapter 7

1   *Asharq Alawsat*, 24 February 2011.

2   Information provided by informant on condition of anonymity.

3   This applies to 2011. On 25 January 2012, the masses who turned up in Tahrir Square exceeded that number.

4   al-Hindy et al., *al-Dustur*, 2011.

5   *al-Dustur*, 2011.

6   Hani Shukrallah, *Ahram Online*, 2011.

7   *Asharq Alawsat*, 24 February 2011.

8   H. Radwan, "The Death of Two Following a Romantic Fitna in Atfeeh," *al-Shuruq*, 6 March 2011 (in Arabic).

9   A much abridged version of this section appeared in the *Arab Reform Bulletin* on 11 May 2011 under the title "Egyptian Democracy and the Sectarian Litmus Test."

10   A. Muhammad, "Egypt Is Not Just Tahrir Square," *Rose al-Yusuf*, 23–29 April 2011 (in Arabic).

11   A. Al Aswany, "When We Speak, You Must Listen," *Al-Masry Al-Youm*, 26 April 2011 (in Arabic).

12   *Al-Masry Al-Youm*, 21 April 2011, and *Watani*, 22 April 2011.

13   Fahmi Huwaydi, "Talk of Lies and Hatred," *al-Shuruq*, 27 April 2011 (in Arabic).

14   A militant Islamist group that recently denounced the use of violence.

15   H. Qandil, "Generals, Make the Decrepit Interior Minister Resign and Hit the Thugs of Saudi Arabia," *Sawt al-umma*, 25 April 2011 (in Arabic).

16   D. Rashwan, "A Vision and Possible Solutions for the Qena Crisis," *al-Shuruq*, 25 April 2011 (in Arabic).

17   *Rose al-Yusuf*, 23–29 April 2011.

18 *al-Shuruq*, 27 April 2011.

19 For a detailed account of the Camillia crisis, see M. Tadros 2010a.

20 K. Muntasir, "Never Mind Camillia, Take 'Abir," *Al-Masry Al-Youm*, 10 May 2011 (in Arabic).

21 *al-Dustur*, 12 May 2011.

22 'A. 'Abd al-Mun'im, "Let Egypt Die and Long Live the Salafis and the Church," *al-Yawm al-sabi'*, 11 May 2011 (in Arabic).

23 Y. Sidhum, "Will the State Quail Before the Terror of the Salafis?" *Watani*, 17 April 2011 (in Arabic).

24 *al-Wafd*, 7 March 2011.

25 *al-Dustur*, 11 May 2011.

26 E. Gad, "The Amiriya [Incident] Is Sectarian, You Philosophers of Denial," *Al-Tahrir*, 21 February 2012 (in Arabic).

27 A. Oreiby, "The Report [Contract] for Expelling Christians from al-Amiriya," *Al Wafd*, 2012 (in Arabic).

28 E. Gad, "The Amiriya [Incident] Is Sectarian, You Philosophers of Denial," *Al-Tahrir*, 21 February 2012 (in Arabic).

29 Mervat Rashad, http://www.youm7.com/News.asp?NewsID=362418

30 S. 'Abd al-'Ati and M. Dunya, "Sulayman li-l-niyaba: 'indama tamma ta'yini na'iban li-l-ra'is hadathat halat istiya' bayn al-shurta," 19 April 2011, front page *al-Ahram*, http://www.ahram.org.eg/508/2011/04/19/25/73713/219.aspx

31 See J. Munir, "Kahin al-qiddisn: al-kanisa lan tatakhalla 'an haqq shuhada'iha," *al-Yawm al-sabi'*, 24 July 2011, http://www.youm7.com/ NewsPrint.asp?NewsID=460822

32 R. Ramadan, "The Alexandria Cathedral Files a Lawsuit against the Field Marshal due to Delays in the Two Saints Investigations," *Al-Masry Al-Youm*, 21 February 2012 (in Arabic).

33 Emergency as in 'fast track.'

34 "Niyabat amn al-dawla takshuf sabab ta'khir al-tahqiqat fi tafjirat Kinisat al-Qiddisin," *al-Aqbat al-yawm*, 1 January 2012, http://www.coptstoday. com/Archive/Detail.php?Id=18373

35 R. Massoud, "Six Presidential Candidates and Nineteen Movements and Parties Announce Their Solidarity with the Activists of al-Massara Church [Case]," *al-Shuruq*, 12 April 2012 (in Arabic).

Notes to Chapter 8

1 E. Habib, "Maspero Youth Union Refuse the Church's Request Not to Protest in Front of the [Ministry of] Interior," *al-Musawwir*, 8 February 2012 (in Arabic).

2 M. Abd al-Latif, *al-Ahram*, "Intense Clashes between Muslims and Christians at the Top of the Muqattam Mountain," front page, 9 March 2011 (in Arabic).

3 M. Abd al-Latif, "The Army Takes Control after Acts of Violence," *al-Ahram*, 10 March 2011 (in Arabic).

4   D. Rashed, "Dumping the Zabaleen," *Al-Ahram Weekly*, 11–17 July 2002,
    home page, http://weekly.ahram.org.eg/2002/594/eg7.htm
5   Rashed, "Dumping the Zabaleen."
6   Commonly referred to as 'swine flu,' the H1N1 influenza virus is a novel
    strain of influenza that first emerged in Mexico and the United States. The
    virus contains a mixture of genes from humans, birds, and pigs. Despite this
    mixture of genetic material, it appeared to spread only between humans
    and no cases of animal-to-human transmission were reported. 'Swine flu'
    proved to be a catchy but misleading nickname for the new virus. Since its
    initial appearance in March 2009, the virus has spread globally. While it
    appeared to cause a relatively mild form of influenza, it infected large num-
    bers of people and, by October 2009, had killed nearly five thousand people
    worldwide. In June 2009, the World Health Organization declared a global
    pandemic of H1N1 as a result of sustained human-to-human transmission
    in multiple countries.

Notes to Chapter 9

1   *Rose al-Yusuf*, 5 October 2011.
2   *al-Yawm al-sabi'*, 12 October 2011.
3   *al-Ahram*, 1 October 2011.
4   *al-Dustur*, 2 October 2011.
5   See *al-Dustur*, 8 October 2011, and *al-Tahrir*, 8 October 2011.
6   The video footage of the beating is online at http://www.youtube.com/wat
    ch?v=3OAYMw25Q2U&feature=youtu.be&skipcontrinter=1
7   Dream 2, "al-Sa'a 'ashira" program, Mona al-Shazly interview
    with Noha al-Zeini, undated, http://www.youtube.com/watch?v=_
    o5gJNIyTw8&feature=fvwrel
8   For a comprehensive collection of all that has been written on Maspero as
    well as documentation of different witnesses' accounts, see Yacoub 2012.
9   *al-Dustur*, 12 October 2011.
10 Live footage of the army raid on al-Hurra is online at http://inagist.com/
    SultanAlQassemi/123262745566117888/Video_of_Al_Hurra_anchor_
    Amro_Khalil_reacting_live_as_Egyptian_army_storms_Al_Hu
11 Nawara Nigm, *al-Tahrir*, 11 October 2011, p. 7.
12 *al-Yawm al-sabi'*, 11 October 2011.
13 A. Ibrahim, "The Military's Statement Emphasizes that It Will Not Abdi-
    cate from Ruling," *al-Tahrir*, 11 October 2011 (in Arabic).
14 Details have been purposely removed for ethical reasons, to protect the
    identity of the informants.
15 S. Meirs, "The Halt of the Implementation of the Court Ruling of Impris-
    oning the Priest of al-Marinab Church," *Watani*, 14 May 2012.
16 N. Shoukry, "Maspero Youth Movement Challenge the Pope: Talk about
    Spiritual Matters Only," *al-Yawm al-sabi'*, 22 October 2011 (in Arabic).

Notes to Chapter 10

1 These were relayed to the author through oral histories of Copts who wish to remain anonymous.

2 *al-Hayat*, "Dialogue between the Copts and the Muslim Brotherhood in Egypt Stops," 23 April 1992 (in Arabic).

3 K. Gabr, "The Dead Alliance between the Copts and the Muslim Brotherhood," *Rose al-Yusuf*, 12 October 1992. According to another press source (R. Hamad, "The Copts and the Brotherhood, Love and Revenge," *Sabah al-khayr*, 8 May 1997), one of the main sticking points in the meetings that took place in 1992 was the Copts' utter refusal of the idea of living under shar'ia.

4 S. 'Abd al-Hadi, "The Brothers' and Copts' Dialogue: Imposed by Delusions and Awaiting Activation," *Al-Masry Al-Youm*, 5 January 2006 (in Arabic).

5 *al-Usbu'*, "Why Do the Copts Fear the Political Ascendancy of the Brothers?" 28 November 2005 (in Arabic).

6 *al-Dustur*, 2 October 2011.

7 *al-Dustur*, 2 October 2011.

8 R. Habib, "The Copts and the Ascendancy of the Brothers," *al-Usbu'*, 26 December 2005.

9 Informal interviews with Church leaders (who preferred to remain anonymous).

10 Interview with Zakhir, March 2011.

Notes to Chapter 11

1 A. Hammouda, "Judges Who Have Lost their Integrity and Nerves in the Copts' Committees," *al-Fajr*, 8 December 2011.

2 See "Ta'arjuh aqbat al-Iskindiriya bayn Musa wa Shafiq . . . wa-l-Sabahi yastahwidh 'ala aswat al-shabab," *al-Yawm al-sabi'*, 20 May 2012, http://www2.youm7.com/News.asp?NewsID=683255

3 R. Nawar and K. Kamil, "al-Jama'a al-Islamiya: al-taswit al-ta'ifi wa amwal fulul al-watani sabab su'ud Shafiq," *al-Yawm al-sabi'*, 25 May 2012, http://www1.youm7.com/News.asp?NewsID=688444&SecID=65&IssueID=0

4 Noha al-Zeini in an interview with Wael al-Ibrashy, Dream TV, http://www.youtube.com/watch?v=vF_B1gwjS6o

5 "Muhallilun: aswat al-Aqbat rajahat kafat Shafiq 'ala hisba murashahiyy al-thawra," *al-Misriyyun*, 26 May 2012, http://almesryoon.com/permalink/9624.html

6 B. Youssef, "Idha kana al-Aqbat mu'athirun li-hadhihi al-daraja fa'alayna waqf naghamat al-aqaliya," *al-Shuruq*, http://www.shorouknews.com/news/view.aspx?cdate=27052012&id=3470ff7f-c30f-4f57-8190-1e3e7cbf7ecd

7 Telephone interview with Robeir el Fares, 18 June 2012.

8   http://www.youtube.com/watch?v=1eUWYgOoiZE&feature=youtube_
    gdata_player

Notes to the Conclusion

1   Translated from the film script, *Hassan and Morcos* (2008), by Youssef
    Mu'ati.
2   http://www.almasryalyoum.com/node/947546

Bibliography

'Abd al-Fattah, N. 2010. *al-Din wa-l-dawla al-ta'ifiya: musahma fi naqd al-khitab al-muzdawaj.* Cairo: al-Masry For Citizenship and Dialogue Publ.

———. 2009. "Ru'ya tahliliya li-waqi' al-'unf al-ta'ifi zil al-irtifa' al-dini." In M. Megahed, ed. *Misr li-kul al-Misriyin.* Cairo: al-Mahrusa.

———, ed. 1995. *al-Hala al-diniya fi Misr.* Cairo: Markaz al-Ahram li-l-Dirasat al-Siyasiya wa-l-Stratijiya.

———. 1984. *al-Mushaf wa-l-sayf: al-sira' al-dini bayn al-din wa-l-dawla.* Cairo: Madbouli.

'Abd al-Hamid, R., and T. Mansour. 2001. *Misr fi al-'asr al-bizantini* AD *284–641.* Cairo: al-Markaz al-Misri al-'Arabi li-l-Nashr wa-l-Tawzi'.

'Abd al-Rahman, A. N.d. (commentary by Mohamed Sobeih). *Futuhat Misr wa akhbaraha.* N.p.: n.p.

'Abd al-Sadek, A. 2011. "Hitafat 25 Yanayir, a Reading in Its Nuances and Inferences. 2011." In A. Rabi', ed., *25 Yanayir: qira'a awaliya wa ru'ya mustaqbaliya.* Cairo: Markaz al-Ahram li-l-Dirasat al-Siyasiya wa-l-Stratijiya.

Abu Ghazi, E. 2009. "al-Hala al-diniya fi Misr bayn al-ta'ayush wa-l-tamyiz." In M. Megahed, ed., *Misr li-kul al-Misiryin.* Cairo: al-Mahrusa.

Abu Ja'far, A. AH 1407 *Tarikh al-umam wa-l-muluk,* 1st ed. Beirut: Dar al-Kutub al-'Ilmiya.

Abu Zeida. 2012. "The Political and Social Composition of Parliament." In Rabi' 2012.

Abu Zulak, A. 1999. *Fada'il Misr wa akhbariha wa khasa'isiha.* Preface by Ali Mohamed Omar. Cairo: Egyptian General Organization for Books.

al-Afani, S.H. 2004. *A'lam wa aqzam fi mizan al-Islam*. 2 vols. Jeddah: Dar Magid 'Usayri.

Afifi, M.1992. *al-Aqbat fi al-ahd al-'uthmani*. Cairo: Egyptian General Organization for Books.

Ali, A. 2005. *al-Ikhwan al-Muslimun wa-l-fatawa 'ala al-aqbat, al-dimuqratiya, al-mar'a wa-l-fann*. Cairo: Al Mahroussa Publ.

Ali, K. 2012. "Precursors to the Revolution." In "The Pulse of Egypt's Revolt," *IDS Bulletin* 43 (1) (January).

Anderson, B. 1991. *Imagined Communities*. London: Verso.

Andrawous, F. 2012. "State Security Investigations Apparatus Reveals the Reason for the Delay in the Investigations in the Two Saints [Church] Bombing." *Copts Today Online*, January 1. http://www.coptstoday.com/Archive/Detail.php?Id=18373

———. 2011. "Ask the Expert." *Pew Research Center*, May 11. http://pewresearch.org/pubs/1770/ask-the-expert-pew-research-center#christians-egypt

———. 2010. *Muslimun wa aqbat*. Cairo: Dar al-Thaqafa al-Haditha.

———. 2007. *Taqrir taqasi al-haqa'iq fi qaryat Bamha, al-Ayat*. Cairo: Andalus Institute for Tolerance and Anti-violence Studies.

Aref, G. 2006. *Dukhul al-Islam Misr*. Cairo: al-Maktab al-Misri al-Hadith.

Armanios, F. 2011. *Coptic Christianity in Ottoman Egypt*. Oxford: Oxford University Press.

Asaf, Y. 1995. *Tarikh salatin bani 'Uthman min awwal nash'atihim hatta al-ann*. 1st ed. Series of pages from Egypt's history. Cairo: Madbouli Press.

Ashmawy, S. 2009. "al-Sha'i'at wa durha fi ta'jij al-sira' al-ta'ifi." In M. Megahed, ed., *Misr li kul al-Misriyin*. Cairo: al-Mahrusa.

Atiya, A. 1968. *A History of Eastern Christianity*. London: Methuen and Co.

Atiya, L. 2010. *An Index to the History of the Patriarchs of the Coptic Church*. Salt Lake City, UT: University of Utah Press.

al-'Awa, M. 2006. *Li-l-Din wa-l-watan fusul fi 'ilaqat al-Muslimin bi ghayr al-Muslimin*. Cairo: Nahdat Misr.

Ayad, H. 2011. "The Position of the Egyptian Church and the Reactions of the Copts." In Rabi' 2012.

al-Bahr, S. 1984. *al-Aqbat fi-l-hayah al-siyasiya al-misriya*. Cairo: Anglo-Egyptian Publ.

al-Banna, H. 1986. *Muzakkirat al-da'wa wa-l-da'iya*. Cairo: Islamic House for Distribution and Publishing.

al-Banna, R. 2001. *al-Aqbat fi Misr wa-l-mahgar*. Cairo: Egyptian General Organization for the Book.

Baraka, M. 2011. *Masihi Muslim dut kum*. Cairo: Dar al-Uyum li-l-Nashr.

Barth, F. 1969. *Ethnic Groups and Boundaries: The Social Organization of Culture Difference in Ethnicity*. Bergen: University of Bergen.

al-Baz, M. 2006. *Didd al-Baba: asrar azmat al-kanisa fi Misr*. Cairo: Kenouz.

———. 2005. *al-Baba Shenouda: al-wajh wa-l-qina'*. Cairo: Kenouz Publ.

Bebawy, L. 2011. *'Ala al-Muslimin hal mashakil ikhwanihim al-Masihiyyin fir itar al-wihda al-wataniya*. Cairo: Dar al-Sa'd Publications.

———. 2006. *al-Baba Shenouda al-thalith wa-l-ashum al-ta'isha al-muwajjaha li-siratu*. Cairo: Dar al-Su'ad.

———. 2001. *Mashakil al-Aqbat fi Misr wa hululiha*. Cairo: al-Ahram Publications.

Beshay, M. 2010. *Dalil al-wifaq fi al-zawaj wa-l-talaq*. Cairo: Pop Professional Press.

al-Bishri, T. 2011. *al-Dawla wa-l-kanisa*. Cairo: al-Shuruq.

———. 2005. *al-Jama'a al-wataniya: bayn al-'uzla wa-l-indimaj*. Cairo: Dar al-Hilal.

———. 1981. *al-Muslimun wa-l-aqbat fi itar al-jama'a al-misriya*. Cairo: General Egyptian Organization for Books.

Butler, A. 1902. *The Arab Conquest of Egypt and the Last Thirty Years of the Roman Dominion*. Oxford: Clarendon Press.

Carter, B. 1986. *The Copts in Egyptian Politics*. London: Routledge.

Cawther, W. 2010. "Introduction." *Contemporary Romanian Politics, Communist and Post-Communist Studies* 43: 1–5.

Davis, S.J., 2004. *The Early Coptic Papacy: The Egyptian Church and Its Leadership in Late Antiquity*. Cairo: American University in Cairo Press.

DFID (Department for International Development). N.d. "Building Peaceful States and Societies. A DFID Practice Paper."

Emara, M. 2011. *Fi al-mas'ala al-qibtiya: al-haqa'iq wa-l-awham*. Cairo: al-Shuruq.

Eriksen, T. 2010. *Ethnicity and Nationalism*. 2nd ed. London: Pluto Press.

Eskarous, T. 1910. *Nawab': al-Aqbat wa mashahirahum fi al-qarn al-tasi' 'ashar*. 2 vols. Cairo: El Tawfik Publ.

Ezzabawy, Y. 2012. "The Role of the Youth's New Protest Movements in the January 25th Revolution." In M. Tadros, ed. "The Pulse of Egypt's Revolt." *IDS Bulletin* 43, no. 1 (January).

Fawzi, S. 2009. "al-Harakat al-islamiya wa qadaya al-muwatana: qira'a fi mawqifhum ittijah al-Aqbat." In A. Shobky, ed., *al-Muwatana fi muwajahat al-ta'ifiya*. Cairo: Markaz al-Ahram li-l-Dirasat al-Siyasiya wa-l-Stratijiya.

Filipescu, C. 2009. "Revisiting Minority Integration in Eastern Europe: Examining the Case of Roma Integration in Romania, Debatte." *Journal of Contemporary Central and Eastern Europe* 17 (3): 297–314.

Gabra, G. Forthcoming. *Coptic Civilization: Two Thousands Years of Christianity in Egypt*. Cairo: American University in Cairo Press.

Gadallah, T. 2005. *al-Aqbat: qadaya sha'ika, ru'ya mustaqbaliya*. Cairo: al-Gazira.

Galal, L.P. 2012. "Coptic Christian Practices: Formations of Sameness and Difference." *Islam and Christian–Muslim Relations* 23 (1): 45–58.

Ghabbour, M., and A. Osman. 2011. *Hadarat Misr al-qibtiya: al-dhakira al-mafquda*. Cairo: al-Madbouli.

Ghobrial, K. 2008. *al-Aqbat wa-l-libiraliya*. Cairo: Haven Publ.

Gouda, B. 1981. *al-Sadat wa-l-aqbat*. USA: American Coptic Association Chapter of Southern California Publ.

Griggs, C.W. 2000. *Early Egyptian Christianity from Its Origins to 451 CE*. Amsterdam: Koninklijke, Brill, NV.

Guindy, A. 2010. "al-'Awa'iq allati tamna' al-Aqbat min al-indimaj fi al-hayah al-siyasiya." *Ruwaq 'arabi*, no. 54. Cairo Institute for Human Rights Studies.

Guirguis, M., and N. Van Doorn-Harder. 2008. *The Emergence of the Modern Coptic Papacy*. Cairo: American University in Cairo Press.

Habib, R. 2010. *al-Wasatiya al-hadariya*. Cairo: al-Madbouli.

———. 2005. *al-Jama'a al-qibtiya bayn al-indimaj wa-l-in'izal*. Cairo: al-Shuruq.

Hanna, M. 1993. *al-A'mida al-sab'a li-l-shakhsiya al-misriya*. Cairo: Dar al-Hilal.

Hanna, S. 1965. *Who Are the Copts?* 4th ed. Cairo: Costa Tsoumas and Co.

Hassan, A. 2010. "al-Muslimun wa-l-Masihiyyin fi Misr." *Ruwaq 'arabi*, no. 54. Cairo Institute for Human Rights Studies.

Hassan, B. 2009. "Sina'at al-tamyiz al-dini." In M. Megahed, ed., *Misr li-kul al-Misriyyin*. Cairo: al-Mahrusa.

Hassan, S. 2003. *Christians versus Muslims in Modern Egypt*. London: Oxford University Press.

Heikal, M. 1983. *Autumn of Fury*. London: Andre Deutsch.

Hirschman, A. 1970. *Exit, Voice and Loyalty*. Cambridge, MA: Harvard University Press.

El Howeiry, M. 2002. *Tarikh al-dawla al-'uthmaniya fi al-'usur al-wusta*. Cairo: al-Maktab al-Misri li-Tawzi' al-Matbu'at.

Hussein, A.S. 2009. *Harakat al-mutaliba bi-l-taghyir fi al-watan al-'arabi*. Cairo: al-Alamiya li-l-Nashr wa-l-Tawzi'.

Ibn Abd al-Hakam. 1922. *The History of the Conquest of Egypt, North Africa, and Spain: Known as the Futuh Misr of Ibn Abd al-Hakam*. Edited by C. Torrey. New Haven, CT: Yale University Press.

Ibn al-Kandi. N.d. *Fada'il Misr al-Mahrusa*, part one. N.p.: n.p.

Ibrahim, S. 1996. *The Copts of Egypt*. Minority Rights Group International Report 95 (6). London: Minority Rights Group.

Isaac, B., 1965. *al-Kanisa wa-l-siyasa*. 1st ed. Alexandria: n.p.

Ishak, K.F. 2001. *Mihnit al-hawiya al-misriya wa mihnit al-lugha al-qibtiya*. Cairo: Theban Bookshop.

———. 1997. *Tarikh al-lugha al-qibtiya*. Cairo: n.p.

———. n.d. *Mihnit al-hawiya al-qibtiya*. Cairo: n.p.

Ishak, S. 2001. *Tarikh al-lugha al-qibtiya wa-istikhdamiha al-mu'asar*. Cairo: n.p.

Iskander, E. 2012. *Sectarian Conflict in Egypt: Coptic Media, Identity and Representation*. London: Routledge.

Jenkins, P. 2008. *The Lost History of Christianity: The Thousand-Year Golden Age of Church in the Middle East, Africa and Asia*. New York: Harper One.

Johnson, C. 2002. "Democratic Transition in the Balkans: Romania's Hungarian and Bulgaria's Turkish Minority (1989–99)." *Nationalism and Ethnic Politics* 8 (1): 1–28.

Kamal, K. 2012. *al-Ahwal al-shakhsiya lida al-Aqbat*. Cairo: Dar Nahdat Misr.

———. 2006. "al-Kanisa al-qibtiya wa-l-dawla al-misriya." Unpublished paper presented at the First Lay Conference, November, Cairo.

Kamil, J. 2012. *Christianity in the Land of Pharaohs: The Coptic Orthodox Church*. London: Routledge.

———. 1998. *Coptic Egypt: History and Guide*. New York: Columbia University Press.

Karas, S.F. 1985. *The Copts Since the Arab Invasion: Strangers in Their Land*. Jersey City, NJ: American, Canadian, and Australian Coptic Associations.

Kassem, K. 1994. *'Asr salatin al-mamalik: al-tarikh al-siyasi wa-l-ijtima'i*. 1st ed. Cairo: Dar al-Shuruq.

Kelada, W. 1993. *al-Masihiya wa-li-Islam fi Misr wa dirasat ukhra*. Cairo: Sina Publ.

———. 1986. *al-Masihiya wa-li-Islam fi ard Misr*. Cairo: Freedom Writers, House of Liberty.

Khalil, M. 2010. "Qira'a fi khasa'is al-'unf al-muwajjah didd al-Aqbat." *Ruwaq 'arabi*, no. 54. Cairo Institute for Human Rights Studies.

———. 1999. *Aqbat Misr: dirasa madaniya hawl humum al-watan wa-l-muwatana*. Cairo: Dar al-Khayal.

El Khemeissy, A. 2012. *al-Bab al-mughlaq bayn al-aqbat wa-l-Muslimin*. Cairo: Egyptian General Organization for Books.

Labib, H. 2012. *al-Kanisa al-misriya wa tawazun al-din wa-l-dawla*. Cairo: Dar Nahdat Misr for Publ.

Lajnat al-Tarikh al-Qibti. 1922. *Khulasat tarikh al-masihiya fi Misr*. Cairo: N.p.

Leach, M., and S. Dry, eds. 2010. *Epidemics: Science, Governance, and Social Justice*. London: Earthscan.

Lijphart, A. 1977. *Democracy in Plural Societies: A Comparative Exploration*. New Haven, CT: Yale University Press.

Mahmoud, M. 1998. *Misr al-qibtiya: al-Misriyyun yu'amadun bi-l-damm*. Cairo: Center for Studies and Legal Information for Human Rights.

Mahmoud, S. 1995. *Ahl al-dhimma fi Misr fi-l-'asr al-fatimi al-awwal*. Cairo: General Egyptian Organization for Books.

———. 1982. *Ahl al-dhimma fi Misr: al-'asr al-fatimi al-thani wa-l-'asr al-ayyubi*. Cairo: Dar al-Ma'arif.

Makari, P. 2007. *Conflict and Cooperation: Christian-Muslim Relations in Contemporary Egypt*. Syracuse, NY: Syracuse University Press.

Mankarious, Y. 1913. *Tarikh al-umma al-qibtiya fi sanawat min 1893–1912*. Cairo: n.p.

al-Maqrizi, Taqi al-Din A., and M. Zeinhom. 1998. *al-Khitat al-maqriziya*, vol. 3. Cairo: Madbouli.

el Masri, I.H. 1982. *The Story of the Copts: The True Story of Christianity in Egypt*, vol. 3. Newberry Springs, CA: St. Anthony's Coptic Orthodox Monastery Publ.

———. n.d. *Tarikh al-kanisa al-qibtiya*. Cairo: n.p.

al-Mas'udi, A. 2005. *Muruj al-dhahab wa-ma'adin al-jawhar*. Ed. K. Hasan Mar'i. Pt. 1. Beirut: al-Maktaba al-'Asriya.

———. 1916. *Muruj al-dhahab wa-ma'adin al-jawhar*. Ed. Tom Premiere. N.p.: Société Asiatique (with Arabic text).

McCallum, F. 2007. "The Political Role of the Patriarch in the Contemporary Middle East." *Middle Eastern Studies* 43 (6) (November): 923–40.

al-Metentawy, I. 2002. *Fath Misr bayn al-ru'ya al-Islamiya wa-l-ru'ya al-nusraniya*. Cairo: Dar al-Bashir li-l-Thaqafa wa-l-'Ulum.

Mihailescu, M. 2008. "The Politics of Minimal Consensus." *East European Politics and Societies* 22 (3): 553–94.

Milad, S. 1983. *Watha'iq ahl al-dhimma fi al-'asr al-'uthmani wa-ahamiyataha al-tarikhiya*. Cairo: Dar al-Thaqafa li-l-Nashr.

Minority Rights Group International. 2012. *People Under Threat 2012*. http://www.minorityrights.org/11337/peoples-under-threat/peoples-under-threat-2012.html.

Mohamed, A.1990. *al-Sadat wa-l-Baba: asrar al-sidam bayn al-nizam wa-l-kanisa*. Cairo: Dar A.M.

Morcos, S. 2006a. "Mawqif al-Ikhwan min al-Aqbat." In *al-Aqbat wa-l-su'ud al-siyasi li-l-Ikhwan al-Muslimin*. Cairo: Markaz Sawaysa li-Huquq al-Insan wa-Munahdit al-Tamyiz.

———. 2006b. *al-Muwatana wa-l-taghyir.* Cairo: Maktabat al-Shuruq al-Dawliya.

Morcos, S., and S. Fawzi. 2012. *Idarat al-ta'adudiya al-diniya: dirasat halit al-Aqbat ka mathal*. Beirut: Arab Reform Initiative.

Moro, M. 1998. *Ya Aqbat Misr intabihu*. Cairo: al-Mukhtar al-Islami.

Mounir, A. N.d. *al-Aqbat wa-l-barlaman: aswat min zujaj*. Cairo: Watani Publications.

Mu'ati, Y. 2008. *Hassan wa Morcos*. 2nd ed. Cairo: The Egyptian Lebanese Publishing House.

Muhyi al-Din, K., ed. 1980. *al-Mas'ala al-ta'ifiya fi Misr*. Beirut: al-Tal'iya Publ.

Mungiu-Pippidi, A. 2006. "Democratization without Decommunization in the Balkans." *Orbis* 50 (4): 641–55.

Nagy, A. 2001. *Lan na'ish ka dhimmiyyin*. 1st ed. Beirut: n.p.

Office of the United Nations High Commissioner for Human Rights. 2010. *Minority Rights: International Standards and Guidelines for Implementation*. New York: United Nations.

Omar, A. 1970. *Tarikh al-lugha al-qibitiya fi Misr*. Cairo: Egyptian General Organization for the Book.

Patrick, T.H. 1996, *Traditional Egyptian Christianity: A History of the Coptic Orthodox Church*. Greensboro, NC: Fisher Park Press.

Philipp, T., and H. Haarmann, eds. 1998. *The Mamluks in Egyptian Politics and Society*. Cambridge Studies in Islamic Civilization. Cambridge: Cambridge University Press.

Protsyk, O., and L.M. Matichescu. 2010. "Electoral Rules and Minority Representation in Romania." *Communist and Post-Communist Studies* 43 (1): 31–41.

Rabi', A. 2012. *al-Intikhabat al-barlamaniya li-2011/2012*. Cairo: Markaz al-Ahram li-l-Dirasat al-Siyasiya wa-l-Stratijiya.

———, ed. 2011. *25 Yanayir: qira'a awwaliya wa ru'ya mustaqbaliya*. Cairo: Markaz al-Ahram li-l-Dirasat al-Siyasiya wa-l-Stratijiya.

Richter, J. 1910. *A History of Protestant Missions in the Near East*. Edinburgh: Oliphant, Anderson and Ferrier.

Riyad, F. 2009. "Huquq al-insan laysat mawdi'an li-l-ra'i wa-l-ra'i al-akhar." In M. Megahed, ed., *Misr li-kul al-Misriyyin*. Cairo: al-Mahrusa.

Roufeilah, Y.N. 1898. *Kitab tarikh al-umma al-qibtiya*. Cairo: n.p.

Rowbotham, S. 1992. *Women in Movement: Feminism and Social Action*. Oxford: Routledge.

Sabry, M. 1985. *al-Sadat: al-haqiqa wa-l-ustura*. Cairo: Al-Ahram Publ.

al-Sadat, J. n.d. *Sayyida min Misr*. Cairo: al-Maktab al-Misri al-Hadith Publications.

al-Sayyid, L. 1945. *al-Muqtatafat*, pt. 2. Cairo: al-Muqtataf and al-Muqattam.

———. 1937. *al-Muqtatafat*, pt. 1. Cairo: Anglo-Egyptian Bookshop.

Scott, J. 1990. *Domination and the Art of Resistance*. New Haven, CT: Yale University Press.

Scott, R. 2010. *The Challenge of Political Islam: Non-Muslims and the Egyptian State*. Stanford, CA: Stanford University Press.

Sedra, P. 1999. "Class Cleavages and Ethnic Conflict: Coptic Christian Communities in Modern Egyptian Politics." *Islam and Christian-Muslim Relations* 10 (2): 219–35.

Seleem, S.A., 2001. *Tarikh Misr fi-l-'asr al-bizanti*. Cairo: Ain House for Humanitarian and Social Research.

Shafik, M. 2011. *al-Kanisa al-qibtiya: al-azma wa-l-masir*. Cairo: Metropol.

Shahin, I. 2001. *al-'Ilmaniya fi Misr wa ashhar ma'arikuha*. Cairo: Dar Harmuni li-l-Nashr.

Shami, S. 2009. "'Aqalliyya/Minority in Modern Egyptian Discourse." In C. Gluck and A. Tsing, eds., *Words in Motion: Towards a Global Lexicon*. Durham, NC: Duke University Press.

Sharkey, H. 2008. *American Evangelicals in Egypt – Missionary Encounters in an Age of Empire*. Princeton, NJ: Princeton University Press.

al-Sheikh, M. 2011. *Kharif al-babawat min al-Vatikan ila al-kursi al-babawi*. Cairo: Beirut Publ.

———. 1999. *Tarikh Misr al-bizantiya*. Cairo: N.p.

Shenouda III (Pope). 1975. *Kitab nazir al-ilah al-injili Murcus al-rasul al-qiddis wa-l-shahid*. 3rd ed. Cairo: al-Anba Ruways.

Shobki, A. 2009. "Malamih al-ta'ifiya al-jadida." In A. El Shobky, ed., *al-Muwatana fi muwajahat al-ta'ifiya*. Cairo: Al-Ahram Centre for Political and Strategic Studies.

Shoukry, G. 1991. *al-Aqbat fi watan mutaghayyir*. Cairo: Dar al-Shuruq.

Shoukry, N. 2009. *Lijan al-sulh wa-l-Aqbat*. Cairo: Watani Publ.

Soliman, H. 1988. *Qissat Fath Misr min al-Qibtiya ila al-Islam*. Cairo: al-Maktab al-'Arabi li-l-Ma'arif.

Sultan, M. 2008. *al-Aqbat wa-l-siyasa: ta'ammulat fi sanawat al-'uzla*. Cairo: al-'Ilm wa-l-Iman.

Swanson, M.N. 2007. *The Coptic Papacy in Islamic Egypt*. The Popes of Egypt 2. Cairo: American University in Cairo Press.

Tadros, M. 2012a. "Backstage Governance." In M. Tadros, ed., "The Pulse of Egypt's Revolt." *IDS Bulletin* 43 (1) (January): 62–71.

———. 2012b. "The Cross and the Crescent in Post-Mubarak Egypt." In J.L. Sowers and C. Toensing, eds., *The Journey to Tahrir: Revolution, Protest, and Social Change in Egypt*. New York: Verso.

———. 2012c. *The Muslim Brotherhood in Contemporary Egypt: Democracy Redefined or Confined?* London: Routledge.

———. 2011a. "Egypt's Bloody Sunday." *Middle East Research and Information Project*, 13 October, http://www.merip.org/mero/mero101311

———. 2011b. "The Qena Conundrum." *The Arab Bulletin*. Carnegie Endowment for International Peace.

———. 2011c. "The Securitization of Civil Society." *Journal of Security, Conflict and Development* 11 (1).

———. 2011d. "A State of Sectarian Denial." *Middle East Research and Information Project*, 11 January, http://www.merip.org/mero/mero011111

———. 2010a. "Behind Egypt's Deep Red Lines." *Middle East Research and Information Project*, 13 October 2010, http://www.merip.org/mero/mero101310#_3_

———. 2010b. "The Sectarian Incident that Won't Go Away." *Middle East Research and Information Project*, 5 March, http://www.merip.org/mero/mero03051

———. 2009a. "The Non-Muslim Other Gender and Contestations of Hierarchy of Rights." *Hawwa* 7 (2): 111–43.

———. 2009b. "Vicissitudes in the Coptic Church–State Entente in Egypt." *International Journal of Middle East Studies* 41 (2): 269–87.

Tadros, R. 1910. *al-Aqbat fi-li-qarn al-tasi' 'ashar*. 5 vols. Cairo: n.p.

Taha, R. 2010. "al-Kanisa al-qibtiya wa-l-dawla al-madaniya." *Ruwaq 'arabi*, no. 54. Cairo Institute for Human Rights Studies.

Tilly, C. 2004. *Social Movements 1768–2004*. Boulder, CO: Paradigm Publ.

Toson, O. 1996. *Wadi al-Natrun: ruhbanaha wa adyuritha*. 2nd ed. Cairo: al-Madbouli.

Van Doorn-Haarder, N., and K. Vogt, eds. 1997. *Between Desert and City: The Coptic Orthodox Church Today*. Oslo: Institute for Comparative Research in Human Culture.

Winter, M. 1992. *Egyptian Society under Ottoman Rule (1517 – 1798)*. London: Routledge.

Yacoub, H. 2012. *Sarkhit damm 'alya*. Cairo: Marmina Publ.

Youannes, Bishop. n.d. *Muzakkirat fi al-rahbana al-masihiya*. Cairo: The Coptic Orthodox Seminary.

Youssef, A. 1978. *al-Aqbat wa-l-qawmiya al-'arabiya*. Beirut: Arab Unity Studies Center.

Yuhanna, M. 1983. *Tarikh al-kinisa al-qibtiya*. Cairo: El Mahaba Publ.

Zakhir, K. 2009. *al-'Ilmaniyun wa-l-kanisa: sira'at wa tahalufat*. Cairo: n.p.

Zaklama, A. 1931. *al-Mamalik fi Misr*. Cairo: al-Majalla al-Jadida.

Zayan, M. 2011. *Maslubun 'ala bab al-kanisa*. Cairo: al-Massah.

Zayed, A. 2007. *Siwar min al-khitab al-dini al-mu'asir*. Cairo: Dar al-'Uyun.

Zukhur, F. 1993. *Qissat al-Aqbat*. Tripoli: Gross Press.

Index

conversion: from Islam 67, 105, 169; to Islam 27, 33, 78–79, 105, 108, 110, 149, 151 (guidance session 58–59); *see also* Constantine, Wafaa; Shehata, Camillia

Coptic Church xi, xii–xiii, xiv, 12–16, 25, 62, 64; accountability xiv, 13, 30, 64; Holy Synod 68, 71–72, 84–85, 253; marriage and divorce xiv, 13, 57–58, 85, 89–90, 91, 108; political role 62, 64, 72, 74–75, 79, 128–29, 159, 207, 221–22, 229–30; reform xi, xiv, 13, 63, 64, 74, 255; *see also following* Coptic *entries*; Majlis al-Milli

Coptic Church, bishop 3, 16, 69; Bachomious, Bishop 77, 256; Bishoy, Bishop 39, 93, 256; Morcos, Bishop 32, 74, 86, 127–28, 255; Moussa, Bishop 95–96, 128, 134; Pachomious, Bishop xii, 159; Samuel, Bishop 69

Coptic Church, Patriarch/Pope 16, 25, 26, 28,62, 63; as political representative of Copts 15, 19, 65, 84, 107; *see also* Kyrollos VI, Pope; Shenouda III, Pope; Tawadros II, Pope

Coptic Church/state relationship xii–xiii, 3, 15–16, 19, 61–81, 83–96; Church as mediator in Coptic citizenry/state relation 19, 61, 64, 65–66, 107, 197; Coptic Church/ SCAF relation 54, 152, 158, 197–98, 225; Coptic Church/SSI relation 19, 20, 54–55, 65, 66, 69, 75–76, 80–81, 83–96, 139, 158; Coptic Church/state entente 19, 61, 62–66, 67, 70–76, 80–81, 87, 94; *see also* al-Nasser, Gamal 'Abd; Shenouda III, Pope

Coptic churches, construction/renovation 27, 65, 75–76, 152, 157; Islamists 55, 97, 152, 155; law on

places of worship 51–54, 67, 76, 253; sectarian incident 19, 20, 51–55, 65, 66, 106–107, 109, 114, 115

Copts 19, 23–43; citizenship 28, 33, 37, 237, 243, 253; Coptic Egyptian history 4, 24–30; Coptic identity 19, 33, 38–43, 142, 168, 192; diaspora xi, xiii, 2, 14, 32, 33, 67, 68, 69–70, 75, 85, 94, 151, 255; a minority 19, 34, 35–38, 48; population xi, 19, 30–35, 47; stratification 29–30; uses of the term 23–24; *see also following* Copts *entries*

Copts, 25 January Revolution 20, 96, 119–38, 243; 2011 January bombing of Alexandrian church xiii, 20, 119, 120–24, 156–57; Coptic Church leadership 128, 134; Coptic youth 107, 119, 124–25, 130, 131, 134; Egyptian identity 119, 131, 132; motives for participation 20, 128–31; *see also* Revolution of 25 January 2011

Copts, civil society xiii–xiv, 4, 12–15, 19, 38, 61, 63, 64, 66, 88–94, 107–108, 142, 201, 243–44; political participation 14–15, 229, 231–33; *see also* Copts, 25 January Revolution; Copts, protests; Majlis al-Milli

Copts, discrimination 19, 26, 27, 28, 29, 35, 38, 51, 75, 177, 182, 194, 224–25, 241, 246–47, 248; *ahl al-dhimma* 26, 37, 150, 230, 242; discriminatory law 52–53, 107, 154, 155, 253; persecution 25, 26, 27, 37, 38, 51, 116, 130–31, 174–77, 241, 248; SCAF 139, 229, 240–41; zero tolerance for religious discrimination 194, 240

Copts, protests 1, 21, 90–92, 124, 125, 130, 154, 161–82, 183–99, 248–49; Coptic protests/Copts in protest

al-Dustur 101, 106; al-Gumhuriya 253; Al Jazeera 93, 133, 143, 188; al-Karama 83; al-Katiba al-qibtiya 13, 40, 169; al-Kiraza 253–54; Maspero Massacre 188–89, 190–93; al-Masry Al-Youm 39, 86, 93, 134, 142, 185; Mayu 67, 68; al-Naba' 78; Nahdat Misr 185; Revolution of 25 January 2011: 121, 133; Rose al-Yusuf 128, 146, 153; sectarian incident 45–46, 99, 111, 121, 124, 238; al-Tariq wa-l-haqq 130; al-Usbu' 79; al-Wafd 154, 185; Watani 59, 167; al-Yawm al-sabi' 156, 184
methodology 3, 16–18, 251
Mihailescu, Mihaela 7, 8
Mina Daniel Movement 182, 195; Daniel, Mina 162, 182, 195, 196
minority 1, 2, 4–8, 19, 35–36, 45, 240; Copts 19, 34, 35–38, 48
Morcos, Samir 125
Moro, Muhammad 36, 52
Morsi, Hani 251
Morsi, Muhammad xi, 10, 34, 206, 229, 227, 231–33, 244; see also Muslim Brotherhood
Moussa, Amr 227, 229
Mubarak, Gamal xii, 14, 124, 157, 159, 162
Mubarak, Hosni 72–73, 124, 155, 228; Mubarak/Shenouda relation 70–76, 81, 86–87, 94–95, 120, 129, 134, 206, 244, 254; sectarian incident 20, 45, 97–118, 121, 139, 156
Muhammad, Abu al-'Abbas 146
Mungiu-Pippidi, Alina 5
Muntasir, Khalid 150
Muntasir, Salah 122
Muslim Brotherhood xi–xii, 11, 21, 106, 136, 143–44, 147, 193, 201, 202–207; al-Banna, Hassan 202–203; Brotherhood/Coptic relationship 21, 202–207, 208–209, lationship 21, 202–207, 208–209,

244–48; Muslim Brotherhood/ SCAF alliance 10–12, 137, 153–54, 210; Revolution of 25 January 2011: 9–10, 126, 127, 132, 136–37, 138; sectarian incident 144, 203; see also FJP; Islamism; Morsi, Muhammad

Nafa', Hasan 123–24
Naguib, Selim 33
al-Nasser, Gamal 'Abd 19, 41, 62, 64–66, 81, 247, 252, 253–54
National Committee against Sectarian Violence 100
NDP (National Democratic Party) xii, 72–74, 88, 129, 255
NGOs (non-governmental organizations) 11, 18, 64, 221
Nigm, Nawara 190–91
Nour Party 210–11, 212, 216, 220, 222, 223, 224, 225, 245; see also Salafis

al-Oteify, Gamal 67; Oteify Report 67, 238, 253

Pan-Arabism 38, 40, 41, 43, 247
Pasha, Ezaby 53
People under Threat report (2012) 2
Pew Research Institute 31
pluralism 38, 238, 240; political pluralism 63, 137; religious pluralism 2, 43, 73, 133, 137–38, 204

al-Qaeda 123
Qallini, Georgette 90, 101
al-Qaradawi, Yusuf 43, 248
Qena case 145–49; 'Mikha'il, Imad 145–48

Rashwan, Diaa 148, 248
revolution: 1919 Revolution 1, 43, 131; 1952 Revolution 30

Kafr Salama 110, 113; 2007 Ayat, Giza 87; 2007 Bamha 109–10, 111, 113; 2008 al-Nazla 108; 2008/2009 Abu Fana monastery 113–14; 2009 Dayrut 99–100; 2009 'Izbit Bushra 114; 2009 'Izbit al-Fuqa'i 115; 2010 Nag' Hammadi 90–91, 97, 98–106, 111, 120, 122, 147; 2010 'Umraniya Church clashes 97, 106–108, 130; 2011 Alexandria xiii, 20, 119, 120–24, 125, 156–57; 2011 Imbaba 141, 149, 150, 152, 167, 173, 242; 2011 al-Marinab 184–86, 194; 2011 Minya 144; 2011 Sol 141, 145, 149, 165, 167, 171; 2011 Wadi al-Natrun 144–45; 2011 *zabbalin* in Muqattam Hills 174–77; 2012 al-Bayada 153–54; *see also* Maspero Massacre

sectarianism 3, 249; denial of 98–99, 100, 101, 102, 108, 111, 121, 122–24, 150, 184–85, 188–90, 227, 238–39; elections 21, 219, 220–22, 227, 229–30, 231–33; narratives on 4, 16, 121–24, 137, 237–38; three-D policy: denial, demonization, distribution of blame 238–39; *see also* sectarian incident

Shafiq, Ahmad 10, 34, 227–28, 230–31, 232, 233

Shahin, Ilham 24

Shami, Seteni 35–36

Sharaf, Essam 146, 154, 171, 184, 197

Shehata, Camillia 19, 56–57, 80, 97, 102–106; public appearance 57, 92, 103, 149, 151; Salafis 92, 104, 117, 149; Shenouda III, Pope 57, 92–94, 103; SSI 92–94, 103–104, 117

Shenouda III, Pope xi, 12, 16, 32, 40–41, 71, 128, 157–58, 190, 197; Constantine, Wafaa 77, 78, 80–81, 104, 256; death 12, 15, 244; house arrest 67, 70, 71, 81, 88, 254; Maspero Youth Movement 190, 197, 198,

199; Mubarak/Shenouda relation 70–76, 81, 86–87, 94–95, 120, 129, 134, 206, 244, 254; Sadat/Shenouda relation 66–70, 81, 253–54; Shehata, Camillia 57, 92–94, 103; SSI 69, 71, 75, 76, 83, 84, 87–88, 92–94; unpopularity 13, 14, 74, 94–95, 105

Shihab, Mufid 98, 102

Shoukry, Nader 111–12, 167

al-Shubaki, 'Amr 125

Sidhom, Yusuf 59, 204–205

slogan xii, xiii, 119, 133, 136, 143, 147, 187, 191

social cohesion 2, 5, 21, 50, 219, 239–44

SSI (State Security Investigations apparatus) xiii, 20, 55, 69, 83–96, 139, 156, 241; as actor of sectarian violence 116–18, 144, 156, 241; Constantine, Wafaa 57, 59, 76, 77–78, 80–81, 84, 92; Coptic Church/ SSI relation 19, 20, 54–55, 65, 66, 69, 75–76, 80–81, 83–96, 139, 158; criticism 78–79, 101–102, 256; manipulation and injustice 112–15, 116, 241; negligence 98–99, 100, 101, 108–109, 111, 115, 116, 121; reconciliation committee 111–15, 116, 117, 152, 241; Shehata, Camillia 92–94, 103–104, 117; Shenouda III, Pope 69, 71, 75, 76, 83, 84, 87–88, 92–94; *see also* Al-Adli, Habib

Suleiman, Omar 9–10, 156

Sunday School Generation 15, 30, 41

Supreme Constitutional Court of Egypt 12, 89, 220, 247

Surur, Fathi 100, 101, 122

Tadros, Ramzy 39

Tagammu' Party 72, 127, 220, 221, 223

Tantawi, Muhammad Hussein 9, 157, 185, 187, 197

Tawadros II, Pope xi, xiv, 206, 244

terrorism 28, 112, 121

al-Thawra Mustamirra 220, 223
Tilly, Charles 167–68
transition from authoritarian regimes
xii, 2, 4–12, 140–41, 240

al-Umma al-Masriya 39
United States 9, 32, 35–36, 245; Coptic diaspora 67, 68, 69–70, 75, 85

vendetta 20, 81, 99–100, 101, 177, 122, 158, 227

Wadi al-Natrun 67, 78, 144–45, 166
Wafd Party 106, 204, 221, 223, 224
Wasat Party 32, 210, 212, 213, 217, 223, 224; Madi, Abu al-'Ila 32, 210, 213, 217

woman 12, 56, 59, 136, 223, 242; 'blue bra woman' 151; exclusion of 10, 12, 224, 241, 246–47; women's rights activists 90, 103, 105–106; *see also* Constantine, Wafaa; gender relations; Shehata, Camillia

youth movements 10, 11, 77, 130, 137, 142, 224, 241; Coptic youth 77, 107–108, 119, 124–25, 130, 131, 134; demonization of 10, 183, 191–92; *see also* Maspero Youth Movement

zabbalin (garbage-collectors) 18, 163, 174–82, 238, 249
Zakhir, Kamal 13, 30, 129–30, 208–209
al-Zeini, Noha 55, 186, 229–30

DT 72 .C7 .T33 2013
Tadros, Mariz, 1975-
Copts at the crossroads